THE KEY OF REMEMBRANCE

THE KEY OF
REMEMBRANCE

A STUDY OF CHAUCER'S POETICS

by Robert O. Payne

PUBLISHED FOR THE UNIVERSITY OF CINCINNATI

New Haven and London, Yale University Press, 1963

Copyright © 1963 by Yale University.
Designed by John O. C. McCrillis,
set in Linotype Baskerville,
and printed in the United States of America by
The Carl Purington Rollins Printing-Office of
the Yale University Press, New Haven, Connecticut.

Library of Congress catalog card number: 63–7944

For Betty

Here, as I pause and stay
Motionless and alone,
The centuries fall away
And, resting on this stone,
I partly understand
The map of Time and know
How poets of this land
Two thousand years ago
Stood here perhaps one day
Reflecting upon Time
And on the endless flow
Of water in the bay,
Translating into rhyme
All that I ever planned
But lacked the skill to say.

—JOHN PRESS

Acknowledgments

IT IS POSSIBLE to acknowledge here only the most pressing fraction of my very real debts for inspiration and assistance in the preparation of this book. Certainly none of my scholarly creditors share in any sense my responsibility for its faults. I am particularly and permanently grateful for the wisdom of Kemp Malone, under whose guidance I began the study of Chaucer's notions of poetic art, and for the encouragement and incisive criticism of Talbot Donaldson. To the Editors of the Yale University Press, and especially to Mrs. Alice Miskimin, I owe thanks for dispatch, skill, and generous diligence in seeing the manuscript into and through the press.

I am also grateful to all those colleagues, and their publishers, whose contributions to my own study are acknowledged in the notes, particularly to the Bollingen Foundation, for permission to quote from Willard Trask's translation of Curtius; to Harcourt, Brace, and World for material quoted from T. S. Eliot; to Houghton, Mifflin, Inc., for quotations from F. N. Robinson's edition of Chaucer's poems, the text used throughout this study; to the Macmillan Co. for passages quoted from W. B. Yeats; to Random House for the lines from W. H. Auden; and to the Oxford University Press for the stanza from John Press' volume *Uncertainties and Other Poems*.

Finally, I gladly acknowledge a double debt to the University of Cincinnati's Charles Phelps Taft Memorial Fund, which has generously aided research for this book and subsidized its publication.

Contents

I. Review and critique of scholarship. II. Various notions of poetry and persuasion. III. Evolution of medieval from classical rhetoric. General cultural and intellectual factors in the change. Literature in the schools. IV. Thirteenth-century rhetorical poetic contrasted with ancient. Analysis of the academic treatises. V. Vernacular adaptations. The treatises of Dante and Deschamps.

Definitions of tradition in relation to the poet. His sense of the obligation of poetry to the past. Poetry and morality. Form, substance, and the reader as problems for the poet. Correlation of "sentence" and "sentement." The past as instructor in the art of poetry. Nature and artifice.

Structural divisions of the Prologue. The problem of books and experience. The vision as re-enactment of the themes of the introduction. Structural relationship to earlier work. Evasive complications of irony.

Introduction

THOSE who are very much involved in the study of Chaucer are undoubtedly aware that in the past two or three decades we have begun to evolve a new general estimate of his accomplishment—one which differs markedly from the one, or ones, worked out during the period between Dryden and Kittredge. It is still true and probably always will be that the old metaphor about building the house of scholarship is occasionally used to justify merely rearranging the accumulated piles of lumber, but in the main the more recent criticism has been trying to see differently and more clearly what the labor of nineteenth-century scholarship has made it possible to see. Certainly there continues to be a healthy asperity in debate over the methods and findings which are producing the new estimate, but the centers of debate are no longer quite the same as they were fifty years ago. And although we have not reached a fully coherent revised critical estimate, I think the fresh questions are producing discussion which will lead us to one more adequate to the subtlety and complexity of Chaucer's poetry.

B. H. Bronson's sensitivity to stylistic nuance, Kemp Malone's insistence on the artfulness of Chaucer's poetry, E. T. Donaldson's determined and intense reading of the poem in front of him, Charles Muscatine's definitions of the vitality of literary conventions, J. A. W. Bennett's skilled correlations of erudition and insight, Raymond Preston's sense of the relevance of the poetry of our own time to the reading of Chaucer's—all these seem to me to work toward giving Chaucer's poetry a personal and "modern" meaning which it properly contains or permits, and which is derived from the art of the poetry rather than from its historical or psychological context.

These men hold no corner on current criticism; I mention them as representing the ways of thinking which have contributed most to forming my own views of what constitutes illuminating analysis of Chaucer's art. With all of them I sometimes disagree, but it is nearly always with particular conclusions rather than with methods or with what they consider important to look for. I think it is unfortunate that a few of them have been identified, as though the label were some kind of warning to the consumer, as New Critics. If the labelers intend thereby to identify their work, or work like it, with the criticism practiced by Tate, Ransom, Brooks, et al., the association is misleading. There is very little (indeed, too little) in any current Chaucer criticism of the close verbal and structural analysis which is characteristic of those New Critics of twenty or thirty years ago. On the other hand, if all that is meant by the reviewers who speak of Muscatine or Preston (for example) as New Critics is that they analyze Chaucer's work with twentieth-century methods or think of it as subject to comparison with the poetry of our own age, the label is equally unfortunate. The *oldest* criticism of Chaucer—what little we have of it— from Lydgate to Dryden, regularly found the major importance of his accomplishment in its relevance to the problems of poetry contemporary to the critic. It is a narrow and deterministic historicism, developed largely in the nineteenth century, which leads to the fragmentation of culture into noncomparable and mutually incomprehensible units. And certainly it is a self-contradictory historicism which labels anachronistic a comparison of Chaucer and Eliot while sanctioning one of Chaucer and Ovid.

In any case, the restrictive argument from the contemporary audience is fallacious. It is far more respectable historical method to judge the fourteenth-century mind by the kind of appeals that were made to it than the other way around, because ultimately we can guess at what a fourteenth-century reader might have understood only by examining the texts he was evidently expected to understand. Any other method reverses usable procedure and leaves us working from inference back to evidence, with nothing from which to derive the inference. It is approximately as valid to restrict the analysis of Chaucer's poetry to what we think were the principles and methods of fourteenth-century criticism as it would be to restrict the study of his Southeast Midland English to the principles and methods of fourteenth-century linguistics.

Then too, the Romantic and Victorian conviction of evolutionary progress still corrupts us in curious ways. "The earlier the simpler" is undoubtedly a maxim that no scholar or critic of the past seventy-five years would consciously subscribe to. Yet the same man who as a textual critic would defend to the last minim the principle of the *durior lectio* may very well, when faced with a medieval statement of aesthetic principle, assert the most superficial of its possible interpretations as its intended meaning. It is particularly important to emphasize that we are talking about matters of interpretation. The kind of argument I wish to advance has too often been dismissed with the unfair *reductio* that it foolishly wishes away the facts of history. But obviously it does not; the facts of history, in this case, are the poems and critical documents, and the questions are what they mean in themselves and what they tell us of the culture in which they were formed. To a considerable extent we must define their surrounding culture in terms of what we find these poems and critical theories to be. It is a peculiarly naïve way of begging the question to assert that it is more properly "historical" to assume a definition of the nature of the culture and legislate by fiat against the subsequent observation of any discordant phenomena within it.

We must know all we can of the language (including a good deal more than phonetics, grammar, and syntax), the social structure, and whatever else is relevant that we can lay hands on. John Crowe Ransom once said that a good critic always writes as though he had a great scholar looking over his shoulder, and probably the ideal association would be even closer than that. But even a perfect knowledge of historical detail would enable us, by itself, to do no more than recognize the materials of the poem. The clearest and most comprehensive criticism would offer us only a *possible* way or ways of describing, interpreting, or analyzing their organization. In short, there is no legitimate way in which to wish off onto the courtiers of Edward III and Richard II the job of understanding Chaucer's poetry for us.

I have two reasons for stating and defending my position on these questions here. First, there has been, in the tradition of Chaucer studies, too little open discussion of fundamental and general critical problems, and no adequate definition of their practical consequences for someone setting out to investigate how Chaucer's poetry works. There are far too few central poetic questions defined by a continuing critical colloquy around them, so that it is easier than it should be to be diverted to tangential matters of psychology or history or language.

Second, these questions are inescapably involved in the present investigation. What I most wish to do is bring together a group of critical insights into the nature of Chaucer's poetry (some of them my own), a fresh inquiry into his explicit statements about poetry, and a reinterpretation of medieval poetic theory, so that they may illuminate and help to define each other. To bend a bit the favorite critical slogan of the late Leo Spitzer, I want to substitute a virtuous circle for what I have just been arguing is the vicious one, of defining the poem by the hypothetically presumed audience. My circle requires that we understand and analyze Chaucer's poetry as best we can by our own wit, knowledge, and intuition, plus any help we can get from his own statements about poetry and from medieval theory, and that we also consider the ways in which his poetry may be a kind of demonstration of what he or the theorists of the rhetorical poetic were talking about in their questions, definitions, and analyses.

The discovery of a discrepancy as great as some critics have pointed to between Chaucer's practice and the poetic theory of that tradition within which he worked should itself be a signal for caution. Critical language always works under a handicap of necessary ambiguity, and it is not uncommon that poetic practice may provide a useful commentary on contemporary critical theory, as well as the other way around. We cannot afford to reject by prior assumption the possibility that Chaucer's poetry may be a kind of maximal illustration of the meaning of the principles which the academic theorists were trying to define.

Criticism is not exclusively the pursuit of more sensitive or accurate readings, nor does it (at least in its intermediate objectives) necessarily imply evaluation. Of course, one applies oneself to Chaucer's poetry in the

first place because of the judgment that it is good enough
to merit the modern reader's serious and careful attention. But the criticism I attempt in this book is directed
at the means by which Chaucer's poetry gets its effects
—how it works and the aesthetic principles out of which
it develops. That is what I mean by "Chaucer's poetics"
in my subtitle. More particularly, I am interested in a
special function of poetics in Chaucer's poetry, one which
I think has been insufficiently explored, although it has
been indirectly recognized by several critics variously
concerned with his irony. I mean the way in which the
problems and operations of poetry and the poet are repeatedly raised into the consciousness of the reader, both
as general questions and as specific ones in the particular
poems. The result is that they add a peculiar dimension
to the other agencies of structure and style, demanding
our deliberate assent to their artifices. Such a thesis, particularly as it is developed in Chapter 7, may suggest
Coleridge's "willing suspension of disbelief," and the
association is not altogether irrelevant, but I think Coleridge's formula describes an agreement to recognize and
then forget artificial techniques in order to concentrate
response on their effects. The characteristic Chaucerian
procedure is to enforce a continuing consciousness of
technique, as a qualifying condition of effect.

It should become clear as this study progresses that
Chaucer's poetry does not reflect any stable, continuing
"solutions" to the questions about writing good poetry
which are so recurrent in his work. The relationship between his poetic practice and the body of orthodox
theory with which my study begins is variously experimental. Consequently, one has always to speak of the
poems in this connection as tentative ways of realizing
the terms, ideas, and theoretical prescripts of the traditional poetic in immediately practical compositional

situations, or as ways of testing the usefulness of the theories. Even the use of one structural stereotype four times (in what will be defined as the "combinative group" of poems) does not represent a decision on a best way, for these poems differ strikingly among themselves. Of these poems, only the *Book of the Duchess* approaches structural and thematic stability, and in his later poems Chaucer all but abandons that notion of structural order. For these reasons, the reader of this book should be prepared to hear a good deal more about "problems" and "questions" in Chaucer's work than about "solutions" and "answers," a situation forced upon the critic by Chaucer's own procedure.

The attempt to analyze such procedure both assumes some prior interpretation and inevitably produces some reinterpretation. Naturally I hope that this discussion will help to establish some more complex and more adequate readings of Chaucer's poems, but I certainly do not intend it to suggest that they are all about poetry, or that poetics is the exclusive theme of any of them. The verification of a hypothesis is as much a process of selective distortion in criticism as it is in the chemistry laboratory, and I have decided not to discuss some very important things in Chaucer's poetry, in order to concentrate on others. One consequence is that several useful and interesting studies are not mentioned in the documentation of this one. There are also points at which I have not paused to take into account differing, tangentially relevant, or conflicting opinion, because I have decided to present my own findings as far as possible in their own terms. "Tempest thee noght al croked to redresse" is as good advice for the critic as for any other pilgrim in this thoroughfare of woe. And it is a vain hope of the specialist that his work will reach or interest many readers who do not have a prior knowledge of the general foundations of previous scholarship on which it rests.

Especially in Chapter 5, on the *Canterbury Tales,* I have worked around and between previous studies. This is partly because there has in general been a good deal more attention given to the *Canterbury Tales,* and partly because their fragmentary incompleteness so limits their usefulness for my purpose. But it is mostly because Ralph Baldwin, in his *The Unity of the Canterbury Tales* (Copenhagen, 1955), has already done so well what I should otherwise have had to try to do. Consequently, I have not summarized or restated his conclusions, but simply consider my own as supplementary to them.

Finally, the order in which I have proceeded may require some explanation. My over-all scheme is first to characterize the rhetorical poetic which seems to have provided Chaucer's fundamental assumptions about the nature of poetry, then to assemble the direct evidence for his concern with the theoretical questions, and finally to indicate how his poems themselves reflect a range of experiments toward answering the questions. My procedure is thus more categorical than chronological; in particular, the Prologue to the *Legend of Good Women* and *Troilus and Criseyde* have been displaced. The Prologue is discussed early because I find it offers a fuller and more open account of the main issues in the Chaucerian poetic than any other single poem. *Troilus and Criseyde* has been left for the last two chapters in order that I might conclude by trying to analyze and define the most nearly satisfactory solution Chaucer seems to have achieved.

1. The Rhetorical Tradition

I

IN 1926 John Matthews Manly delivered an address[1] to the members of the British Academy, directing the attention of students of Chaucer's poetry to the operation in that poetry of a peculiarly medieval tradition of poetic style. Manly's paper did not pretend to be more than an exploratory examination of the subject (principally in connection with the *Canterbury Tales*), but it did attempt a general characterization of the rhetorical theory of composition and it suggested a developmental pattern in Chaucer's applications of that theory. For Manly, the art of poetry as conceived by the medieval rhetoricians was "purely mathematical in character, and seldom if ever conscious of basic aesthetic problems."

> The questions they raised were not questions of methods by which the writer might most perfectly develop his conception or of the means by which he might convey it to the audience. The elaborate system of technical devices was discussed only with reference to the form and structure of each device, never with reference to its emotional or aesthetic effects.[2]

1. "Chaucer and the Rhetoricians," *Proceedings of the British Academy, 12* (London, 1926).
2. Ibid., p. 10.

In accord, one most suppose, with his mathematical estimate of the rhetorical theory of poetry, Manly produced a chart of the "percentages of the larger rhetorical devices" in the major *Canterbury Tales*. The method by which these percentages were calculated is not discussed in the paper. The figures range from nearly 100 per cent in the Monk's tale to less than one per cent in the Friar's and Summoner's tales. These results are not precisely what one might have expected, in the light of the characterization quoted above, and Manly (as elsewhere in the lecture) suggests further investigation.[3] He does, however, state tentative conclusions which his own survey of the problem seems to indicate would be confirmed by further study. First, it is his opinion that Chaucer's poetic development is characterized by "the gradual replacement of formal rhetorical devices by methods of composition based on close observation of life and the exercise of creative imagination."[4] Second, the employment of the rhetorical devices which do remain in the later poetry is a greatly richer and more effective employment than would be possible on the sole basis of the philosophy of composition implicit in the rhetorical treatises.[5]

3. ". . . That some of Chaucer's freest and most delightful work should contain twice as much rhetoric as some of his least inspired work is a puzzle that demands investigation" (ibid., p. 16).

4. Ibid., p.5.

5. Manly apparently feels that the *House of Fame* was some sort of turning point in this growth of conscious powers. He quotes,

> O Thought, that wrot al that I mette,
> And in the tresorye hyt shette
> Of my brayn, now shal men se
> Yf any vertu in the be,
>
> . . . .
>
> And yif, devyne vertu, thow
> Wilt helpe me to shewe now
> That in myn hed ymarked is,

and then comments, "These passages, although the first is translated

Manly's lecture, then, is at bottom the recognition of a basic critical problem: the operation of literary convention upon the genius of the individual artist, or upon the structure of the particular work. It is perhaps only a subsidiary complication of that basic problem to consider the progressive changes in the effect of conventions upon the individual poet. Certainly, as the structure of Manly's lecture indicates, any discussion of such a critical problem must begin with an accurate characterization of the operative convention; it must also, of course, demonstrate the existence of significant traces of that convention in the work in question.

While Manly's lecture, tentative and exploratory as it was, depended largely upon assertion and representative example for the demonstration of the influence of rhetorical theory on Chaucer's style, the work of a later investigator has given chapter and verse to that text. Traugott Naunin,[6] sharing Manly's opinion of the character of the rhetorical tradition, though differing with him on the questions of relationships between it and Chaucer's poetry, makes a somewhat fuller statement of this evaluation of the aesthetic implications of medieval

---

from Dante, seem to me to express Chaucer's growing conviction that narration and description, instead of being mere exercises in clever phrasing, depend upon the use of visualizing imagination" (p. 17). And a few paragraphs further on he says that Chaucer grew to recognize that "the right way to amplify a story was not to expand it by rhetorical devices, but to conceive it in terms of the life he had observed so closely. . . . It is the dramatic use of the rhetorical devices which we must learn to recognize in the later and more artistic poems, and which must be taken into account in our examination of the percentages of rhetoric in the separate tales of the Canterbury pilgrimage" (p. 18).

6. *Der Einfluss der mittelalterlichen Rhetorik auf Chaucers Dichtung* (Bonn, 1929).

rhetoric,[7] and his constant emphasis is upon its "mathematical character":

> Poetry is thus a rational process, an art that can be learned.

> When the material was very familiar, the poet attempted to enliven the work by means of such occasional interpolations.

> Since rhetoric comprehends only the outer shape of poetry, it provides no proper definitions for figurative language. The rules which are given for making metaphors come nowhere near the heart of the problem. And if we recognise in Chaucer a development in the handling of metaphor, from the traditional forms to those of artistic boldness and power, we could find in this the evolution of a poet from within himself, but never the influence of rhetoric.[8]

The last of these statements is simply the logical extreme of the position taken by Manly: the principles of medieval rhetoric were so mechanical and nonpoetic in character that whatever is effective in Chaucer's poetry cannot possibly have resulted from their operation.[9]

Naunin then proceeds to catalogue the stock rhetorical devices in Chaucer's poetry, giving documentary sub-

7. Both Manly and Naunin relied almost exclusively upon Edmond Faral's famous study, *Les Arts poétiques du XIIe et du XIIIe siècle* (Paris, 1924); Faral prints, at the end of his study, the texts of four major medieval rhetorical treatises.

8. Naunin, pp. 2, 25, 30. Translation mine.

9. This is essentially the argument raised by William Empson in his "Donne and the Rhetorical Tradition," *Kenyon Review, 11* (1949), 571–87, written in reply to the attempt of Rosamond Tuve to demonstrate a strong rhetorical influence in the poetry of some sixteenth- and seventeenth-century English poets; see her *Elizabethan and Metaphysical Imagery* (Chicago, 1947).

stance to Manly's assertions about the extent to which such devices had become a part of Chaucer's poetic vocabulary. I suspect, however, that this list is rather different from the one Manly might have produced, since Naunin refuses to count as "rhetorical" any figures he feels to have genuine "poetic" functions.

> And we confront characters taken indeed from life, such as Nicholas, Alison, Absolon, and the Carpenter in the Miller's Tale, the two students and the Miller in the Reeve's Tale, the merchant's wife and John the monk in the Shipman's Tale, the Wife of Bath in her Prologue, ailing Thomas in the Summoner's Tale, the Summoner and Friar in their accounts of each other, January and May in the Merchant's Tale, Harry Bailey in the frame-story! These have nothing to do with the rhetorical prescriptions for *descriptio*.[10]

When all the figures have been compiled and catalogued, Naunin presents a picture quite different from Manly's. Chaucer was never, even in his earliest works, very deeply indebted to the rhetoricians, says Naunin. Furthermore, the degree to which he is indebted to them remains fairly constant throughout his poetic career. When Naunin encounters what Manly had characterized as "the more richly dramatic use of rhetorical devices," he simply does not admit any connection with the mathematical and unpoetic principles of the thirteenth-century formulators. French models, real life, the general literary taste of the Middle Ages, and Chaucer's "dramatic sense" are all invoked to explain away much of what Manly had ascribed to the influence of rhetoric. Late in his study, however, Naunin seems more willing to ac-

10. Naunin, p. 29.

knowledge some poetic value in what he does grant to
be the "rhetorical element" in Chaucer's poetry:

> In the master hand of Chaucer, rhetoric became an
> inevitable and necessary constituent of his poems.
> If one were to cut it out of them, one would have
> more dramatically effective, but not intrinsically
> more valuable poems.[11]

But in the end, Naunin re-emphasizes that throughout
his career what Chaucer did not get from the rhetoricians
was far more and more important than what he did get
from them, that little of his best poetry is explainable in
terms of the rhetorical discipline, and that Chaucer's development cannot be significantly measured in terms of
his attitudes toward the rhetorical doctrines.

> Chaucer's development proceeds not as a disen-
> tanglement from rhetoric, but as a transition from
> the medieval spirit to modern ideas. What is mod-
> ern is the Individual that we find in his poems, and
> the high humor that everywhere prevails. His spir-
> itual outlook is modern, and his critical attitude to
> what was in his time universally accepted. But the
> form he uses is medieval indeed . . . So his modern
> ideas often appear in medieval form. Exactly in that
> may we recognize his transitional character. He
> stands at the borders of two worlds.[12]

It must be apparent that both Manly's and Naunin's
studies raise questions which neither answers satisfactorily. Perhaps the most obvious of these arises from the
fact that neither Manly's percentage tables nor Naunin's
catalogue of rhetorical figures tells us anything about the
operation of particular stylistic devices in their poetic

11. Ibid., p. 54.
12. Idem.

contexts. Such a question, in turn, presupposes the larger
one of whether a particular device or technique can be
rhetorical and poetically functional at the same time.
That is, can a literary convention be genuinely and per-
vasively operative in the work of a poet without either
losing its own character or destroying the individual
character of the work in question? Manly's explanation,
that Chaucer was outgrowing the influence of the convention when he came to use it more effectively, is no
more satisfactory, on these terms, than Naunin's simpler
assertion that the convention itself could not have produced much of genuine poetic worth.

But at the least we should ask that such a characterization of medieval rhetorical theory be supported and
justified. Both Manly and Naunin refer to Faral as the
immediate authority for their statements concerning
medieval rhetoric, and yet Faral himself is certainly more
moderate in his judgments, despite the fact that he introduces his discussion with some adverse criticism:

> À la base, une définition insuffisante des facultés de
> l'intelligence; à l'application des vues très incer-
> taines sur les fonctions de l'art; un ordre superficiel,
> dénué de logique profonde; un classement des
> principes qui, faute d'une analyse préalable assez
> poussée du genre d'opérations qu'ils concernent,
> sent le faux; bref, pas de philosophie satisfaisante:
> voilà les défauts que, sans sévérité excessive, on est
> en droit d'accuser.
>
> [But] on aura saisi un des ressorts importants de la
> création artistique: le métier, à côté du génie—le
> métier qui au moyen âge, a eu une importance aussi
> grande qu'à n'importe quelle époque.[13]

13. Faral, pp. xv–xvi.

Furthermore, some six years after the publication of
Manly's lecture, a more careful reader of the rhetorical
treatises had pointed out that the very statements in the
House of Fame upon which Manly had based his assertion of Chaucer's displacement of the older rhetorical by
the new psychological method "were themselves only restatements (in rhetorical form!) of common ideas in
many of the rhetorical treatises."[14] Miss Hamilton help-
fully quotes, as a supporting parallel, five lines from
Troilus and Criseyde which are translated from Geoffrey
of Vinsauf:

> For everi wight that hath an hous to founde
> Ne renneth naught the werk for to bygynne
> With rakel hond, but he wol bide a stounde,
> And sende his hertes line out fro withinne
> Aldirfirst his purpos for to wynne.   (1.1065–69)

This is the only serious statement of general aesthetic
principle that Chaucer takes directly from the rhetorical
theorists. It is also a sufficiently general one to allow a
wide range of practical inferences as to the imaginative
as well as the technical aspects of the art of composition.
But wherever such a statement is encountered, in living
poetry or in dead theory, we are obligated to consider
the possibilities for reconciling the practical inferences
with the general statement, and perhaps to revise our
estimate of the relationships between the theory and
the poetry. It is true, as Miss Hamilton points out, that
this statement, though unique in Chaucer's work, is not
the only one of its kind among the rhetorical treatises. It
may be debatable whether such declarations are merely
introductory flourishes by the rhetoricians, or whether
they actually constitute an attempt to give a broader

14. Marie P. Hamilton, "Notes on Chaucer and the Rhetoricians,"
PMLA, 47 (1932), 403–09.

aesthetic basis to the manuals of style; it is certain that
the question cannot be debated honestly if we approach
it with a presupposition that any such statement is not
to be taken seriously.[15] Neither is it necessary, of course,
to conclude that because Chaucer shares with the rhetoricians principles like the one mentioned above, the
rhetoricians must be solely and directly responsible for
"teaching" him those principles. One of the most useful
lessons that modern criticism has learned is that literary
influences are seldom or never that neatly (or superficially) formulated. An aesthetic theory may be as much a
product or an expression of the principles of its age as it
is a formulator of them. It may also, even as formulator
of literary principles, promulgate those principles as effectively through general impact upon the standards and
practices of the period as through immediate influence
upon particular poets. Miss Hamilton, in her regrettably
sketchy criticism of Manly's lecture, voices this warning
quite precisely:

> Such theories about writing as Chaucer did not find
> merely in the rhetoricians were doubtless strength-
> ened for him when he met them there—the doc-
> trine, for example, that the artist must vividly con-
> ceive his creation before giving it bodily form.[16]

If such questions as have been raised in the preceding
few pages be admitted, it becomes necessary both to
state the problem of "Chaucer and the rhetorical tradition" in different terms and to seek a different kind of
solution for it. For if the medieval rhetorical tradition

15. The point I am making here was developed a good deal more
fully by Dorothy Everett in her Gollancz Memorial Lecture, "Some Reflections on Chaucer's 'Art Poetical'," *Proceedings of the British Academy, 36* (Oxford, 1950).
16. Hamilton, p. 406.

contains even a possibility of genuinely poetic application, then conclusions based on the more or less quantitative measurement of Chaucer's development in terms
of how much or little of that tradition is discernible in
his poetry are of little use. Those who have criticized the
medieval rhetoricians so severely for their failure to deal
with basic affective relationships between language, image, and structure have too often been guilty of the same
fault themselves, producing catalogues rather than criticism. The real question is not whether Chaucer employs
occasional stylistic devices which the rhetoricians happen
to have tabulated, but whether whole poems—good or
even great poems—can be produced in the aesthetic tradition which the rhetorical manuals represent.

Certain qualifications must be made if the question is
to be considered in such terms. Most obviously, many
details of the rhetorical system will become meaningless
if applied to vernacular poetry. Perhaps this stricture
should be asserted more positively: the rhetorical manuals are primarily pedagogical devices produced by
schoolmasters whose whole literary orientation was
Latin. They are codifications of the responses of those
men to Latin poetry—largely classical Latin poetry.
Hence any influence they may have had upon subsequent
vernacular poetry is more or less indirect, and certainly
not intended by their authors. More important, however, is the fact that generations of medieval university
students were taught from these manuals, and by the men
who wrote them; the teachers themselves were products
of the same culture, the same educational system. That
is, if we are to come near to understanding the importance of such writings, we must see them whole, not only
as formulative, but as representative of a way of thinking
about poetry. It is a way of thinking about poetry which
Dante and Chaucer and Geoffrey of Vinsauf shared alike,

however incongruous those three names might seem if
we were speaking in terms of their personal attributes
or of the qualities of the art they produced. It is a way
of thinking which does not exist only in the specific
rhetorical documents that survive the age, and when I
speak of the rhetorical tradition, the reference is not
limited to the contents of a handful of school texts produced in the thirteenth century. It is a relatively simple
matter to demonstrate that Chaucer knew some of those
texts,[17] but it is useless to try to distinguish what he
learned there from what Guillaume de Lorris or Dante
or Machault may have taught him if the aesthetic lessons
are the same.

II

Yeats said "Out of the quarrel with others, we make
rhetoric; out of the quarrel with ourselves, we make
poetry." This modern and essentially romantic view
makes poetry and rhetoric both fundamentally demon-
strative arts, but it distinguishes them in terms of the
public as against the *private* nature of the demonstration.
W. H. Auden, in his "Elegy for W. B. Yeats" expresses
a similar estimate of the essentially private nature of
whatever demonstration poetry makes:

> . . . mad Ireland hurt you into poetry
> Now Ireland has her madness and her weather still
> For poetry makes nothing happen: it survives
> In the valley of its saying where executives
> Would never want to tamper; it flows south
> From ranches of isolation and the busy griefs,
> Raw towns that we believe and die in; it survives
> A way of happening, a mouth.[18]

17. Cf. Manly and Naunin.
18. Quoted from *The Collected Poetry of W. H. Auden* (New York,
1945), p. 50.

Poetry, in such a view, must therefore be sharply separated from rhetoric, in that rhetoric, in any of its common historical senses from Platonic through Ramistic, must make something happen. Even leaving intent aside, the management of language (which we might expect, following Aristotle, to be similar in the two arts) must be very different in the poetic projection of the private vision from what it is in the affective public demonstration of the better and the worse choice. For instance, the latter must to a considerable extent deal in clichés (both of substance and of structure), since it seeks a community of response, from common motives toward a generally approved (i.e. "ethical") choice.

But there does remain, behind this sharp distinction between rhetoric and poetic a point of contact, or a kind of sense of mutual responsibility, between rhetoric as it was classically defined and poetry as Yeats and Auden defined it. This common responsibility is probably best stated as a question to be resolved by theorists of the two arts: What sorts of ethical compulsion are laid, either separately or in common, upon the two arts? Yeats' formula called poetry "a quarrel with ourselves," an attempt to resolve some conflict of possibilities within the poet's own nature. This pursuit (or creation) of one's private vision of the good is, not only in Yeats but through much romantic and modern poetry, essentially a moral pursuit, and the extreme anti-rhetorical, anti-rational, anti-systematic character of the style of some modern poetry follows the transfer of the biting ethical questions from the domain of public decision to that of individual vision.

Aristotle's system of rhetoric fairly clearly defined two sorts of ethical force operative in persuasion: "ethics"— the system of right actions, defined in terms of the general order of ideas and of society; and "ethos"—the particular nature of a man, as determined by his individual capabilities and the particular motives, beliefs, and choices those capabilities have led him to. But for Aristotle, the former operated upon the whole art, especially in establishing its purposive norms; the latter operated only as a technique in the individual's practice of the art. The romantic (and often the modern) poet, in his distrust of publicly defined ethical systems, also comes to distrust the orderly system of persuasion, rhetoric, which had historically claimed to mediate between the general truths of systematic ethics and general human emotional response.

So if we define rhetoric and poetic as two arts concerned primarily with the management of language; and if, like Yeats and Aristotle, we distinguish them basically in terms of purpose (from which differences in form follow); then we must logically conclude that as the purposes defined for the two arts by various value systems move closer together, the formal analyses offered for the two arts will tend more and more to coincide. Further, even in the two extreme views I have mentioned (extreme in their separation of poetry from rhetoric) the problem of the relation of art to ethics is central, and we may start from that observation in examining some of the various alignments of poetry, rhetoric, and ethics. Generally, I think there are three archetypical alignments, which may help to identify and limit the one we are to be particularly concerned with:

1. The "Aristotelian" view,[19] in which poetic and rhetoric are distinct largely because rhetoric is *essentially* an ethical art and poetry is committed

---

19. I label this an "Aristotelian" view in full awareness that no one quite understands what ideas about the relationships between poetry and truth are bound up in Aristotle's terms "mimesis" and "catharsis."

to mimetic and emotional functions which seem
to be only indirectly, if at all, ethical.

2. The Horatian–Medieval Christian–Renaissance
   Rationalist view, in which poetic and rhetoric are
   identical, being only alternative terms for the
   ordered use of compelling language (eloquence)
   in ethical demonstration. Both have the single
   function of mediating between man's desires and
   his moral sense.

3. The romantic view (which I have represented
   above in Yeats' aphorism), in which poetry is distinct from rhetoric because bound to the private
   ethos, the imaginative creation of a better self,
   while only rhetoric has any persuasive efficacy
   relative to systematic social conduct.

Rhetoric and poetic become more and less related arts
as their separate relationships to ethics become more and
less similar.

III

In his monumental survey of the formative influence
of medieval Europe's Classical heritage,[20] Ernst Robert
Curtius begins by characterizing the broad philosophical
and theological concepts which underlie many of the
phenomena of medieval culture. Since the rhetorical
theory of composition is one of these phenomena, and
since it is itself so excellent an example of a medieval
reconstruction out of classical ruins, it will be necessary
to consider rather carefully here some of Curtius' conclusions. The point of departure for his whole study is a

20. *Europäische Literatur und lateinisches Mittelalter* (Bern, 1948);
Eng. trans. Willard R. Trask, *European Literature and the Latin Middle
Ages* (New York, 1953). All quotations in the text are from the Trask
translation.

somewhat modified and expanded statement of the familiar medieval historical perspective:

> "medieval Antiquity." Which means Antiquity as the Middle Ages saw it. The concept is as valid for literature as it is for the visual arts. Antiquity has a twofold life in the Middle Ages: reception and transformation. This transformation can take very various forms. It can mean impoverishment, degeneration, devitalization, misunderstanding; but it can also mean critical collecting (the encyclopedias of Isidore and Raban Maur), schoolboyish copying, enthusiastic empathy.[21]

While it is no longer necessary to point out that this qualitative rather than chronological sense of history was not simply the result of inordinate naïveté in medieval thinkers, it may be useful to consider the relation of such a perspective to other areas of thought. Such an attitude is rooted in the central Christian doctrines of creation as wholly a manifestation of the Divine Will, and of ultimate reality as eternally existent in that Will. As early as Augustine, the consequent view of the historical past is foreshadowed in his often-cited claim, in the *Confessions* (Book VII), that whatever is good and true among the ancient writings belongs to Christian doctrine. Curtius traces this view directly, through medieval commentaries, to the Bible.

> The Bible furnished medieval historical thought with yet another theological substantiation for the replacement of one empire by another: "Regnum a gente in gentem transfertur propter injustitias et injurias et contumelias et diversos dolos" (Ecclesiasticus 10:8). "Because of unrighteous dealings, injur-

21. Ibid., p. 19.

ies, and riches got by deceit, the kingdom is transferred from one people to another." The word
transfertur ("it is transferred") gives rise to the concept of *translatio* (transference) which is basic for
medieval historical theory. The renewal of the Empire by Charlemagne could be regarded as a transferal of the Roman *imperium* to another people.
This is implied in the formula *translatio imperii*,
with which the *translatio studii* (transferal of learning from Athens or Rome to Paris) was later co-ordi-
nated. The medieval Empire took over from Rome
the idea of world empire; thus it had a universal,
not national, character.

Meanwhile, let us not forget that the "Latin Middle
Ages" is nowise limited to the idea of Rome in the
sense of a glorification of Rome or of an effort to
renew it. The concept of *translatio,* indeed, implies
that the transference of dominion from one empire
to another is the result of sinful misuse of that dominion.[22]

This particular expression of the pervasive Christian
idealism of the Middle Ages casts a rather different light
upon the concept of "classical authority," in the name of
which much in medieval literature has been dismissed
without explanation. It is apparent from many sources
that the orthodox attitude is an ambivalent one. Augus-

22. Ibid., pp. 28–29. Chaucer paraphrases the Biblical Latin in *Troilus and Criseyde:*

> Fortune, which that permutacioun
> Of thynges hath, as it is hire comitted
> Thorugh purveyaunce and disposicioun
> Of heighe Jove, as regnes shal be flitted
> Fro folk in folk, or when they shal be smytted,
> Gan pulle awey the fetheres brighte of Troie
> Fro day to day, til they ben bare of joie. [v. 1541–47]

tine and Jerome, in their famous struggles with con-
science over pagan classical thought and literature, simply record another sort of experience of the same feelings
which Curtius discusses in the passage just quoted. At
a later date, and in a context perhaps more immediately
pertinent to the present study, a scholarly cleric characterizes the poetry of Vergil, in the same ambivalent
terms, as a "beautiful vase full of vipers."[23] In these, or
any number of similar examples, one is in constant danger of disturbing what must have been a rather delicate
balance of emphasis. Just as the medieval theologian (or
historian) saw no contradiction in the idea of a power
which was intrinsically good but embodied in evil or
corrupt institutions, so the medieval critic could respond
to the formal perfection of an art the substance of which
was abhorrent to him. The problem became one of separating the vase from the vipers, at the same time preserving it intact for the conveyance of venomless viands.

But to return to the argument at hand, there are two
pertinent inferences to be made from the above data.
First, medieval thinkers were constantly aware of and
influenced by the traditions of classical philosophy and
art, especially Roman, which lay behind them. Second,
and more important for this discussion, they felt no compulsion to be concerned for the historical integrity of
those traditions. What was important in them was whatever they might offer which would be true and useful—
that is, whatever the necessarily half-blind pagans might
have been able to perceive of eternal verities. And what
the medieval world was most quick to grant and admire
in the classical tradition was the perfection of form,

---

23. Quoted in J. L. Paetow, "The Arts Course at Medieval Universities,
with Especial Reference to Grammar and Rhetoric," *Univ. of Illinois
Studies, 3,* 20. See also Kemp Malone, "Beowulf," *English Studies, 29*
(1948), 161–72.

method, technique—such virtues as the reason might achieve without the aid of revelation. The types of perfection, at least insofar as human institutions are concerned, became for the orthodox the embodiment of the ideal substance of medieval Christianity in the perfect or near-perfect forms of classical antiquity: a Christian philosophy with the logical and metaphysical solidity of Aristotle; a Holy Roman empire with the legal and administrative cohesion of Augustan Rome; a Christian epic of the formal perfection of the *Aeneid*. Even in such an attitude, the medieval thinker could find scriptural support.

> From the verse in the Psalms, "in omnem terram exivit sonus eorum" (Vulg. Ps. 18:5): "their sound went out over all the earth." In the Authorized Version this is Psalm 19, beginning: "The heavens declare the glory of God . . . There is no speech nor language, where their voice is not heard." The reference is to the speech of the heavens, which declare the glory of God throughout the world. But Cassiodorus reads the words of the Psalm allegorically as meaning that the Old Testament was known to all peoples. *Thus the pagans could learn all the arts of rhetoric and reduce them to a system.*[24]

It is the medieval sense of order and system in classical art and philosophy, and the closely related desire to construct new, Christian systems equally satisfying to the reason, which are most significant to the present discussion. For it is that belief in the unified, ordered, and systematic character of reality, and hence of all human knowledge, which gives to the medieval educational

24. Curtius, p. 41; italics mine.

system its particular character, and it is within the universities that the aesthetic theory under discussion was conceived and nurtured.

The bare outlines of the medieval university are probably themselves part of the legacy of the crumbling fourth- and fifth-century Roman culture. Through Martianus Capella, who first specifically separates and defines the seven liberal arts,[25] there descends into the Middle Ages the well-known outline of an educational system divided according to seven clearly designated areas of knowledge, which areas in turn fall into the two groups of preparatory and advanced studies, the *trivium* and the *quadrivium*. It is not so much the division of learning into separate, regularized disciplines which is noteworthy in that system, although the divisions are significantly revelatory of the rational and analytical character of the medieval intellectual world. Far more striking is the integration of the separate disciplines (in the ideal, if not always in practice) into a single, grandly conceived program with the single, lofty purpose of opening to the industrious student the two great textbooks of the body of pagan classical learning and of the universe around him. To the liberally educated man who has learned to distinguish aright, the heathens and the heavens alike declare the glory of God. As one of the greatest of medieval educators put it, *Totius philosophiae unicum ac singulare instrumentum*.[26]

Nor should we lose sight of the fact that the system itself—the pattern of its organization—was more than a pedagogical convenience. Just as the several "arts" were more than merely "subject matters" in the modern

25. *De nuptiis Mercurii et Philologiae.*
26. Theodore of Chartres, quoted in L'Abbé Clerval, *Les Écoles de Chartres* (Chartres, 1895), p. 225.

sense,[27] so the systematic arrangement of them was somehow felt to correspond to the natural order of things.[28]
It was the necessary arrangement of knowledge and the
only adequate one. The only matters which lay outside
the range of that organization of knowledge were matters
of divine revelation—matters eternally beyond the reach
of human reason, even though humans might possess a
certain kind of awareness of them. Thus of the two areas
of knowledge so clearly marked off by Scholastic philosophy, the medieval university claimed as its exclusive
province the lower one, the ordered universe perceptible
to rational man.

Not that truths existing in the lower area could ever
contradict those evident in the higher; indeed, the first
test of right reason was its compatibility with the self-
evident truths of revelation. Or to put it in a manner
closer to the heart of medieval Christian idealism, the
lower order of knowledge (which *could* be perceived independent of revelation) was simply a dim reflection, a
cruder, material symbol, of the higher. And we have here
come back to a question bearing upon the attitude of
the medieval world toward the classical. It was a fact that
much of what Greece and Rome had accomplished was
eminently and eternally true and useful, and the question of historical integrity was simply an irrelevant one.
The giants of the pre-Christian era were to be respected
and studied, the more so for the fact that so much of the
order of the universe had been perceived by them without the aid of revelation. The obligation of Christian

27. "Der Begriff *ars* . . . bedeutet 'Lehre' in dem Sinn, den das Wort
in 'Sprachlehre' hat." Curtius, p. 45.
28. "Die *artes* sind für das Mittelalter bis zum 12. Jahrhundert die
Fundamentalordnung des Geistes. Nur das zentrale Ereignis der Heils-
geschichte, die Inkarnation, konnte, ja musste, sie durchbrechen." Ibid.,
p. 50.

education was to equip the thinking man with the tools
perfected by classical civilization in order that he might,
in the light of divine revelation, discover the whole
truth. Gilson has summed up these attitudes in a famous
defense of Scholastic philosophy:

> Ils [Aristotle and Plato] n'ont pas erré dans leurs
> questions, car c'est bien le problème de l'être qu'ils
> posaient et c'est pourquoi leurs formules restent
> bonnes; la raison des penseurs du XIIIe siècle s'y
> retrouvait, non seulement sans peine, mais avec joie,
> parce qu'elle y pouvait lire des vérités qu'elles con-
> tiennent, bien que ni Platon ni Aristote lui-même
> ne les y aient déchiffrées. . . . Platon et Aristote ont
> construit une arche magnifique dont toutes les
> pierres montent vers cette clef de voûte, mais elle
> n'a été mise en place que grâce à la Bible et ce sont
> des chrétiens qui l'ont posée.[29]

Even at intellectual altitudes well below the frosty
peaks of Saint Thomas, medieval schoolmen were clearly
aware of their place and function in the order of Christian knowledge, and of their relationships to the great
classical culture of which they were conscious heirs.
While it is perhaps an anachronism to speak of an "educational philosophy" in the thirteenth century, still we
can discover some revealing statements of principle by
men actively engaged in the organization and administra-
tion of universities. Theodore of Chartres, again, affords
one of the most revealing of such statements, reminiscent
of Dean Swift or Messrs. Temple and Wotton:

> We are dwarfs seated on the shoulders of the an-
> cients as on the shoulders of giants. If we see more

29. Etienne Gilson, *L'Esprit de la philosophie médiévale* (Paris, 1932),
pp. 85–86.

and farther than they, it is not because of the pene-
tration of our sight, nor of our grandeur; it is because we are elevated by them, and borne to a
gigantic height.[30]

What had been achieved before the thirteenth century
was a rationally ordered discipline of learning, based
upon whatever the Middle Ages could salvage out of the
wreckage of classical antiquity, and supplemented by the
Christian revelation. Each of the carefully graded *artes*
which composed the hierarchy of learning was itself as
carefully systematic as the whole; what was not reasonable was simply not teachable,[31] and what was reasonable
must be systematic, ordered, subject to analysis. Perhaps
the most important point to be made here in preparation
for the discussion of rhetorical theory is that literature,
insofar as it was a part of this major phase of medieval
intellectual history, was so by virtue of its inclusion in
the lower levels of this systematic hierarchy.[32]

When Paetow[33] states that the arts course at medieval
universities contained no study of Latin literary classics,
he should be taken to mean that there was no specified
section of the arts course exclusively devoted to formal
study of Latin literature as literature. His statement is
misleading, however; a quick glance at the records of
curricula at any medieval school or university (at least as

30. Quoted by Clerval, p. 227; translation mine.
31. This included the mysteries of revelation, e.g. the Incarnation,
which could be "known," but not analyzed or taught. "Als der Schöpfer
Geschöpf wurde *(factor factus est factura)*, waren alle *artes* ausser Kraft
gesetzt; *in hac verbi copula stupet omnis regula.*" Curtius, p. 50.
32. "Seitdem [sixth century] ist die Literatur Schulfach, und die
Kontinuität der europäischen Literatur ist an die Schule gebunden.
Das Bildungswesen wird Träger der literarischen Tradition: ein Tat-
bestand, der zur Charakteristik Europas gehört, der aber nicht wesens-
mässig bedingt ist." Curtius, p. 44.
33. "Arts Course," ch. 1.

far back as the tenth century) will confirm the fact that
Latin poetry was the substance upon which pupils in
the elementary courses, grammar and rhetoric, constantly worked.[34] Quintilian's definition of the twofold purpose of the study of grammar is everywhere adopted and
applied: *recte loquendi scientiam et poetarum enarra-
tionem.* During the peak period of literary interest, in
the latter half of the twelfth century, students of grammar and rhetoric were getting healthy doses of Vergil,
Horace, Statius, and Ovid, among others.

Two important conclusions are to be reached. First,
and most significant, literature was being read in the
schools; what the student in the twelfth or thirteenth
century knew of poetry, he knew in the systematic terms
in which knowledge was possible. Second, literature was
read in order to perfect other sorts of knowledge; it was
the primary substance of the two most elementary disciplines in the liberal arts curriculum, and those two disciplines had a common end: the fluent and accurate use
of the Latin language. The second half of Quintilian's
much-quoted definition had become simply another step
in the mastery of the language and in training for the
fullest use of it. Even as the Augustinian distrust relaxes
into a more permissive attitude toward Christian poetry,
it is always Christian first and poetry second. In a round-
about way, the orthodox theory of literature had, well
before the twelfth century, developed a close counterpart of the Aristotelian concept of the persuasive art of
rhetoric, dependent upon things outside itself for substance and purpose.[35] Just as Aristotle, in the first book

34. See Clerval, pp. 222–23, for a list of authors whose works were
used in these courses at Chartres in the eleventh and twelfth centuries.
35. Augustine, *De doctrina Christiana*, Bk. IV: "Such is the message
that the words in which it is expressed seem not to be sought by the
speaker but to subserve that message naturally, as if one saw philosophy

of the *Rhetoric,* had been careful to point out that if men were as reasonable as they ought to be there would be no need of an art of rhetoric, so there was a constant feeling (often explicitly stated) among the medieval schoolmen that poetry was useful mainly in discourse to those who were incapable of coming at the truth more directly. Vincent of Beauvais offers a typical statement of this view:

> *Poetica* is the lore of ordering meters according to the proportion of words [*dictiones*] and the times of feet and of their rhythms [*numeri*]. . . . It belongs to *poetica* to make the hearer through its locutions image something as fair or foul which is not so, so that he may believe and shun or desire it. Although certainly it is not so in truth, nevertheless, the minds of the hearers are roused to shun or desire what they image. . . . The function of the poet, then, is this, that with a certain beauty he converts actual events into other species by his slanting figures.[36]

If we put Vincent's statement, and others like it, back into their contexts, the place of literary studies in general and of poetry in particular becomes even more evident. The *Speculum doctrinale* is the second part of Vincent's compendium of universal knowledge, two books of which

---

issuing from her own home in the heart of the philosopher, and eloquence following as an inseparable servant even when not called." Cf. the greater tolerance of stylistic polish in Rabanus Maurus' statement concerning the same question: "Nevertheless [rhetoric] is not outside the scope of training for the church. For whatever an orator or preacher of the divine law sets out capably and fitly in teaching, whatever he expresses aptly and elegantly in letters, conforms to this art." (*De clericum institutione,* III.xix.)

36. *Speculum doctrinale,* Ch. 108–09; translated in Charles Baldwin, *Medieval Rhetoric and Poetic* (New York, 1928), pp. 175–76; cited hereafter as Baldwin, *MRP.*

are devoted to the *trivium*. In these two books, ninety-eight chapters are given over to *logica,* ten to *rhetorica,* twenty-three to *poetica;* parts of the section on *rhetorica,* together with most of *poetica,* seem to be intended to cover the area of *grammatica.* Perhaps the pertinence of such statistical evidence can be borne out best by a glance at some more general discussion of the functions of the trivial arts.[37] In the thirteenth century, the *Anticlaudianus,* a sprawling doctrinal allegory by the indefatigable Alanus de Insulis, has as its central motif the function of education in the redemption of mankind. Each of the particular *artes* is defined according to the contribution it makes to that function. Baldwin summarizes the pertinent sections:

> The seven arts are summoned to provide Prudentia with a chariot for her quest on behalf of man. *Grammatica* supplies the pole; *Logica* the axle, which *Rhetorica* adorns with gems and gold; the *Quadrivium,* the four wheels. The horses, the five senses, are then harnessed by *Ratio.* When the upward journey has reached the term of human powers, *Prudentia,* leaving her chariot, is conducted by *Theologica* into the empyrean, to the saints, to Mary, to God himself.[38]

Rhetorica and poetry have become practically equivalent in the thirteenth century, save for that branch of rhetoric which split off and developed separately in the *ars dictaminis.* Textbooks for rhetoric are beginning to appear under such titles as *Poetria nova.* It is therefore doubly

37. The sense of modern English "trivial" no doubt exaggerates one aspect of "trivium," but at least the possibility for the modern meaning was there, in that the group of three was, from the beginning, the elementary or lesser group.
38. Baldwin, *MRP,* p. 173.

interesting to note that for Alanus, *rhetorica* is the only
one of the seven liberal arts which is given no direct
function in the process of education for salvation.

Even so great a "humanist" as John of Salisbury reflects a similar sense of the relative unimportance of
literature in the whole scheme of things. His *Metalogicus*
sets forth a reasoned survey of the *trivium,* which is defined as the total body of teaching dealing with words.
The organization of the discussion, and the primacy of
logica throughout, speak for themselves. Baldwin outlines the contents:[39]

$$
logica \begin{cases} grammatica \begin{cases} scientia\ recte\ loquendi\ scribendique \\ poetica \end{cases} \\[2em] ratio \\ disserendi \end{cases} \begin{cases} demonstrativa \\ \dots probabilis \begin{cases} dialectica \\ rhetorica \end{cases} \\ sophistica \end{cases}
$$

The purpose here is not to prove that the schools
scorned poetry—which is palpably not the case—but
rather to place poetry as precisely as possible in the medieval scale of educational values. If we are to understand
at all properly or sympathetically the theory of poetry
which the schoolmen produced, we must know that poetry did not have the importance, officially at least, to
John of Salisbury and Geoffrey of Vinsauf that it had
to later Christian-humanist-idealists like Sidney and
Milton. It should be increasingly clear that the inclusion
of reading, criticizing, and composing poetry among the
lowest of the scholastic disciplines had a direct and pervasive effect upon the character of medieval poetic the-

39. Ibid., p. 158.

ory, and a considerable though probably less direct effect on medieval poetry.

Before looking closely at the literary theory embodied in the *artes* of grammar and rhetoric, however, we should note that the fully developed rhetorical concept of the art of poetry does not appear until late in the twelfth century, although most of the principles of which the "new" theory is composed are discoverable in preceding centuries. What is most new about such works as Geoffrey of Vinsauf's *Poetria nova* is the assembly and codification of these scattered principles into an art of poetry.

According to Faral's datings,[40] nearly all the important rhetorical *arts poétiques* appeared in the last quarter of the twelfth century and the first half of the thirteenth, and according to Paetow, these are the years of the peak and decline of interest in classical literature in the grammar and rhetoric courses.[41] They are also the years of a running battle in the universities between the "ancients" and the "moderns"—those who prefer to teach the elementary arts by precept and example from the best classical authors, and those who would place them on a thoroughly logical and speculative basis.[42] The rhetorical treatises, almost as though in conscious compromise, offer a thoroughly scholastic, dialectical analysis of poetic theory and practice, everywhere supported with quotation and example from classical (and sometimes medieval) Latin poetry.

40. Faral, Preface and Ch. I. He lists ca. ten "arts of poetry" (as distinct from the also rhetorical *artes sermocinandi* and *artes dictandi*) as of major importance.

41. ". . . Chartres was a truly humanistic center [in the middle of the twelfth century] where flourished the belles lettres based on a sympathetic study of the ancient classics" (Paetow, p. 13). But with the rapid rise of the universities in the first half of the thirteenth century, classical interest falls off; see ibid., p. 16, for Jean de Garlande's lament of the decay and plea for the revival of the classical tradition.

42. Duns Scotus actually composed a *Grammatica speculativa*.

This battle of ancients and moderns, however, is probably not the primary cause for the particular character of these early thirteenth-century documents. Of deeper significance is the development, mentioned above, of a kind of orthodox point of view toward literature, and the absorption of literary study and production into the scholastic system, first of the monastic and cathedral schools, and later of the universities. To the extent that the thirteenth-century rhetorical theories are based on classical poetry, they are so in full consciousness that it is the *technique* of that poetry which is of importance to Christian education. If the substance has any value, it is only when it is susceptible of allegorical interpretation, or where it has typical or exemplary value. In theory itself, of course, the ancients (or such of them as the Middle Ages knew) were trustworthy enough, for such theoretical abstractions were works of the rational and analytic faculties. Hence, the two books of Cicero's *De inventione* which the Middle Ages knew, the pseudo-Ciceronian *Auctor ad Herennium,* and (to a considerably lesser extent) Horace's *Ars poetica* provide the framework and terminology for all their medieval successors. But without the development of attitudes toward the classical past and the Christian present which are essential to the medieval educational ideal, the theory of poetry with which we are dealing would scarcely have emerged at all.[43]

43. The remainder of this discussion of the rhetorical doctrines is based on the texts printed by Faral in the second part of his volume. These include Matthieu de Vendome, *Ars versificatoria;* Geoffrey of Vinsauf, *Poetria nova, Documentum de modo et arte dictandi et versificandi, Summa de coloribus rhetoricis;* Gervais de Melkley, *Ars versificaria* (résumé only); and Evrard l'Allemand, *Laborintus.* For the text of Jean de Garlande's *Poetria,* I have used G. Mari's edition in *Romanische Forschungen, 13* (1902), 883 ff. Subsequent references to these works refer to these editions.

IV

The first and probably the most important problem presented by medieval literary theory is simple, obvious, and by no means easily solved: just how did what had been two clear and distinct sets of ideas for Aristotle—rhetoric and poetic—come to be confused and merged in a hybrid that often seems to be neither one nor the other? Certainly the functions and provinces of each are clearly indicated in Aristotle's discussions, although the *Poetics* is much less satisfactory than the *Rhetoric,* in this as well as in other respects. The distinction goes a good deal deeper than the level of style; it is most clear, in fact, with respect to modes and purposes of composition. Rhetoric was, for Aristotle, an art which had its scientific counterpart in dialectic; its function was in public debate, and its legitimate effect, persuasion to action. Poetry (or at least epic and tragedy) was an art of the imagination with no scientific counterpart; its legitimate effect was emotional response and it moved men not to action, but to joy, pity, fear, contemplation, etc. In both cases, Aristotle's attack is at the compositional level, in terms of over-all structure, and in the *Poetics* he scarcely touches on questions of style at all. In the *Rhetoric,* where he does devote half of Book III to style, he refers frequently to the *Poetics,* and repeatedly points out that in matters of style, rhetoric and poetic have much in common. Even though he maintains a constant distinction between the utilitarian affectiveness of prose style and the emotional efficacy of poetry, Aristotle is clear in his implication that the techniques of style (which had long been the province of poets) were the same for, and equally the concern of, both. Herein lay the seeds of confusion—and of a long and significant development in late Rome and the early Middle Ages.

Aristotle treats rhetoric itself under two general head-
ings, style and arrangement, although he has in Book I
considered the question of "invention," or gathering and
analysis of material. The question of delivery is handled
more or less digressively throughout Book III. By the
time of Cicero, however, a fivefold division had evolved
which was to provide the basis for all subsequent development: 1) *inventio,* gathering and analysis; 2) *dispositio,*
arrangement, sequence, and structure; 3) *elocutio,* diction, choice of words, phrases, clauses, sentences, figures;
4) *pronunciatio,* delivery, "elocution" in the modern
sense; 5) *memoria,* sheer memory.[44] Yet for Cicero, rhetoric was still the art of public address necessary to an
educated man of affairs, although in Book III of *De ora-
tore,* he indicates in the dialogue with Crassus that the
Sophistic idea of rhetoric as principally a technique of
adornment was already (ca. 46 B.C.) in evidence.

By A.D. 81, Tacitus indicates, the Sophists have taken
over almost completely, and rhetoric is well on the way
to becoming a literary study.[45] The Republic has passed
out of existence, and with it that form of government and
jurisprudence in which a private citizen needed rhetorical skills for direct participation. Study, speculation, and
practice of rhetoric survived largely in school exercises
called *declamatio,* a sort of set piece in which the speaker
elaborated on conventional themes. Seneca's *Controver-*

44. Cicero, *De inventione,* VII. 9: "Quare materia quidem nobis rhe-
toricae videtur artis ea quam Aristoteli visam esse diximus; partes autem
eae quas plerique dixerunt, inventio, dispositio, elocutio, memoria, pro-
nuntiatio. Inventio est excogitatio rerum verarum aut veri similium
quae causam probabilem reddant; dispositio est rerum inventarum in
ordinem distributio; elocutio est idoneorum verborum ad inventionem
accommodatio; memoria est firma animi rerum ac verborum perceptio;
pronunciatio est ex rerum et verborum dignitate vocis et corporis moder-
atio." Ed. H. M. Hubbell (Cambridge, Mass., 1949), pp. 18–20.

45. See Charles S. Baldwin, *Ancient Rhetoric and Poetic* (New York,
1924), pp. 95 ff.; cited hereafter as Baldwin, *ARP.*

siae is a collection of *declamationes* made by famous orators and preserved as models of style. In his discussion of the art of *declamatio,* Seneca says nothing of the old Ciceronian divisions of rhetoric; he analyzes, rather, according to a threefold division: *sententiae, divisio,* and *colores.* The *colores* include descriptive amplification and dramatic characterization.

> The interpretations demanded by *sententiae* and *divisio* were at least intellectual; but the main interpretation, the goal and measure of skill was imaginative. The surest way to fame was through *colores.* Through *colores,* what had once been useful as a school exercise was artificially extended, and forensic was turned into a kind of occasional oratory.[46]

Though we need not share Baldwin's horror at the encroachment of the imagination upon the provinces of rhetoric, we cannot overlook the importance of the development in late classical Rome which made a new discipline out of what had been in Aristotle an almost accidental association. By Plutarch's time, poetic and rhetoric have become practically indistinguishable. Quintilian and Horace are late exceptions, the more notable because of the degree to which they differ in attitude from their contemporaries and successors.

> The process of conceiving of poetic in terms of rhetoric was so much more a preoccupation of ancient thought that the conception of poetic as a distinct movement seems to have become less and less active. Though a few critics, even under the Empire, held the Aristotelian distinction, generally ancient poetic was more and more warped toward rhetoric.[47]

46. Ibid., p. 100.
47. Ibid., p. 225.

The rhetoricians of the third century, however, are still to be clearly distinguished from those of the thirteenth, and in several ways. First, the former represent the last stages of a dying tradition, which had never really widely influenced literary production. Second, they existed exclusively in a school system which never achieved either the systematic clarity of purpose or the broad influence of the medieval schools. Finally, they have behind them nothing even faintly resembling the solid doctrinal support of a great religious orthodoxy which gave purpose and function to the work of the medieval schoolmen. The most significant heritage of early medieval students of literature from the late Roman rhetoricians was one of which the later Middle Ages was scarcely even conscious: the impress left upon the schools of Gaul, in the fourth and fifth centuries, by the Roman practice of quasi-literary rhetoric. In the three succeeding centuries, as the concept of the seven liberal arts was being formulated and worked out in these same schools, the association of literature with rhetoric and grammar became fixed and institutionalized. When medieval criticism finally did become articulate, it looked (perhaps only by the accidents of manuscript survival) to Cicero for terms in which to speak, but it spoke them in the tongue of Martianus Capella.

Yet even for Martianus, rhetoric had not yet become the art of poetry alone, however closely the two may be associated in his work. In his *Liber de arte rhetorica*,[48] he devotes considerable attention to the decorative aspects of style, including a rather unsystematic treatment of the figures,[49] but his definition of the nature and pur-

---

48. Text in Halm, *Rhetores latini minores* (Leipzig, 1863).

49. First a scattered list of "figures of sense," and then a more detailed work on what he labels *elocutionium figuras*.

pose of rhetoric reflects the Ciceronian emphasis upon its
oratorical function.

> I am that same Rhetorica, whom some call an art,
> others a quality, and others a discipline. An art, in-
> deed, because I am taught, wherefore Plato is pleased
> to oppose this term: those call me a quality who
> take me to be primarily skill in speaking well: those
> who do not ignore the necessity of rightly and
> thoroughly committing the oration to memory truly
> call me a discipline.
> 5. My proper function is effective persuasion; my
> end, to convince of that which is contended in the
> speech. Which words, indeed, I confirm from Cic-
> ero; by whose model, furthermore, I insinuate my-
> self everywhere with precepts suitably guiding prac-
> tise. Moreover, the basic categories ["matters"] for
> making a speech are two: the "whither" and the
> "whence"; the "whither," so that the question may
> be approached through the proper divisions; and
> the "whence" so that words and the things of the
> [speaker's] invention may be rightly joined.[50]

Just how much of this is mere echoing Cicero and how
much represents Martianus's estimate of the nature of
things in his own day is a dubious question. Certainly
there is no surviving forum for the Ciceronian type of
rhetoric. It is most probable that the splitting up of the
functions of rhetoric, apparent in the organization of
the later cathedral schools, is already beginning. The
ars dictaminis moves away in one direction, and eventual-
ly dominates in the professional schools; the ars sermocinandi got a vigorous send-off from Augustine in the
fourth book of De doctrina christiana, but was not to be

50. Halm, p. 454 (translation mine).

picked up and fully developed until the era of the preaching orders; the *ars poetica* is implicit in the association of poetry with the analytic methods of teaching advanced grammar and what is left to the *trivium* of rhetoric. It should also be noted that through the period of growing influence of the schools, the boundary between grammar and rhetoric grows increasingly vague. From a relatively early period, certain classes of verbal figures are considered to be in the province of grammar, and in later centuries the overlap becomes even greater. The school rhetoric, separated from public address in the sermon, and even from the ornate *ars dictaminis,* becomes increasingly preoccupied with style—a sort of upper-level advanced grammar. Late in the twelfth century, under the impetus of that reappraisal of classical poetry by educated Christians which has been labeled the "twelfth-century renaissance," rhetoric formally declares itself *Poetria.*[51]

When the "new poetic" does assume form and system, its modifications of its Ciceronian basis are numerous and significant. In fact, although the later rhetoricians claim descent from Cicero, they probably knew only the early and incomplete *De inventione.* The *Auctor ad Herennium,* known to the schoolmen as *Cicero nova* or *Rhetorica nova,* has been proven a forgery.[52] About all they actually retain of the *De inventione* is the doctrine of

51. Curtius sees one other influence entering during this formative period: "[Aldhelm] fordert klassische Bildung in bloss formalem Sinne und erweist sich damit als Vertreter eines kirchlichen Rigorismus. Das Empfinden für klassisches Latein war schon den Iren abhanden gekommen und ging auch ihrem Schüler Aldhelm ab. Aber er fand eine neue Autorität für Stil und Komposition in der Vulgata. Zwar hatten schon Hieronymus, Augustin, Cassiodor und Isidor auf sprachkünstlerische Entsprechungen zwischen der Bibel und dem heidnischen Schrifttum aufmerksam gemacht. Aber diese Männer standen doch der antiken Sprachkultur noch zu nahe, um die Kluft zwischen deren Masstäben und dem Bibellatein zu übersehen" (p. 54).

52. See Faral, ch. 4.

the three styles, some technical terms, and the form, at least, of the five-part division of the art of rhetoric. The most revealing indication of the changed concept of rhetoric—or poetic—is the interpretation of those five parts.

Cicero had listed *inventio, dispositio, elocutio, memoria,* and *pronunciatio* as the components of the art of oratory. Geoffrey of Vinsauf, the most prolific as well as the most famous of the thirteenth-century theorists, lists five essential points in the art of poetry: 1) *inventio et dispositio,* 2) *amplificatio et contractio,* 3) *elocutio,* 4) *actio,* and 5) *dictio.* This revision of the system shows first of all the tremendous decrease in importance of that component which the modern critic would probably consider the most transferable from rhetoric to poetic—*inventio.* The hasty paragraph in which Geoffrey disposes of *inventio* in order to get on with the major business of his treatise indicates not only a decrease in its importance, but practically its disappearance from the system. But before we accept Baldwin's irritation[53] at this shift in emphasis, it would be well to remember what had been happening in the intervening centuries.

Ciceronian oratory would have been a good deal sillier and more aridly academic in the thirteenth-century schools than the poetic derived from it was. Even more pertinent is the fact that, within the Christian orthodoxy of thirteenth-century Europe, and within the theory of knowledge supported by that orthodoxy, there was no place for the classical *inventio* in the art of poetry. Curtius[54] and Baldwin[55] seem to concur in the explanation

---

53. See Baldwin, *MRP,* p. 189: "The sophistic of the ancient encomium, walking the schools once more, is now called *Poetria,*" and other such judgments.

54. *European Literature,* pp. 68 ff.

55. Baldwin, *MRP,* pp. 171 ff.

that, in the division of the arts of the *trivium, dialectica* had absorbed the activities denoted by Cicero's *inventio.* That is, no doubt, a part of the explanation, but I think the change is also only indicative of some even more basic ones. *Inventio* had been, for Aristotle and Cicero alike, a genuine process of discovery through rational activity. It is, in both, the link between rhetoric and dialectic. But the theory of knowledge which orthodox Christianity produced placed rigid limits on what man could discover, even through the best exercise of his rational faculties. Poetry, at the same time, never quite emerged from the Augustinian stigma, or if it did, it did so only because it came to be regarded as a medium for conveying—not discovering—the highest truths. One of the many medieval developments which all but necessitated the confusion of poetic and rhetoric is the evolution of an attitude which relegates poetry to directly communicative and persuasive functions.

Classical rhetoric had always involved, in its very categorical processes, questions of the nature of knowledge and moral value. Plato, in the *Gorgias* and the *Phaedrus,* had rejected rhetoric (or at least the early Sophists' definition of it) on grounds that there was nothing insuperable in the nature of knowledge or of man to prevent man's knowing the good and the true, and once he knew them he would follow them with no further persuasion. Dialectic, then, was its own agency of persuasion, and both rhetoric and poetry were at best unnecessary, at worst promoters of illusion. Aristotle, and Cicero following him, had argued rather that there are questions about which, because of the nature of man and the universe, certainty is impossible or practical application of it open to doubt. The first step in the useful art of persuasion, therefore, is making the best or most useful decision about such questions, and this decision (which was most of the activity denoted by *inventio*) was the standard by which all subsequent questions about the agencies of persuasion were decided. The Sophists, in their insistent separation of knowledge from morality, had produced a purely formalistic rhetoric, its operational validity resting on no prior commitments whatever. Quintilian, finally, had straddled the fence, agreeing with the Sophists that rhetoric per se was concerned only with the "science of writing well," but then commenting that only the good man could write truly well.

In all of this variety of classical attitudes, however, there is no pervasive, established doctrine about the substance or source of truth; only a variety of convictions (most of them essentially rationalistic) about the means for arriving at it. Consequently, in none of these attitudes does history or an authoritative tradition play much part beyond providing some of the data reason works on, or an occasional precedent or illustration.

But beginning perhaps even before Augustine's *De doctrina,* and certainly clearly systematized in that document, Christianity had bound knowledge and moral value inseparably together and subjected both to a priori determination, doubly based on direct revelation (the Passion) and indirect revelation (the pattern of history and the created universe). Augustine thus stands very near the head of a new traditionalist and institutionalist theory of knowledge, which leads at once (already in Augustine's writing, as well as in Jerome's) to the separation of useful from useless knowledge; with salvation at stake, the distinction of useless from useful knowledge in turn demands authoritarian and systematic enforcement. So, the rhetoric which Augustine defines in Book IV of *De doctrina* is a system of persuasion which specifically does *not* involve its user in any choices about the content or direction of argument. Those are already determined—for Augustine, by the Scriptures alone, for later analysts (who also have relaxed enough to consider poetry a legitimate extension of rhetoric, as Augustine did not) by Scripture plus tradition as corrected and illuminated by orthodox authority.

Tradition itself—both as meaningful historical pattern or accurate literary constructs by previous observers, and as workable analyses of means—becomes a pattern for imitation and a substitute for the ancient "invention." Tradition, in its common medieval sense, implied what was nearest to stability in human knowledge: the preserved record of what is constantly meaningful to all men in all times and places, and therefore a record of the way in which temporal events reflect eternal purposes. Post-Augustinian rhetoric, then, assumes on the one hand a constant human psychology and on the other a constant supra-human order of value. It is the business of the rhetorician-poet to choose from the variety of possible inconstant linguistic means the ones which will successfully connect the two.

Poetry as an art must remain, as long as the framework of medieval belief stood, a process of arousing favorable response to a fittingly dignified statement of pre-existing truths. At least those were the only terms in which its theoricians could discuss it. Thus *inventio,* if it remains in the discussion at all, becomes a process of verbal ingenuity or a search for a theme.

Jean de Garlande, one of the most scholarly of the theorists,[56] treats *inventio* under five heads, and in so

---

56. Jean de Garlande's list of the parts of the art of poetry is the most inclusive to be found in such analyses. The opening section of his *Poetria* lists seven: "Primo tradetur doctrina inveniendi; II. deinde docebitur de modo eligendi materiam; III. postea, de dispositione et de modo inchoandi materiam; IV. deinde, de partibus dictaminis; V. postea, de vitiis vitandis in quolibet genere dictandi; VI. consequenter consti-

doing gives us the most precise definition we have anywhere in the rhetorical treatises of this new concept of it.
Ubi, quid, quale, ad quid, qualiter? These are the questions to be answered in the process of invention. Jean's
answer to the first—*ubi?*—is an explanation in principle
of one of the dominant characteristics of medieval poetry.
Among persons, examples, and proverbs, he tells us, one
finds the substance for poetry. *What* one is to find in them
is: in persons, merits and faults; in examples and proverbs, morals or traits or means of praising and blaming.
There are two sorts of ideas *(quale?)*, to be discovered
thus: direct expressions of fact, and implications or insinuations. The end toward which the poet collects subject matter is, of course, always the establishment of the
honestum et utile. The last question is most indicative.
To *qualiter?*, Jean replies: by the use of the seven "colors" of beautification and amplification. That is, the poet
"discovers," or makes clear, the particular truth which
he wishes to extract from his subject matter[57] by elaborating and strengthening the portions upon which he
wishes the emphasis to fall.

Such a theory obviously shifts the major burden in the
composition of poetry to the specific techniques of amplification and abbreviation, and primarily to the former,
for the latter is only a device for making room for one's
own restatements. This in turn demands an equally
heavy emphasis upon the labor of style, for it is through
style that particular affectiveness is given to the rearrange-

---

tuitur tractatus de rhetorico ornatu, necessario tam in metro quam in
prosa, utpote de coloribus materiam abbreviantibus et ampliantibus ad
scribentis electionem; VII. septimo et ultimo subjiciuntur exempla lit-
erarum curialium et dictaminum scholasticorum, et versum et rhythmo-
rum ornate compositorum et diversorum metrorum."

57. In all the rhetorical treatises, it is assumed that this subject matter
may already be in some literary form.

ment of emphasis achieved by amplification and abbreviation. That is, returning to Geoffrey of Vinsauf's parti-
tion of the art, the function of *inventio et dispositio* has
become primarily the choice of a theme or source and
the decision as to how to get under way with it; the function of *dispositio,* as the ancients had conceived it, is as
a consequence transferred to the process of *amplificatio*
and *contractio;* these in turn are carried out in detail
through the labor of style, *elocutio.*

The result, if we consider it as a whole system, is actually a tripartite analysis of the process of composition,[58]
with each of the parts closely related to the others. As a
whole system, it tends to reverse almost precisely the relative importance of the elements in the ancient formulation; stylistic elaboration becomes the effort whereby the
poet actually accomplishes what he sets out to do in his
poem. Hence the heavy weighting, in all the treatises, of
the categories of figures, colors, tropes, etc. It is a danger-
ous oversimplification to attribute this pervasive interest
in the devices of style exclusively to the theorist's predi-
lection for categories and catalogues when they ought to
have been concerned with larger issues. The conclusion
seems to me inescapable that the consistent arrangement
of the *poetriae* represents a kind of aesthetic formulation,
and whether or not the individual compilers discuss directly the aesthetic bases of their systems, we must recognize them if we are to avoid the arrogance of dismissing
a group of serious scholars as a generation of shallow
muddleheads. Furthermore, on the assumption that in
scholarship understanding is even more important than
professional courtesy, we must perceive the integration

58. *Actio* and *dictio* always appear, if at all, only in a few sentences at
the ends of discussions. They are obviously a concession to the half-
understood prescripts of *De inventione,* and they turn abruptly away
from the process of composition to the process of oral reading.

of the system of rhetorical criticism in order to realize that a legitimate kind of poetry *is* possible in such terms, even though those terms may not necessarily describe to our satisfaction the reasons for the effectiveness of the poetry. In fact, a good deal of the kind of poetry possible on such terms had already been written before the compendia appeared. Prescriptive though they may be in intent (and this has no doubt been overemphasized by adverse critics), their method is descriptive, and the great majority of illustrative examples in them are gathered from the best poetry, medieval as well as classical Latin, available to their authors. The *poetria nova* is "new" primarily in treating *poetria* as an art separate from grammar and rhetoric; it does not create the theory of poetry which it embodies.

The details of the system built upon these foundations are not so important to this study, and they have been treated exhaustively elsewhere.[59] What still remains to be said about the *summae* of rhetorical colors, the three-level codifications of stylistic decorum, and the catalogues and categories of figures, is that if we allow the premises from which they proceed, they too are consistent and integral parts of the system within which they exist. The distinctions between tropes and schemes, figures of sense and figures of words, figures pertaining to structure and those pertaining to style, simply establish a series of parallels at the various levels of structure (proceeding always from the more general to the more particular). The order and scope of the treatments of figures are direct reflections of the manner in which the weight of poetic statement is passed down through the supporting members of the structure to rest ultimately upon style. The five prin-

59. By Faral with most sympathy and understanding; also by Baldwin, although his prejudice against the adoption of rhetorical methods in poetic theory weakens his study.

cipal figures of amplification, for example, which Geoffrey of Vinsauf and Jean de Garlande list in common,[60] are all either themselves expanded tropes or colors,[61] or have precise counterparts at the more particular levels. Clearly, the system is coherent, and its parts mutually interdependent. The fact that we find separate treatises containing discussions of only one or two of the parts—e.g. the colors—does not leave us free to conclude that the other parts are purely perfunctory graces.

There remain two serious criticisms to be considered. Both have been directed frequently at the rhetorical compendia, and both are made much of in the early studies of Chaucer's relationship to the rhetorical theories. First, is it not possible that, however coherent the system may be, it is arbitrarily and artificially so? To a certain extent, this is true, but only if we insist that all discussions of poetic art must consider it in terms of its effects upon the reader or of the psychological processes of its authors. The analysis made in the rhetorical treatises is an analysis of causes in the structure of poetry, rather than of effects in the reader. Its ultimate aim was, of course, to instruct in the art of producing a poetry which *would* move its readers, and it is no doubt a limitation in the instruction that it has so little to say about how those effects follow from the causes listed, or what effects may follow. It is also the case that some—perhaps even many —of the causes analyzed are falsely observed or described. Even so, I cannot see that this invalidates the procedure of trying to observe systematically what forces are opera-

60. *Circumlocutio* (paraphrase), *exclamatio* (apostrophe), *digressio, prosopopoeia, descriptio.*

61. *Circumlocutio,* or *circuito,* for example, is discussed at all three levels—under amplification, difficult ornament, and simple ornament— in Geoffrey, although we must go from the *Poetria* to the *Summa de coloribus* to complete the information.

tive in the structure of a poem. For that is what the best of the rhetoricians were attempting, and like critics in any age, they brought to the task the epistemology they had accepted.

The second, and more practical criticism which has been brought against the rhetorical system is that it offers the poet only the possibility of verbal embroidery upon established themes or outdated poems. I think the preceding discussion has in part answered this objection, but to reconsider it may provide the opportunity for a useful summary. The charge rests ultimately upon a misunderstanding of the tripartite division of the art of poetry, as we have seen it in Geoffrey of Vinsauf, and of the truly re-creative nature of the labor of style. "Verbal embroidery," if carefully and thoughtfully applied, can radically alter not only the color but the pattern of the original. It seems to me a great deal more than coincidence that the age which produced the "verbal embroidery" theory of poetry is also the age of triumphant robberies in the practice of poetry, including those of Chaucer.

V

Discussing the twelfth-century renaissance, J. L. Paetow says: "If this movement had not been checked, there probably would have been a steady increase of interest in the Latin and later in the Greek classics, without any of the brilliance and éclat of the later Italian revival, but also without many of its excesses."[62] But the twelfth-century movement *was* checked, partly by a new and rapid development in the universities themselves, partly by the advent of what Curtius has called "die Hochscholastik." The thirteenth-century rhetorical compendia are

62. Paetow, p. 92.

themselves almost the last flickerings of the flame of literary interest which had burned brightly though briefly at Chartres and Orléans. John of Salisbury and Jean de Garlande are just about the last remaining spokesmen for the strong literary emphasis in the *trivium*. By the middle of the thirteenth century, the discipline of the seven liberal arts is itself beginning to crumble, and whether it is a matter of cause and effect or of simple coincidence, it is significant that it is in the twelfth and thirteenth centuries that the vernacular literatures are reaching a state of development in which they can compete with Latin for serious attention.

But in the collision of the Latin and the vernacular traditions of poetry, and in the triumph of the vernaculars, the clash is not between two completely distinct modes of composition. The first formulations of a vernacular poetry on the continent, and its continuations in England, are carried out on the general lines established by Latin poetry. From such basic and obvious characteristics as accentual and syllabic meters to such inclusive and generic ones as the development of allegory, most of the significant formal features of the new poetry (and many of the thematic ones) derive from its Latin exemplars.[63]

63. These generalizations will not apply to the poetry being produced in Iceland, where Romance influence strikes very late and then not deeply enough to alter the formal character of Icelandic poetry. See Margaret Schlauch, *Romance in Iceland* (New York, 1934). Welsh and Irish poetry also preserve strong native traditions, but their contributions to the rest of European poetry are thematic rather than formal. Helpful studies of these contributions are to be found in A. T. Nutt, *The Influence of Celtic upon Medieval Romance* (London, 1904); Roger S. Loomis, *Celtic Myth and Arthurian Romance* (New York, 1927); and Tom Peete Cross, "Celtic Mythology in Arthurian Romance," in *Philologica: Malone Anniversary Studies*, ed. T. A. Kirby and H. B. Woolf (Baltimore, 1949).

Inevitably, the ideas about poetry embodied in the Latin exemplars found their way into the vernacular poetry and took effect there, regardless of whether the poets of the vulgar tongues had heard of those ideas directly. That is to say, it is perfectly possible to speak of the relation of the rhetorical theories of composition to early vernacular poets who may never have seen or heard of any of the rhetorical formularies, because medieval Latin poetry was being produced by men who not only knew the theories, but were in several cases helping to compile them.[64] And we may well even find poets in the vernacular absorbing these same standards of composition from two or three different sources: quite indirectly, through their predecessors in the vernaculars; at second hand, through Latin poetry; or directly from the sources themselves. Such is demonstrably the case with Dante and Chaucer, who, despite their differences in poetic personality, have a common consciousness of their own art and of the traditional bases upon which it rests.

But an interesting paradox develops when the serious and artistically self-conscious vernacular poets, sharing in general the rhetoricians' assumptions about the nature and values of poetry, realize at the same time that the Latin-oriented analyses of the *particulars* of style are usually not transferable to the management of the vernaculars. The weight of the rhetorical poetic rested solidly on a doctrine of the persuasive efficacy of style; hence the tendency of the academic treatises to turn into *summae de coloribus*. Thus the vernacular poet had somehow to construct his own equivalent of the worthy poetry defined in Latin by the schoolmasters of Paris, Chartres, and Orléans. Dante and, somewhat later, Eustache Des-

---

64. Jean de Garlande and Geoffrey of Vinsauf, to name two of particular interest, were both poets of considerable reputation in their own time.

champs, are sufficiently concerned with the problem that
they provide us with theoretical expositions as well as a
body of poetry to help bridge the gap between Latin
theory and vernacular practice.

A little less than a century after the flourishing of
Geoffrey of Vinsauf, Dante bases his discussion of poetry
in *De vulgari eloquentia* on the statement that poetry
"is nothing else but a rhetorical composition set to
music."[65] And speaking of the authority of the poetry
to be written in the illustrious vulgar tongue, he says
"for what is of greater authority than that which can
sway the hearts of men, so as to make an unwilling man
willing, and a willing man unwilling, just as this language has done and is doing?"[66] For Dante, as for the
school rhetoricians a century before him, language
which could both worthily adorn its theme and sway the
hearts of men could only be a language of disciplined
artifice. The illustrious vulgar tongue is not the Italian
men speak in the streets; it is the Italian which can be
created by the art of poets. The models upon which it
is to be constructed are the grammar and rhetoric which
have been codified by the schoolmen, and the practice
of those whom Dante called "Regular Poets"—those who
wrote in Latin the poetry which men like Geoffrey of
Vinsauf and Jean de Garlande were trying to analyze.
Dante's own treatise was intended to supplement those
models, spelling out at least some of the rules which the

65. Liber secundus, III, p. 393, lines 16–20: ". . . quod procul dubio
rationabiliter eructare praesumpsimus, quia prorsus poetae sunt, si
poesim recte consideremus: quae nihil aliud est quam fictio rethorica,
in musicaque posita." In *Tutte le opere di Dante Alighieri*, ed. E. Moore
(Oxford, 1894), (translation mine).

66. Ibid., Liber primus, XVII, p. 389, lines 26–31: "Quod autem sit
exaltatum potestate, videtur: et quid maioris potestatis est, quam quod
humana corda versare potest; ita ut nolentem, volentem; et volentem,
nolentem faciat, velut ipsum et fecit et facit?"

vernacular required, but which could not be found in stylistic manuals for Latin composition.

The result, in Dante's case, is not a manual of style so much as a survey of prosody. The reason, I think, is that he saw two kinds of order in the artful language of poetry —orders which might loosely be called meaning and music.[67] Since the order of music is most closely and distinctively determined by the particular language, it is there that the critic beginning the construction of a vernacular aesthetic must begin. Once he has demonstrated that the same decorative management of language is possible in the vulgar tongue and in Latin, Dante's principal concern becomes those particulars in which vernacular art will prove most different from Latin.

It is likewise with the music of the vernacular that Deschamps is concerned in his *L'art de dictier et de fere chançons.*[68] His is a much thinner poetic than Dante's, both in that he takes up only one kind of poetry, and in that he has next to nothing to say about the moral commitment which for Dante gave rational consistency to the theory and affective power to the practice of poetry. But Deschamps' treatise remains an interesting example of what happens when the moral passion which had converted rhetoric to poetic weakens, while the consequent sense of regular artifice and rational discipline in poetry remains.

He begins with a list of the seven liberal arts, which has no connection that I can discover with the rest of the treatise, except that it reveals how strongly the connection had become fixed between the intellectual disci-

67. I also think that this sense of orders parallels the rhetoricians' distinction between "tropes" and "schemes," or figures of sense and figures of words.

68. *Oeuvres complètes de Eustache Deschamps,* ed. Gaston Raynaud, *Société des anciens textes français,* 7 (Paris, 1891), 266–92.

plines of the schools and the art of poetry—even the lighter kinds of poetry that Deschamps was talking about. And when, under Music, he comes to his discussion of poetry, there remains a kind of faded and indirect moral apology for it. "Its delectable and pleasant songs," he says, "medicine and recreate those who are fatigued, heavy, or bored by thought, imagination, or labor," so that they may return profitably to the pursuit of the liberal arts.[69] Like Dante, he reminds the vernacular poet of the school disciplines, and then, after remarking on the need of the vernacular for formal rules, proceeds to the same kind of analysis of prosody as Dante had been occupied with in the last two thirds of the *De vulgari*. Like both Dante and the school rhetoricians, he attempts no consideration of why or how the particular orders of language which he defines produce the effects which he imputes to them; it is simply to be assumed that they do. Fit decoration becomes the norm of the beautiful, and in medieval poetic theory, analysis proceeds no further in that direction, but turns back upon itself to classify means.

With Chaucer, all these questions assume a somewhat different character. He has left us no single treatise on the art of poetry, although the Prologue to the *Legend of Good Women* comes close to being one. At the same time, there is scarcely a poem in which he does not somewhere stop for at least a few lines to reflect about the formal problems of his art. However much the nineteenth-century critics (and some more recent) may have revered Chaucer as an earthy realist, the two constant concerns in his scattered reflections about poetry are the

69. Ibid., p. 269: ". . . par sa melodie delectable les cuers et esperis de ceuls qui auxdiz ars, par pensee, ymaginaison et labours de bras estoient traveilliez, pesans et ennuiez, sont medicinez et recreez, et plus habiles a estudier et labourer aux autre .VI. ars dessus nommez."

formal traditions established by past writers and the good, useful, or moving matter which poetry may embody. In the earliest of his long poems, the *Book of the Duchess,* these concerns—central to the old rhetorical poetic—are already evident. Late into the *Canterbury Tales,* the same concerns still occupy him.

If what I have been arguing for Dante and Deschamps holds for Chaucer also, we should not expect that in the particulars of his style his poetry would reflect exactly the stylistic prescriptions of the school rhetoricians. When Chaucer laughs at the rhetoricians—as he does, for instance, in the Nun's Priest's tale—he laughs at particular stylistic practices or pretensions. When he quotes them in all seriousness—as he does, for instance, in *Troilus and Criseyde*—he accepts their basic premises about the formal, ordered nature of art and its double commitment to the moral order and to human feelings. The fact that Chaucer was an impersonal and ironic moralist, while Dante was a personal and passionate one, makes real differences in the effects of their poetry, but it should not blind us to their common assumption that their poetry was to be ordered in terms of their moral perceptions.

It is undoubtedly true that the vernacular literatures were growing gradually, and with increasing rapidity, away from the specific doctrines of rhetorical composition during the period under consideration. However, I am not so concerned here with specific techniques as with the central belief, in rhetorical theory, that poetry is the art of clothing the already discovered truth in fitting language. The doctrines of disposition, amplification, and stylistic elaboration provided the medieval poet with a compositional technique for insinuating into the work of a previous writer, or for extracting from a general concept, the particular statement he himself desired to convey. Depending upon whether he was a good or a poor poet, he might produce by these means either superficially elaborated plagiarisms or genuinely recreated poems. The Middle Ages offers us large amounts of poetry of both sorts, but it offers us strikingly little poetry shaped directly out of original experience. Such seems to me to be the basis upon which Curtius' doctrine of the *topoi* rests, although his statement of it is in terms of substance rather than of form:

> But we have seen that the two most important oratorical genres, the judicial and the political, disappeared from political reality with the extinction of the Greek city-states and the Roman Republic, and took refuge in the schools of rhetoric; that eulogy became a technique of praise which could be applied to any subject; that poetry too was rhetoricized. This means neither more nor less than that rhetoric lost its original meaning and purpose. Hence it penetrated into all literary genres. Its elaborately developed system became the common denominator of literature in general. This is the most influential development in the history of antique rhetoric. By it the topoi too acquire a new function. They become clichés, which can be used in any form of literature, they spread to all spheres of life with which literature deals and to which it gives form. In late Antiquity we see the new ethos give birth to new topoi.[70]

For those who still believe that this is a necessarily mechanical and sterile method of analyzing poetry, it might be well to recall that the two greatest vernacular poets of the Middle Ages mastered their craft in the schools of

70. Curtius, pp. 70–71.

poetry which were most consciously and directly experimenting with such formalistic and intellectualized notions: Dante, with the earlier poets of the *dolce stil nuovo,* and Chaucer, with the school of Machault.[71] It is perhaps indicative of the much greater extent to which Dante's vision encompasses the coming Renaissance, as well as of the vast differences in temperament, that Dante chose to appoint as master of his school, Vergil; Chaucer's choice was Ovid.

71. It is difficult, in the light of these facts, to understand Naunin's argument that it is often French poetry and not rhetorical treatises which produce certain effects in Chaucer's work. He himself agrees (*Einfluss,* pp. 51–52) that the French poetry of Chaucer's exemplars was strongly rhetorical in character.

2. Chaucer on the Art of Poetry

WILLIAM BUTLER YEATS wrote of the relationship
between artistic tradition and the individual talent:

> An aged man is but a paltry thing,
> A tattered coat upon a stick, unless
> Soul clap its hands and sing, and louder sing
> For every tatter in its mortal dress;
> Nor is there singing school but studying
> Monuments of its own magnificence.[1]

In the metaphor of the last two lines, Yeats comes very
close to the definition of the literary past implicit in
Chaucer's introductory comment in the *Parliament of
Fowls:*

> Of usage—what for lust and what for lore—
> On bokes rede I ofte, as I yow tolde.
> But wherfore that I speke al this? Nat yoore
> Agon, it happede me for to beholde
> Upon a bok, was write with lettres olde,
> And therupon, a certeyn thing to lerne,
> The longe day ful faste I redde and yerne.
>
> For out of olde feldes, as men seyth,
> Cometh al this newe corn from yer to yere,
> And out of olde bokes, in good feyth,
> Cometh al this newe science that men lere.   (15–25)

1. *Sailing to Byzantium,* stanza 2.

Chaucer's is the more general of the two statements, since it includes all knowledge, and we must recall its context in order to see its particular application to the art of poetry. But both poets insist on a necessary and vital relationship between the human spirit and the processes of art and history. It is that relationship—and the moral and aesthetic and epistemological problems attendant upon it—which constitute the central theme of the recurrent discussions of the problem of the poet throughout Chaucer's work. Art, for him as for Yeats, takes form in intellectual activity, an activity which has as its principal substance the traditions which embody the past. But where Yeats, at least in the Byzantium poems, leaves us a definition of art all but cut off from utility or effect in any present nonliterary actuality, Chaucer sees poetry as a part of knowledge and therefore measurable ultimately only in terms of utility or effect. However, there are many possible kinds of utility and effect, and a confusing variety of means of achieving them, so that as Chaucer sees the rhetorical poetic, it is not nearly so monolithic as it might appear when reduced to its simplest formulation. It will be the purpose of the next several pages to trace out the line of argument Chaucer follows in considering these problems, and to outline the principles which seem to remain constant in his aesthetic thinking. I do not intend to suggest, at this point, anything about the chronology of development of the Chaucerian poetic, or about its specific sources. Rather, I wish to move at will through all the writings, arranging materials according to their point and degree of relevance. Such procedure undoubtedly produces some topical over-emphasis,[2] but not, I think, any serious distortion.

2. At the same time, perhaps the over-emphasis itself is desireable. I find it very difficult to understand how recent critics such as Paull F. Baum, *Chaucer: A Critical Appreciation* (Durham, N. C., 1958), can still

There are several ways in which the term "tradition" may be used in literary criticism, and it is necessary to distinguish some of them before proceeding. I intend to speak of three distinct uses of the word, although the number "three" has no particular metaphysical necessity. First, we may mean by "tradition" simply the series of linguistic, substantive, and perceptual habits—largely inherited from the past—which a poet necessarily acquires if he is to write at all. In this sense, "tradition" is roughly equal to "language." Second, "tradition" may mean those particular literary acts, in the past, to which the poet turns in the attempt either to create or to justify his creation; that is, "tradition" as model or specific source. Finally, it may indicate the total continuity of the past, contemplated by the poet as a process, in the attempt to establish its significance in toto and relate himself and his art to it—approximately the sense in which Eliot uses the term in his *Tradition and the Individual Talent*. It should be noted that all three of these distinctions are phrased in terms of a possible significance of the past to the poet, and also that the first indicates a much less conscious relationship between the poet and his past than the others do. It is with the second and third senses of "tradition" that I shall deal most, since I am interested here mainly in the aesthetic ideas which affect the structure and content of Chaucer's poetry directly.

Chaucer was much concerned with those two senses of the term, and some of his finest poetry grew out of his attempts to specify them and relate them to his indi-

---

seriously advance the notion that Chaucer was a casual amateur, writing more or less left-handed with no very serious concern for what he was doing. It is hard to open a volume of Chaucer at random without hitting upon a passage concerned in some way with the sort of problem under discussion here.

vidual acts of composition. In nearly every one of his major poems there appears some variant of the "old fields—new corn" metaphor quoted above from the *Parliament of Fowls,* usually employed as a part of the machinery introducing some acknowledged plagiarism through which we are to be conducted to the heart of the poem. The kind and the extent of the development Chaucer gives these ideas vary widely. The next chapter will present an argument to the effect that the whole Prologue to the *Legend of Good Women* is a complicated consideration of the apparent opposition between "books" and "experience," terms which are in that context very nearly synonymous with "past" and "present." But it will be necessary and useful here to anticipate some of the substance of that argument, in slightly different terms, in order to correlate it with key passages from the other poems.

The central issues in the Prologue, from the point of view of the poet, are concerned with establishing a stance, a moral and aesthetic "location," from which he can take adequately sure bearings to produce good poetry. And in the first part of the Prologue (G Text) he tries to locate himself with respect to three cardinal points: the past as a whole (lines 17–28); particular artists in the past (lines 61–65); and the particular work he is engaged upon, especially its intention and effect (lines 81–88).[3] The key term in Chaucer's attempted synthesis of art, experience, and history is "remembrance."

3. But wherfore that I spak, to yeve credence
    To bokes olde and don hem reverence,
    Is for men shulde autoritees beleve,
    There as there lyth non other assay by preve.
    For myn entent is, or I fro yow fare,
    The naked text in English to declare
    Of many a story, or elles of many a geste,
    As autours seyn; leveth hem if yow leste! (G. 81–88)

> And if that olde bokes weren aweye,
> Yloren were of remembrance the keye.   (G. 25–26)

Both the reason for art and its purpose derive from the relationship between the past and present consciousness expressed in the word "remembrance." It is necessary for two reasons to note that old books are the key of remembrance.[4] First and most obvious, for Chaucer and his contemporaries books were very nearly the sole source of historical knowledge, so that the past is inevitably the literary past. Second, by implication in the second of the three passages in the Prologue referred to above (lines 61–65), the books in which the past is preserved for remembrance are not simply storehouses. They have—whether rightly or wrongly—selected and evaluated the past. To the extent to which "olde bokes" have "lad awey the corn" rather than the chaff, they supply the remembrance with a history unified and significantly ordered. History had its most real and its only fruitful existence in the minds of men, so that the first thing we must note in considering Chaucer's uses of the past is that the past was for him primarily an intellectual phe-

---

4. Cf. Dante's parallel but slightly different concern with memory as a kind of synecdoche for human limitation, and closely involved with the question of his two guides, one literary and one spiritual, in the *Commedia*.

> Nel ciel che più della sua luce prende
>   Fu'io, e vidi cose che ridire
>   Nè sa, nè può chi di lassù discende;
> Perchè, appressando sè al suo disire,
> Nostro intelletto se profonda tanto,
>   Che retro la memoria non può ire.   (*Paradiso*, I. 4–9)

And again, in the letter to Can Grande: "Ad quae intelligenda sciendum est, quod intellectus humanus in hac vita, propter connaturalitem et affinitatem quam habet ad substantiam intellectualem separatam, quando elevatur, in tantum elevatur ut memoria post reditum deficiat, propter transcendisse humanum modum" (lines 531–38). Both quotations from Moore, *Dante*. See Ch. 1, n. 65.

nomenon which continued in remembrance just so long
as it could be made meaningful to experience. Even the
Parson, scornfully distrustful as he was of the literary
niceties of the old books, would not dispense with the
past as a kind of encyclopedia of moral experience:

> Stondeth upon the weyes, and seeth and axeth of
> olde pathes (that is to seyn, of olde sentences) which
> is the goode wey, / and walketh in that wey, and ye
> shal fynde refresshynge for youre soules.
>
> (CT, x. 77–78)

Neither should we miss the fact that the Parson's figure
is itself lifted from the old book of Jeremiah. In remembrance begins morality.

> For seint Paul seith that al that writen is,
> To oure doctrine it is ywrite, ywis;
> Taketh the fruyt, and lat the chaf be stille.
>
> (CT, VII. 3441–43)

The Knight's tale, lines 2443–49, gives another sort of
synthesis of memory, experience, art, and wisdom, rather
parallel to that offered in the Prologue to the *Legend of
Good Women,* although here the application is not just
to poetry, but to all life:

> . . . the pale Saturnus the colde,
> That knew so manye of aventures olde,
> Foond in his olde experience an art
> That he ful soone hath plesed every part.
> As sooth is seyd, elde hath greet avantage;
> In elde is bothe wysdom and usage;
> Men may the olde atrenne, and noght atrede.
>
> (CT, I. 2443–49)

Saturn, however, has obvious advantages over mortals;
his conventional mythic values make of him a symbol in

which experience and remembrance are concurrent and coincident. He is a poetic fact embodying the moral possibility of the proverb in line 2449, and unlike visionary, bookworm poets, has no need of books to unlock his memory.[5]

But the irony which in the Prologue to the *Legend of Good Women* nearly obviates all available doctrinaire solutions is also reflected in the range of attitudes expressed at various points in Chaucer's other work. If Saturn suggests a synthesis of experience and knowledge (present and past) so complete as to require no assistance from the conventionalized "memory" of literary tradition, the Wife of Bath argues so complete a separation and opposition of experience and book knowledge, and so absolute a superiority of the former, that she too would dispense with the memory to which books are the key.

> Experience, though noon auctoritee
> Were in this world, is right ynogh for me.
>   (*CT*, III. 1–2)

> Glose whoso wole, and seye bothe up and doun,
> That they were maked for purgacioun
> Of uryne, and oure bothe thynges smale
> Were eek to knowe a femele from a male,
> And for noon oother cause, —say ye no?
> The experience woot wel it is noght so.
>   (*CT*, III. 119–24)

The Prologue to the Wife's tale is a complicated play on experience and book learning, running first through the

5. And the tale over the outcome of which Saturn presides is typically full of Chaucer's reminders to the reader of his own need for the old books, both for the substance of the story and for expansion and commentary on it if the reader wishes. See lines 859–88; 1462–64; 2036–40; 2073–74; 2155–56.

scholarly lore and then moving on to the "experience"
which confutes it—her five husbands. Then, in her account of the last husband, Janekyn, it is again book learning (the husband and his proverbs) versus experience
(the Wife and her good right arm). And for her, in the
end, "memory" is not a storehouse of wisdom, morality,
and art. Neither does it have any useful connection with
books. In fact, the substance of memory, as far as the
Wife of Bath is concerned, is wholly emotional—sentimental—and to a considerable degree personal.

> But, Lord Crist! whan that it remembreth me
> Upon my yowthe, and on my jolitee,
> It tikleth me aboute myn herte roote.
> Unto this day it dooth myn herte boote
> That I have had my world as in my tyme.
>
> > > > (*CT*, III. 469–73)

The Monk, at the end of his prologue and in the opening lines of his tale, expresses the flatly conventional,
orthodox view, occupying the middle ground between
the mythic divinity of Saturn and the human individuality of the Wife.

> Tragedie is to seyn a certeyn storie,
> As olde bookes maken us memorie,
> Of hym that stood in greet prosperitee,
> And is yfallen out of heigh degree
> Into myserie, and endeth wrecchedly.
>
> .   .   .   .   .   .
>
> I wol biwaille, in manere of tragedie,
> The harm of hem that stoode in heigh degree,
> And fillen so that ther nas no remedie
> To brynge hem out of hir adversitee.
> For certein, whan that Fortune list to flee,
> Ther may no man the cours of hire withholde.

Lat no man truste on blynd prosperitee;
Be war by thise ensamples trewe and olde.

(CT, VII. 1973–98)

Perhaps in all these instances—certainly in some of them—there is not only the common, recurrent concern about art and wisdom as related to the past; there are further implications about Art and Nature which ought to be explored at least briefly. Truth, as the Parson and the Nun's Priest and the Monk all knew—and as the Wife tried hard to deny—was ordinarily visible to fallen man in time only as clothed in one of the two garments which it always wore in order to walk decently among men: Nature and Art. To Nature belonged all the phenomenology of experience, largely as it could be perceived in the present; to Art belonged the significance of experience as it could be recloaked in the more durable (though more artificial) garment of language. Beyond these lay only revelation.[6] But if Nature, as a guise of Truth, could be transient, illusive, arcane, too vast for human comprehension, language—in some ways a more durable garment—was always slipping backward into the past, and was in danger of slipping ultimately out of remembrance.

"But al shal passe that men prose or ryme; / Take every man hys turn, as for his tyme," Chaucer wrote to his friend Scogan. And, perhaps with more serious intent, he says in the introduction to *Anelida and Arcite:*

> For hit ful depe is sonken in my mynde,
> With pitous hert in Englyssh to endyte
> This olde storie, in Latyn which I fynde,
> Of quene Anelida and fals Arcite,
> That elde, which that al can frete and bite,

6. See above, Ch. 1.

> As hit hath freten mony a noble storie,
> Hath nygh devoured out of oure memorie. (8–14)

These, as any reader of Chaucer's poetry knows, are examples of a common minor theme in it. Even the language, particularly "memorie," has multiple echoes, including those I have already noted in the Prologue to
the *Legend of Good Women*. One might even see in such
lines an application of the familiar *ubi sunt* theme to
poetics, with a consequent obligation of the poet to re-
enact—to revivify in the memory—not only ancient
deeds but ancient words as well.[7] That is at least one of
the critical grounds upon which the pilgrims base their
favorable judgment of the first Canterbury tale.

> Whan that the Knyght had thus his tale ytoold,
> In al the route nas ther yong ne oold
> That he ne seyde it was a noble storie,
> And worthy for to drawen to memorie;
>
> $\qquad\qquad\qquad$ (*CT*, I. 3109–12)

And although Chaucer is certainly more constantly,
variously, and fundamentally concerned with this nexus
of questions than most of his contemporaries were, there
are striking parallels in the introductory verses of *Sir
Orfeo* and particularly in the opening of the *Destruction
of Troy*.[8]

> Off aunters ben olde of aunsetris nobill,
> And slydyn vppon shlepe by slomeryng of Age:
> Of stithe men in stoure strongest in armes,
> And wisest in wer to wale in hor tyme,
> That ben drepit with deth and there day paste,

---

7. Cf. also *LGW* 616–23; 924–29; 1139–45, et passim.
8. *"The Gest Hystoriale of the Destruction of Troy:" An Alliterative
Romance Translated from Guido de Colonna's "Hystoria Troiana,"* ed.
George A. Panton and David Donaldson, *EETS,* nos. 39 and 56 (London,
1869 and 1874).

And most out of mynd for there mecull age,
Sothe stories ben stoken vp, and straught out of mind,
And swolowet into swym by swiftenes of yeres,
Ffor new that ben now, next at our hond,
Breuyt into bokes for boldyng of hertes;
On lusti to loke with lightnes of wille,
Cheuyt throughe chaunce and chaungyng of peopull;
Sum tru for to traist, triet in the ende,
Sum feynit o fere and ay false vnder.
Yche wegh as he will warys his tyme,
And has lykyng to lerne that hym list after.
But olde stories of stithe that astate helde,
May be solas to sum that it segh neuer,
Be writyng of wees that wist it in dede,
With sight for to serche, of hom that suet after,
To ken all the crafte how the case felle,
By lokyng of letturs that lefte were of olde.   (5–26)

But to return to Chaucer—I spoke earlier of three
senses of the term "tradition," and in the passage quoted
above from *Anelida and Arcite* (lines 8–14) Chaucer considers all of them. Tradition as "language"—a set of
local historical accidents that determine the particular
materials with which a poet builds—is the least stable,
the least permanent of the three. That means, among
other things, that a part of the legitimate activity of the
poet may be simple translation:[9] "With pitous hert in
Englyssh to endyte / This olde storie, in Latyn which I
fynde." The assertion may be verified, if it needs to be,
from the disclaimer which opens Book II of *Troilus and
Criseyde:*

Ye knowe ek that in forme of speche is chaunge
Withinne a thousand yeer, and wordes tho

9. In which case Deschamps' praise of Chaucer as a "great translator"
is both more particular and higher praise than might at first appear.

That hadden pris, now wonder nyce and straunge
Us thinketh hem, and yet thei spake hem so.

(II. 22–25)

And Chaucer, like Dante, is able to see the application
to the future life of his own work:

And for ther is so gret diversite
In Englissh and in writyng of oure tonge,
So prey I God that non myswrite the,
Ne the mysmetre for defaute of tonge.
And red wherso thow be, or elles songe,
That thow be understonde, God I biseche!

(T&C, v. 1793–98)

Tradition as the specific source or sources is so evident
throughout Chaucer's work that one finds acknowledg-
ments of it on almost every page. In the passage from
Anelida and Arcite which I have been examining here,
the general acknowledgment, "This olde storie, in
Latyn which I fynde, / Of quene Anelida and fals Arcite," is specified a few lines further on: "First folowe
I Stace, and after him Corynne." The fact that the attribution here (as occasionally elsewhere in Chaucer's
work) is false and misleading has little or no bearing, I
think, on the point at issue: Chaucer knew his story had
an ancient source, and wanted us reminded of it. I think
also that at least a part of the explanation for the whole-
sale plagiarism so characteristic of much medieval poetry
might be found in the medieval poet's sense of the instability of the forms of the past, and his obligation to
"clepen into memorye" those fables, as Chaucer put it
in the *Book of the Duchess*,

That clerkes had in olde tyme,
And other poets, put in rime

To rede, and for to be in minde,
While men loved the lawe of kinde.   (53–56)

Tradition becomes the whole of the past in meaningful
relation to the poet and his art when we reach the proverbial generalization of the last three lines of the passage from *Anelida and Arcite*. "Many a noble story"
places before us a shadowy procession of lost literature,
mainly to sharpen our awareness of the value of the
noble stories which do survive in the memory, and to
which Chaucer is about to attempt another contribution.
Then too, it was "with pitous hert" that he set about the
work. His poem is to be a record of something still living
out of the past.[10] I do not think Chaucer was very far,
even in the terms in which he chose to discuss it, from
T. S. Eliot's view of the artist's relation to the traditional
past:

> This historical sense, which is a sense of the timeless
> as well as of the temporal and of the timeless and of
> the temporal together, is what makes a writer tra-
> ditional. And it is at the same time what makes a
> writer most acutely conscious of his place in time,
> of his own contemporaneity. . . . The existing monu-
> ments form an ideal order among themselves, which
> is modified by the introduction of the new (the real-
> ly new) work of art among them.[11]

10. *LGW*, again, provides a confirmatory statement:

> And, as to me, so grisely was his dede
> That, whan that I his foule storye rede,
> Myne eyen wexe foule and sore also.
> Yit last the venym of so longe ago,
> That it enfecteth hym that wol beholde
> The storye of Tereus, of which I tolde.   (2238–43)

11. "Tradition and the Individual Talent" in *Selected Essays* (New
York, 1932), p. 5.

Most of the discussion in this chapter so far has been
concerned with relatively passive relationships between
art and the past in Chaucer's poetry, and if that were all
there were to be discovered, we should probably have
to conclude that much of his best poetry lay outside of
his formal theories of art and beyond them. We certainly
expect more of poetry than that it provide metrical moral
appendices to history. I think Chaucer's poetry certainly
offers us a good deal more than that, too. But I also think
it reflects a kind of certainty about the necessity of his
relationship to the past which convinced him that if his
poetry were to live at all, it had to grow out of the past
in such a way as to keep the past alive in it. He was repeatedly troubled and uncertain about precisely how
such a growth might take on substance and structure in
particular poems, but for Chaucer poetry began and
ended in remembrance. The trouble for the practicing
poet, however, is that remembrance is not a passive concept, and neither is the formal art which serves it.

In the first book of *Troilus and Criseyde,* introducing
the first *canticus Troili,* Chaucer writes:

> And of his song naught only the sentence,
> As writ myn auctour called Lollius,
> But pleinly, save oure tonges difference,
> I dar wel seyn, in al that Troilus
> Seyde in his song, loo! every word right thus
> As I shal seyn; and whoso list it here,
> Loo, next this vers he may it fynden here.
>
> (I. 393–99)

What I am most interested in here is the implied distinction between the content of the past—the "sentence"
—and its form. From this passage and others like it, it
seems that Chaucer felt he was expected to record the
"sentence," but that the added care of reproducing the

form was a grace beyond expectation. Later the problem
comes up again, and we get a somewhat fuller statement,
this time negatively put, of the same principle:

> But now, paraunter, som man wayten wolde
> That every word, or soonde, or look, or cheere
> Of Troilus that I rehercen sholde,
> In al this while unto his lady deere.
> I trowe it were a long thyng for to here;
> Or of what wight that stant in swich disjoynte,
> His wordes alle, or every look, to poynte.
>
> For sothe, I have naught herd it don er this
> In story non, ne no man here, I wene;
> And though I wolde, I koude nought, ywys;
> For ther was som epistel hem bitwene,
> That wolde, as seyth myn autour, wel contene
> Neigh half this book, of which hym liste nought write.
> How sholde I thanne a lyne of it endite?   (III. 491–504)

The principle of composition, somewhat differently put
in the two passages, is clearly that the poet's greatest freedom is with the forms in which he reclothes the truths
of the past. In exercising that freedom, the poet does
work within limits, limits set on the one hand by the
necessity to deal with the expectations and responses of
his readers and on the other hand by what he wants to
do with what the old books provide. That the freedom
also implies a responsibility for the poet and possible
troubles for the reader is evident in Chaucer's prefatory
remarks to his tale of Melibeus, although here the irony
lingering from the Sir Thopas fiasco complicates interpretation.

> "As thus: ye woot that every Evaungelist,
> That telleth us the peyne of Jhesu Crist,

Ne seith nat alle thyng as his felawe dooth;
But nathelees hir sentence is al sooth,
And alle acorden as in hire sentence,
Al be ther in hir tellyng difference.
For somme of hem seyn moore, and somme seyn lesse,
Whan they his pitous passioun expresse—
I meene of Mark, Mathew, Luc, and John—
But doutelees hir sentence is al oon.
Therfore, lordynges alle, I yow biseche,
If that yow thynke I varie as in my speche,
As thus, though that I telle somwhat moore
Of proverbes than ye han herd bifoore
Comprehended in this litel tretys heere,
To enforce with th'effect of my mateere,
And though I nat the same wordes seye
As ye han herd, yet to yow alle I preye
Blameth me nat; for, as in my sentence,
Shul ye nowher fynden difference
Fro the sentence of this tretys lyte
After the which this murye tale I write.
And therfore herkneth what that I shal seye,
And lat me tellen al my tale, I preye." (*CT*, VII. 943–66)

Another passage from *Troilus* reveals clearly how Chaucer felt the simultaneous privilege and obligation to illuminate, activate, even to add to what remembrance provided for him.

But soth is, though I kan nat tellen al,
As kan myn auctour, of his excellence,
Yet have I seyd, and God toforn, and shal
In every thyng, al holy his sentence;
And if that ich, at Loves reverence,
Have any word in eched for the beste,
Doth therwithal right as youreselven leste.

For myne wordes, heere and every part,

> I speke hem alle under correccioun
> Of yow that felyng han in loves art,
> And putte it al in youre discrecioun
> To encresse or maken dymynucioun
> Of my langage, and that I yow biseche.
>
> *(T&C,* III. 1324–36)

The "sentence" Chaucer claims to have preserved "all
wholly," but he hopes also to have "added some words
for the best." Those last six lines are particularly interesting, and I am not sure which of two interpretations
to give them. Perhaps they will bear both. The submis-
sion of the poem to the "correction, increasing, and
diminution" of those who have "feeling" for its subject
matter may be an attempt to indicate the part the reader's response is to play in the total efficacy of the poem.[12]
It probably ought to be pointed out also that Chaucer
was quite aware of the difficulty consequent upon basing
critical standards on the readers' responses:

> For to thi purpos this may liken the,
> And the right nought, yet al is seid or schal;

12. Similar suggestions occur in *T&C,* II. 255–62 and 267–72, in Pandarus' oft-quoted remarks on the craft of fiction:

> ". . . Nece, alwey, lo! to the laste,
> How so it be that som men hem delite
> With subtyl art hire tales for to endite,
> Yet for al that, in hire entencioun,
> Hire tale is al for som conclusioun.

> And sithen th'ende is every tales strengthe,
> And this matere is so bihovely,
> What sholde I peynte or drawen it on lengthe . . ."

> Than thought he thus: "If I my tale endite
> Aught harde, or make a proces any whyle,
> She shal no savour have therin but lite,
> And trowe I wolde hire in my wil bigyle;
> For tendre wittes wenen al be wyle
> Theras thei kan nought pleynly understonde;"

> Ek som men grave in tree, some in ston wal,
> As it bitit; but syn I have bigonne,
> Myn auctour shal I folwen, if I konne.
>
> ($T&C$, II. 45–49)

The Second Nun puts together similar ideas in a similar
aside to the reader before beginning her tale:

> Yet preye I yow that reden that I write,
> Foryeve me that I do no diligence
> This ilke storie subtilly to endite,
> For bothe have I the wordes and sentence
> Of hym that at the seintes reverence
> The storie wroot, and folwen hire legende,
> And pray yow that ye wole my werk amende.
>
> (CT, VIII. 78–84)

On the other hand, if we note how precisely Chaucer's
"to encresse or maken dymynucioun / Of my langage
. . ." translates the technical terms of the rhetoricians,
amplificatio and *abbreviatio,* lines 1324–36 from Book
III might be taken to suggest the possibility that some
subsequent poet may do with Chaucer's poem what he
has done with the old books of Benoit de Ste. Maure and
Boccaccio. At least, Robert Henryson may have read
them that way.

But whichever way we choose to read the lines, what
is most interesting in them in this connection is their
clear implication that the poet, as he re-forms the old
story to repair the "fretyng and biting" of time, is actually heightening its value by adding to its emotional effect.
The whole invocation to Book II of *Troilus* (much of
which has been quoted in the immediately preceding
pages) develops clearly the distinction between the primarily intellectual character of remembrance per se, and

the emotional efficacy which style can restore to it in the recreated poem. "Restore" may not be quite accurate, because Chaucer indicates his awareness in this invocation (and elsewhere) that the poet can, out of his own "sentement," correct or re-emphasize the effects latent in his materials. After invoking the historical Muse alone ("Me nedeth here noon other art to use"), he excuses himself to lovers and critics on the grounds that he is not writing out of "sentement," implying clearly that his readers probably do expect him to. But the various metaphors in the next twenty-five lines or so, all of them somewhat ambiguous in application, offer a series of sententious explanations and exceptions so that in the end the proem just *may* be taken to read, "be careful—the sentiment and a lot else may be here, all right, but my way of presenting it may not square with your expectations, or with earlier authors' methods."

The blind man who cannot judge of hues certainly does some subtle generalizing about the various colors of love in lines 21–49, in spite of his repeated implication that anybody is likely to have difficulty distinguishing them through the double veil of time and language difference. And this proem is a plea for tolerance of the poet's own "forme of speche" (which he is having a hard time patterning after his ancient exemplar), as well as of the speeches and actions of the characters in the old story. At least a recognition of the "sentement" is expected to follow from the successful cooperation of the ancient author and the modern one and his audience, since we are presumably able to judge whether these antique lovers "spedde as wel in love as men now do."

And, before proceeding with this discussion of "sentence" and "sentement," we should recall that Chaucer is aware of and occasionally states the nearly opposite, puritanical, and anti-poetic view of those who hold that

the attempt to beautify truth is only foolish pride. As
the Parson expressed it:

> "Thou getest fable noon ytoold for me;
> For Paul, that writeth unto Thymothee,
> Repreveth hem that weyven soothfastnesse,
> And tellen fables and swich wrecchednesse.
> Why sholde I sowen draf out of my fest,
> Whan I may sowen whete, if that me lest?
>
> .   .   .   .   .   .
>
> I wol ful fayn, at Cristes reverence,
> Do yow plesaunce leefful, as I kan.
> But trusteth wel, I am a Southren man,
> I kan nat geeste 'rum, ram, ruf,' by lettre,
> Ne, God woot, rym holde I but litel bettre;"
>
> (*CT*, x. 31–44)

Yet even for the Parson, the problem of effect was real
and serious, and for Chaucer generally it was a recurrent
one which almost always led him into some ironic considerations of the relation of his own experience and
that of his readers with what is recorded of the past.
While it is generally Chaucer's view that remembrance
precedes knowledge and wisdom, remembrance is never
by itself quite adequate to produce the most active virtue
or the best art, and it usually falls short in one of two
ways, both of them immediately involving effect. The
past may simply have lost its persuasive value, and therefore its applicability to experience. "My spirit feeleth
noght of swich mateere," the Franklin said. Or, as the
Squire more artfully put it,

> Who koude telle yow the forme of daunces
> So unkouthe, and swiche fresshe contenaunces,
> Swich subtil lookyng and dissymulynges

> For drede of jalouse mennes aperceyvynges?
> No man but Launcelot, and he is deed.
>
> (*CT*, v. 283–87)

On the other hand, the past may have remained all too persuasive, in the wrong ways. The poetry of Vergil, as one thirteenth-century cleric read it, was "a beautiful vase full of vipers." "Yit last the venym of so long ago," Chaucer complained of the story of Tereus; and later, in *Troilus and Criseyde:*

> Lo here, of payens corsed olde rites,
> Lo here, what alle hire goddes may availle;
> Lo here, thise wrecched worldes appetites;
> Lo here, the fyn and guerdoun for travaille
> Of Jove, Appollo, of Mars, of swich rascaille!
> Lo here, the forme of olde clerkis speche
> In poetrie, if ye hire bokes seche.   (v. 1849–55)

The argument about the balance between the intellect and the emotions in poetry may lead in almost any number of directions, and it lies somewhere near the center of nearly every serious and important critical theory, from Aristotle's on. But "intellect" and "emotion" may be quite reasonably interpreted to associate with various apparently irreconcilable elements in the aesthetic formula: "sentence" and "sentement," convention and originality, society and individuality, form and effect, the artificial and the natural, order and disorder, among many others. Depending on what grouping of these antinomies particular theorists make, and on how they attach values to each, they will produce justifications for art ranging from the moralistic or utilitarian at one extreme to the purely expressive (or perhaps therapeutic) at the other. Chaucer, like the aesthetic theorists of the earlier Middle Ages, followed the argument from a set of

predispositions which lead to a heavily utilitarian, or
rhetorical, definition of poetry. And I think one of the
most compelling of those predispositions was the aspect
of medieval idealism which made of history an intellectual and symbolic order, rather than a physical and
chronological one. The past, by becoming a series of illus-
trations of intellectual abstractions, lost its length—its
distance. At least, it lost them whenever it was considered
in the last two of the three senses of tradition I outlined
earlier. As a body of source material and as a significant
process, the past was immediately available to be amplified and animated in the best art so that it might become
a part of present moral experience. When Chaucer tells
us in the Prologue to the *Legend of Good Women* that
he is going "to declare in English the *naked text*" of the
legends, he is writing a disclaimer of his responsibility to
clothe the past in the animating amplifications of poetry,
and we should know what to expect. That may not be
the explanation a modern critic would give, but it is one
kind of explanation of why most readers, after the mag-
nificence of the Prologue, do not manage to persevere
very far into the flatlands of the legends themselves. Repeatedly in the course of retelling the legends, Chaucer
re-states his point:[13]

> The weddynge and the feste to devyse,
> To me, that have ytake swich empryse
> Of so many a story for to make,
> It were to longe, lest that I shulde slake
> Of thyng that bereth more effect and charge;
> For men may overlade a ship or barge.
> And forthy to th'effect thanne wol I skyppe,
> And al the remenaunt, I wol lete it slippe.   (616–23)

13. Cf. also *LGW*, 924–29; 1002–03; 1020–22; 1139–45; 1678–79.

But, if he occasionally tarries to develop an effect, we
may get a statement as revealing as this one at the opening of the tale of Lucretia:

> Now mot I seyn the exilynge of kynges
> Of Rome, for here horible doinges,
> And of the laste kyng Tarquinius,
> As seyth Ovyde and Titus Lyvius.
> But for that cause telle I nat this storye,
> But for to preyse and drawe to memorye
> The verray wif, the verray trewe Lucresse,
> That, for hyre wifhod and hire stedefastnesse,
> Nat only that these payens hire comende,
> But he that cleped is in oure legende
> The grete Austyn, hath gret compassioun
> Of this Lucresse, that starf at Rome toun;
>
> (1680–91)

That is, he will partly alter the purposes of one set of
earlier writers and combine them with more material
out of remembrance, all to heighten an effect that is at
once sentimental and moral.[14]

Once more, we probably should not leave the point
without noting the occurrence of an opposed set of notions, again set in a half-humorous passage which just
blurs their precise significance:

> For this ye knowen al so wel as I,
> Whoso shal telle a tale after a man,
> He moot reherce as ny as evere he kan
> Everich a word, if it be in his charge,
> Al speke he never so rudeliche and large,
> Or ellis he moot telle his tale untrewe,
> Or feyne thyng, or fynde wordes newe.
>
> (*CT*, I. 730–36)

14. Cf., in much more sketchy fashion, *LGW*, 1886–93, 2238–43.

Most commonly, however, even when he is speaking ironically or humorously, Chaucer associates emotional effectiveness with "fynding wordes newe," i.e. with deliberate verbal elaboration, which is one of the senses in which he uses the term "rhetoric."

> I dar nat undertake so heigh a thyng.
> Myn Englissh eek is insufficient.
> It moste been a rethor excellent,
> That koude his colours longynge for that art,
> If he sholde hire discryven every part. (*CT*, v. 36–40)

> Youre termes, youre colours, and youre figures,
> Keepe hem in stoor til so be that ye endite
> Heigh style . . .   (*CT*, iv. 16–18)

> Fraunceys Petrak, the lauriat poete,
> Highte this clerk, whos rethorike sweete
> Enlumyned al Ytaille of poetrie.   (*CT*, iv. 31–33)[15]

Yeats, in the lines from *Sailing to Byzantium* quoted at the beginning of this chapter, spoke of the artistic monuments of the past collectively as a source of instruction in the techniques of art—a "singing school"—as well as a source of inspiration. So, for Chaucer, the techniques of poetry were in a large part to be recovered from the past. They, too, were part of the substance of remembrance. In the *Complaint of Venus*, he apologizes to the "Princesse" to whom the poem is addressed for whatever faults she may find in it:

> For elde, that in my spirit dulleth me,
> Hath of endyting al the subtilte
> Wel nygh bereft out of my remembraunce;
>   (76–78)

---

15. Cf. also *CT*, iv. 1145–48; *CT*, iv. 2030–33; *CT*, v. 98–109; *CT*, v. 709–28.

Clearly, it was one function of remembrance to retain
the "subtleties of enditing." That those subtleties were
derived from the past can also be learned from other
passages of Chaucer's poetry. In the fifth book of *Troilus,*
for instance, he consigns his book to a critical posterity
with the injunction:

> But litel book, no makyng thow n'envie,
> But subgit be to alle poesye;
> And kis the steppes, where as thow seest pace
> Virgile, Ovide, Omer, Lucan, and Stace.

(v. 1789–92)

Here the past functions as artistic norm in two ways.
"Alle poesye" summons up an abstract body of aesthetic
principle, the sources or examples of which are specified
in the representative catalogue "Virgile, Ovide, Omer,
Lucan, and Stace." The literary past is a significant
whole, with a normative relationship to the individual
poet's work. Or if we take the last line as a list of indi-
viduals, rather than as a representative catalogue, then
we have the past as specific sources, although as far as
stylistic norms are concerned, that is a fairly rare attitude
in Chaucer. Occasionally, with a few poets—Vergil,
Ovid, Dante, and Petrarch—he seems to acknowledge
individual obligations in technique, but most commonly
it is a rationalized system of principles that Chaucer,
with the help of the scholastic rhetoricians, discovers in
the past.[16] I think it is pertinent that the Franklin, in
the prologue to his tale, lumps together the art and song
of the Breton lays with the Mount of Parnassus and the

16. Whitney H. Wells, "Chaucer as a Literary Critic," *MLN, 39* (1924),
255–68, provides an exhaustive list of citations of Chaucer's specific references to the work of previous and contemporary writers, and to the
particulars of stylistic technique, and I have relied heavily on his article
for materials in developing my argument here. However, he makes little

rhetoric of Cicero—clearly as though they were all the same thing—and concludes by excusing himself from the whole business of heightening his tale by any art. And Chaucer almost never manages (or even tries) to reproduce the specific forms of his originals, even though he repeatedly reminds his readers that

> folk han here-beforn
> Of makyng ropen, and lad awey the corn;
> And I come after, glenynge here and there,
> And am ful glad if I may fynde an ere
> Of any goodly word that they han left.
>
> (*LGW*, G. 61–65)

There is in these critical ideas about the poetics of tradition also an incidental irony for modern critics. Chaucer would certainly not have agreed with—and indeed scarcely understood—the insistence of some Victorian and post-Victorian critics that poetry of the past (Chaucer's, for instance) is somehow immune to contemporary standards of critical analysis and evaluation or impossible to measure by them. For Chaucer, although the agencies of poetic effect were sadly inseparable from language and therefore also from linguistic erosion, the art of poetry itself—not a language but a way of managing language —was a weapon in the eternal human battle against time.

But it was, again sadly, a weapon exclusively of man's own forging, and wrought of materials whose nature was itself of time, and therefore treacherously corruptible. Much has been written of Chaucer's irony and it will appear again in later chapters of this study, but here,

---

or no attempt to coordinate and interpret Chaucer's comments in the light of any aesthetic generalizations or to relate them to any contemporary body of theory, so I have added citations which I consider revelatory of basic principles and attitudes, even where they do not contain specific comments on details of technique in his own work or that of others.

insofar as that irony reflects fundamental artistic convictions, I think we are very close to one of its sources.
T. S. Eliot wrote:

> Men's curiosity searches past and future
> And clings to that dimension. But to apprehend
> The point of intersection of the timeless
> With time, is an occupation for the saint . . .[17]

Chaucer knew that the point of intersection was always
now, and that an occupation for the poet was to make
something timeless out of time, knowing all the while
that it was an impossibility. The future Chaucer searched
was often a future in which his own work had become
past, a part of the same partly illegible record which
his own remembrance supplied him of Virgile, Omer,
Lucan, and Stace. I think that is a large part of the significance of this curious passage late in the *House of
Fame* which has drawn some comment, but never to my
mind a wholly satisfactory interpretation:

> Sufficeth me, as I were ded,
> That no wight have my name in honde.
> I wot myself best how y stonde;
> For what I drye, or what I thynke,
> I wil myselven al hyt drynke,
> Certeyn, for the more part,
> As fer forth as I kan myn art.   (1876–82)

It is at least a very good possibility that these lines should
be read as a kind of contrast between the personal mortality of the man and the potential durability of that part of
his experience and intelligence ("what I drye or what I
thynke") which he can convert into poetry. But he will

17. "The Dry Salvages," *Four Quartets* (New York, 1943).

accept responsibility for that self which will survive in his poetry with a reasonable though limited confidence ("certeyn, *for the more part*"), dependent precisely upon the extent to which he has successfully mastered the craft. I would thus translate the last three lines, "I will face the consequences with considerable confidence, to exactly the degree to which I know—am skilled and able in—my art."

Chaucer knew, too, that a sufficient degree of artifice could increase the durability and affective intelligibility of that record, but artifice was always bought at the price of a kind of deliberate separation from actuality.

> Lo! I, Nature,
> Thus kan I forme and peynte a creature,
> Whan that me list; who kan me countrefete?
> Pigmalion noght, though he ay forge and bete,
> Or grave, or peynte; for I dar wel seyn,
> Apelles, Zanzis, sholde werche in veyn
> Outher to grave, or peynte, or forge, or bete,
> If they presumed me to countrefete.
> For He that is the formere principal
> Hath maked me his vicaire general,
> To forme and peynten erthely creaturis
> Right as me list, and ech thyng in my cure is
> Under the moone, that may wane and waxe;
> And for my werk right no thyng wol I axe;
> My lord and I been ful of oon accord. (*CT*, VI. 11–25)

However, human limitation being what it is, the law of nature may be as concealed in the opaque aberrancies of matter as art often is in the artifact; act and art may be contradictory or mutually explanatory, and man always the uncertain and often comical juggler of the two, never quite finally assured which proves the other.

> And than thoughte y on Marcian,
> And eke on Anteclaudian,
> That sooth was her descripsion
> Of alle the hevenes region,
> As fer as that y sey the preve;
> Therfore y kan hem now beleve.   (*HF*, 985–90)

On the other hand:

> For al be that I knowe nat Love in dede,
> Ne wot how that he quiteth folk here hyre,
> Yit happeth me ful ofte in bokes reede
> Of his myrakles and his crewel yre.   (*PF*, 8–11)

> For out of olde feldes, as men seyth,
> Cometh al this newe corn from yer to yere,
> And out of olde bokes, in good feyth,
> Cometh al this newe science that men lere.
>   (*PF*, 22–25)

That vision may illuminate the relations among art, experience, and truth, is one of the assumptions being tested in several of the pre-Canterbury poems, but since the form of the testing is by structural manipulation more than by overt commentary, I shall have to postpone consideration of it until a subsequent chapter. However, Chaucer does occasionally speak out directly on the subject, perhaps most pertinently in the hopeful but noncommital conclusion to the *Parliament of Fowls:*

> And with the shoutyng, whan the song was do
> That foules maden at here flyght awey,
> I wok, and othere bokes tok me to,
> To reede upon, and yit I rede alwey.
> I hope, ywis, to rede so som day
> That I shal mete som thyng for to fare
> The bet, and thus to rede I nyl nat spare.   (693–99)

Yet, as many critics have noted (particularly in the *House of Fame* and the Nun's Priest's tale), Chaucer is as aware of the uncertainty and possibility for error in interpreting dreams as he is in interpreting experience or literature.

In summary, Chaucer started from (and never grew away from) the primary definitions of purpose and method in art as laid down by the orthodox tradition in medieval aesthetics: poetry is a process of manipulating language so that the wisdom evolved in the past will become available, applicable, and operative in the present. Its most distinctive characteristic as poetry is its ability to stir emotion—to move knowledge into operation. However, I also think that Chaucer's reading of other poets, and his own practice of the art, rapidly convinced him that these ideas were problems in the practice of poetry more than they were rules for the conduct of it. Theories, even when they are sound ones, do not write poems. To know that artful language may move men to desire the good does not of itself guarantee that the poet rightly perceives the good, or that what he intends to be moving will actually be so, or that he may not betray the ends of art to its means and please to no purpose.[18] Such implications in the vein of commentary on the nature of poetry running throughout his work make the "retraction" at the end of the *Canterbury Tales* perhaps less contradictory than it might otherwise seem.

To observe that these are conventional ideas is less important than to observe that they came alive for him as artistic problems and led him into complex poetic

18. Cf. the Pardoner's remark:

Thanne telle I hem ensamples many oon
Of olde stories longe tyme agoon.
For lewed peple loven tales olde;
Swiche thynges kan they wel reporte and holde. (*CT*, VI. 435-38)

structures—several of which he became dissatisfied with
and abandoned—in which he tried to fix in remembrance
some emotionally effective synthesis of his sense of moral
values and past and present experience. I think that
Chaucer would have understood, in his own way, the
prayer to the past with which Yeats gives purpose to his
voyage to art's other kingdom:

> O sages standing in God's holy fire
> As in the gold mosaic of a wall,
> Come from the holy fire, perne in a gyre,
> And be the singing-masters of my soul.
> Consume my heart away—sick with desire
> And fastened to a dying animal
> It knows not what it is—and gather me
> Into the artifice of eternity.

3. The Prologue to the *Legend of Good Women*—A Re-examination of Principles

IN THE SPRING OF 1386, very probably, Chaucer had just completed his longest work to date, his greatest poem, *Troilus and Criseyde*. But both the Prologue to the *Legend of Good Women* and what are apparently later revisions and alterations of *Troilus and Criseyde* seem to indicate that he was not altogether satisfied with it.[1] From 1387 on, most scholars assume, he was engaged principally on the framed collection of narratives, the *Canterbury Tales*. In between the two—that is, between *Troilus* and the *Canterbury Tales*—he wrote the Prologue to the *Legend of Good Women*, the "F" version possibly in the summer of 1386 and the "G" version possibly some eight or ten years later. The Prologue is more immediately concerned with the subject of poetry than any other single work of Chaucer's, and it seems to me to reflect in a number of ways the uncertainty and searching of the transition from the *Troilus* kind of narrative to the *Canterbury Tales* kind, although that way of putting it makes a formula rather too neat to be perfectly accurate. The *Canterbury Tales,* as they survive to us, show unmistakable signs that Chaucer never clearly worked out what he intended them to be. And if the

1. Robert Kilburn Root, *Chaucer's Troilus and Criseyde* (Princeton, 1926), Introduction; see especially pp. lxx–lxxxi.

generally accepted datings are correct, then he was also revising the Prologue to the *Legend of Good Women* well after he had started on the *Canterbury Tales*. But we have no evidence to indicate that after *Troilus and Criseyde* he ever tried that kind of narrative poetry again, nor any to indicate experimentation with the framed collection before the *Legend of Good Women*, so that it remains fair to speak of the Prologue as taking shape during a transitional period. It will be the purpose of this chapter to point out how the Prologue brings together for extended reconsideration a scattering of aesthetic topics and themes from his earlier work to provide a kind of re-evaluation of the premises from which the earlier poems had proceeded. And because the Prologue to the *Legend of Good Women* does so concentrate Chaucer's basic poetic problems into a continuous discussion, it should provide useful illumination of the suggestions developed in the preceding chapter.

Questions attendant upon differences between the two versions of the Prologue are, to a certain extent, involved in an attempt to describe its treatment of aesthetic problems. The fact of revision is itself important evidence in the consideration of Chaucer as aesthetician, but how such evidence can be used depends finally on *certainty* about the order of variant versions, and most of the argument supporting the priority of one or the other version is presumptive or circular. None of it achieves final certainty. Fortunately for my purposes here, there is little significant difference between the two versions insofar as the attitudes they express toward the problems of poetry are concerned. The only two points at which differences in their structures will materially affect my argument are the placement of the *balade,* and the conclusion of the dream. In the "F" version, of course, the transition from introduction to vision begins at line 196, so

that we have 195 lines of introductory comment, as compared with 88 in "G." In the quotations (unless otherwise specified) I follow the "G" version, assuming it to
be the later, revised form of the poem.

We should begin by recalling the division of the Prologue into two parts: an 88-line introduction, followed
by a traditional love vision. Although it is customary to
regard the two parts as rather loosely connected, I pro-
pose to consider them as two closely correlated treatments, the first discursive, the second figurative and symbolic, of a common primary theme, the art of poetry.
After all, the charge on which Chaucer is haled into
court by the God of Love in the vision is that his poetry
isn't all it should be; the argument of his case produces
a critical bibliography of his work to date; and his sentence, finally, is to compose another, better poem. So the
two parts of the Prologue might also be described as a
general consideration of poetry as an art, followed by a
particular consideration of Chaucer's own practice of
the art.

In the introductory discourse, after an initial assertion
of the general authority of literary tradition ("olde
bokes"), the poet tells us that the one "experience" which
can draw him away from his "olde bokes" is the contemplation of the daisy in the spring meadows.

> Thanne mote we to bokes that we fynde,
> Thourgh whiche that olde thynges ben in mynde,
> And to the doctryne of these olde wyse
> Yeven credence, in every skylful wyse,
> And trowen on these olde aproved storyes
> Of holynesse, of regnes, of victoryes,
> Of love, of hate, of othere sondry thynges,
> Of which I may nat make rehersynges.
> And if that olde bokes weren aweye,

Yloren were of remembrance the keye.
Wel oughte us thanne on olde bokes leve,
There as there is non other assay by preve.
    And as for me, though that my wit be lite,
On bokes for to rede I me delyte,
And in myn herte have hem in reverence,
And to hem yeve swich lust and swich credence
That there is wel unethe game non
That fro my bokes make me to gon,
But it be other upon the halyday,
Or ellis in the joly tyme of May,
Whan that I here the smale foules synge,
And that the floures gynne for to sprynge.
Farwel my stodye, as lastynge that sesoun!   (G. 17–39)

The books—what survives to us from the past—are
indeed records of what we do not experience directly,
although the love, hate, and other sundry things which
they may cause to be in mind are, as ideas, things we
recognize in the old books partly because they are susceptible of "other assay by preve." And note too that it
is "to the *doctryne* of these olde wyse" that we are to
give credence, a credence which itself is qualified by that
phrase blandly implying so much of the sources of Chaucerian irony, in every *skylful* wise. Whence the "skyl,"
if there is "non other assay by preve"? Presumably it
should be from experience, from direct exposure to the
physical fact of nature, if we accept the statement in lines
29 to 39 of the poet's desertion of his books for the joys
of the May morning.

But *because* it can attract him so powerfully, the daisy
drives him back to his books again, seeking adequate
means to praise it artfully. The specific fact in nature
which had drawn him away from the general abstractions
of literary tradition becomes not exactly an abstraction,

but a sort of apotheosis—"flour of alle floures"—until it also is almost an idea. And that idea, in a nearly Platonic invocation of desire, demands his reverential praise and so leads him back to the particulars of tradition—the specific facts in art of borrowing, choosing, taking sides, adapting, ordering, etc.:

> Fayn wolde I preysen, if I coude aryght;
> But wo is me, it lyth nat in my myght!
> For wel I wot that folk han here-beforn
> Of makyng ropen, and lad awey the corn;
> And I come after, glenynge here and there,
> And am ful glad if I may fynde an ere
> Of any goodly word that they han left.
> And if it happe me rehersen eft
> That they han in here freshe songes said,
> I hope that they wole nat ben evele apayd,
> Sith it is seyd in fortheryng and honour
> Of hem that eyther serven lef or flour. (G. 59–70)

From this point, the familiar "flower and leaf" passage announces the general problem of the particular poem in the offing and makes a transition back to an almost verbatim recapitulation of the opening lines on the general authority of traditional knowledge.

> But wherfore that I spak, to yeve credence
> To bokes olde and don hem reverence,
> Is for men shulde autoritees beleve,
> There as there lyth non other assay by preve.
> For myn entent is, or I fro yow fare,
> The naked text in English to declare
> Of many a story, or elles of many a geste,
> As autours seyn; leveth hem if yow leste! (G. 81–88)

So the thematic pattern of the first 88 lines (during which, by the way, we have no inkling that any vision is forthcoming) is a movement back and forth between "experience" and "books," which might be roughly equated with pragmatic and traditionalist approaches to knowledge, and their respective attractions for the poet. At first this movement seems to be between wholly differentiated and apparently irreconcilable opposites, but in the epideictic apotheosis of the daisy, the pragmatic and the traditional become complementary, through the implication that tradition preserves at the level of generalized (universal) applicability the meanings or values of the facts of experience, so that the poet may identify them, may rightly order and direct his responses to them. Then too, the very lines in which Chaucer sketches this theory of literature are a working demonstration of it; scholarship credits Froissart, Deschamps, and Machault, among others, with contributions of various sorts to the language and ideas of this introductory passage.[2]

But apparently one can never have things in Chaucer quite so direct, so clear and simple, as this analysis of the first 88 lines of the Prologue might make it look. His whole discussion is framed in that troublesome defensive irony—the self-revealing pose of naïveté—which provides him simultaneously with a sub-liminal awareness of the limitations of human certainty, and with a pre-arranged escape from having to face up finally to the profundity of the aesthetic problem which his poetry constantly raises.

The irony certainly complicates interpretation here, as it so often does in Chaucer's poetry, but something should probably be said to forestall the objection that this irony, as well as the humor and frequent whimsicality of the narrator-poet's manner, make it impossible to take seriously the matters discussed in the Prologue. Set-

2. Robinson's explanatory notes to the Prologue, pp. 839–46, document the specific borrowings.

ting aside the easiest (and not very helpful) answer that jokes often have serious points, a more appropriate thought might be, "Why bring up these particular matters to be ironical or humorous or whimsical about?" The question is especially pointed in the light of the frequency of recurrence of many of these notions about art and knowledge in Chaucer's other works, sometimes with accompanying irony and sometimes without it. The narrator in the Prologue opens his discourse with a completely tongue-in-cheek assertion of the unverifiable "authority" of old books, then proceeds immediately to a finely sensitive statement of their contribution to the life of the mind, and then with jocular equanimity dismisses them in favor of the May flowers and birds. Yet surely the contradictory sequence, since it is *all* there, cannot add up to the conclusion that Chaucer is *not* talking at all about books and the inherent difficulties they present to the fallible mind of man, or about the conflicting claims literature and present actuality make upon his emotions. Neither does the carefully framed presentation of the sequence of divergent attitudes leave us any ground for saying that one is the "right" or "intended" attitude and the others just playfulness. Rather, the humorous irony is itself a way of projecting the perplexity that follows from taking the questions seriously enough to realize their inherent contradictions. And there could scarcely be a better vehicle for expressing it than the old, familiar *persona* of the naïve, slightly baffled, slightly incompetent academic poet with one eye always gazing out the window.

In this ironically complicated frame of aesthetic-epistemological considerations, Chaucer proceeds to recount his vision, a vision which figuratively re-enacts and develops to new tension the thematic problems of the introduction. The vision, Chaucer tells us, came to him

one May evening. He had been spending the day in the
meadow admiring the daisy, and decided, when he got
back home, to sleep in a summer house in the garden.
There the dream occurs to him, opening in an otherworldly and perfected version of the meadow of his day's
stroll. In this enchanted meadow, the God of Love and
his entourage, including Alceste, appear and their discussion of Chaucer's merits or demerits as an artist gets
under way.

Alceste provides the most obvious means of unifying
the two different parts of the Prologue. She is, first of
all, the figurative transformation of the daisy; she is also
the maiden of all maidens, as it had been the "flour of
alle floures"; but most significantly, her relation to the
poet is the same: she is to provide the "cause," the compelling attraction for the reverential poetry of the legend
which Chaucer is to write in penance for his "bad" poetry. Finally, we ought to observe that these transmogri-
fied qualities of the daisy find their physical personage in
a character from an ancient legend. As a thirteenth-century rhetorician would have put it, through an invented
figure of the poet's, the fact of experience and the values
of tradition become identified. As a critic in the newest
current vogue might put it, Chaucer has projected the
rational problems of the introduction into a myth which
may allow them to act out their solutions. But Chaucer
as dreamer, the poet on trial in this ideal visionary world,
neither clearly recognizes the complex image of Alceste,
nor is to be permitted to begin his reverential act which
will be a work of art, until he is cleared before the God
of Love of the charge of unworthiness through incompetence. It is true that the God of Love's initial charge is
that Chaucer has sinned against love, but the substance
of the sin is that he has written bad poetry, and its expiation must be by the composition of good poetry.

Of course, "good" and "bad" here must be defined in terms of the God of Love's critical standards, and they are heavily moralistic standards, as his subsequent comments make clear. Yet the fact remains that Chaucer is in trouble with the God of Love not because of anything he has done (or not done) as a lover, but because what he has *written* has been taken to be harmful to the cause of love, and therefore "bad" poetry. Perhaps if we sense here an ironic disagreement between Chaucer and the God of Love, and certainly if we take the initial charges together with Chaucer's (and Alceste's) later plea that he intended only to further truth in love, then there is an implication of a problem in correlating technique with intention so that effects can be accurately controlled. And the expiation, by a kind of law of counterpoise, must be for the poet to solve that problem—to write poetry the effects of which the God of Love will judge "good." But first, the dreamer-poet's art must be perfected by the perfecting of his perceptions, both formal and substantive.

Early in the vision, the beautiful ladies, of whom Alceste is the summation and apotheosis, perform the perfect act of reverence, in the traditional art of the *balade*.[3] Act and art, intention and effect, are perfectly combined (as they had been in the "natural lays" of the birds at the opening of the dream), but the poet cannot yet really

3. Only in the "G" version, of course, does it occur just that way. In "F," Chaucer sings the *balade* himself, rather awkwardly inserting it as a kind of footnote to the vision. The language does not make it at all clear whether Chaucer means the dreamer-poet thought of the *balade* at the time, within the vision, or whether the poet reporting later on his vision thought: "It seems to me I might say these verses in praise of this lady free." The ritual adoration of the lovely ladies comes twenty lines further on in "F," 291–301. But it is there, and serves precisely the same purpose as it does in its rather different circumstances in "G."

comprehend what the vision allows him to watch. It remains only a somewhat imperfectly understood model for him. In fact, the God of Love must considerably later identify Alceste for the dreamer-poet, who has not recognized her. And even though he apparently had the wit to observe and record her daisy-like costume and her daisy crown carved of a single great pearl, he also apparently fails to associate her with the daisy of his waking wanderings. The *balade* of the beautiful ladies actually reconciles, in the ideal world of the dream, what remain for the dreamer-poet apparently divisive ambiguities. Although it is to Alceste that their song is directed, they sing it kneeling around a real daisy in an ideal meadow, so that it becomes a realization and identification, and therefore didactic as well as reverential.

> Now whether was that a wonder thyng, or non,
> That ryght anon as that they gonne espye
> This flour, which that I clepe the dayesye,
> Ful sodeynly they stynten alle atones,
> And knelede adoun, as it were for the nones.
> And after that they wenten in compas,
> Daunsynge aboute this flour an esy pas,
> And songen, as it were in carole-wyse,
> This balade, which that I shal yow devyse.
>
> (G. 194–202)

> Whan that this balade al ysongen was,
> Upon the softe and sote grene gras
> They setten hem ful softely adoun,
> By order alle in compas, enveroun.   (G. 224–27)

In a way, then, the ritual of the lovely ladies has certified through its art the continuity inherent in a series of transformations: the real daisy of the poet's own world becomes the ideal daisy of his visionary version of that

world and then becomes, in turn, the Alceste who combines the natural and the ideal with the traditional past.
Or perhaps the formula can be put another way: the
ladies' recognition of Alceste is recognition of a possible
identity of experience, vision, and books—an identity
which Chaucer had troubled himself about continuously
in his earlier poetry and which he chose to discuss at the
opening of the Prologue.

Only after this ideal ballet (in which aesthetic-moral
ideal becomes ritual act) does the God of Love notice
the dreamer-poet, the human seeker and intruder whose
own art had been striving, but nonetheless imperfect.
And his first charge against the poet is not against his
intent, but against the effects of his poetry:

> "For thow," quod he, "art therto nothyng able.
> My servaunts ben alle wyse and honourable.
> Thow art my mortal fo and me werreyest,
> And of myne olde servauntes thow mysseyest,
> And hynderest hem with thy translacyoun,
> And lettest folk to han devocyoun
> To serven me . . ."   (G. 246–52)

Chaucer is unworthy to come before the God of Love
because he is "therto nothyng able"; that is, he lacks some
capability that a poet ought to possess to merit such an
audience. And the capability, negatively specified in lines
249–52, is obviously to write well and properly about
love. He is judged unable because of the effect of his
"missaying" and "translation." It is Alceste, the intercessor, who pleads his intentions, and at the same time
ironically doubly damns him by adding to the charge of
bad art the charge of "innocence" of its proper substance
and ends.

Some interesting variations evolve as the God of Love's
charge runs its 70-line course. (By now, incidentally,

there have been 88 lines in the introduction and 70 lines within the vision, of direct discourse about the problematic relationships among knowledge, tradition, experience, and art.) First, note that the God of Love, in assuming that the matter of poetry is in the main traditional (bookbound), takes us straight back to the center of the introductory discussion. But there, the question had been general: whether and why books (tradition) as a whole had relevance to knowledge and art. At the close of the introduction, the question had received a flat affirmative answer: yes, because books supplement practical experience with selection and interpretation, and they correct (by expansion) the limits of individual perception. The old books—literary tradition—in part simply contain matter that can no longer be "seyn with ye," but they also contain matter (and manners?) useful in interpreting and praising what *is* directly experienced, for the poet had turned gratefully to them for help in his praise of the daisy. And since they are to be used and believed "in every skylful wyse," one is also obligated to select and choose among them properly and carefully, although the difficulties of choice are not explored in the introductory section of the poem. In the God of Love's brief against Chaucer, the question of books becomes, openly, *which ones* ought the seeker to select and how should he decide? By this time, the "ability" of the God of Love's opening lines has become not only the ability to order language so that it does effectively what it ought, but also the ability of the poet to choose rightly the substances and purposes which his artful language is to activate. In the introduction, the poet had been driven from actuality back to books because he lacked skill to praise what he perceived. Here he is charged with a lack of perception which the lack of skill may imply.

Chaucer himself never answers the God of Love's

charges, or the aesthetic questions implied by them. Alceste, of course, intercedes for him as she must. For this poem, she is the figure for the "attractive cause" of his desire for perfection in his art, and for her to deny him would be, figuratively, for Chaucer to renounce the motivating attraction of ideal beauty for the forms of poetry—an attraction he had affirmed as basic at the first mention of the daisy. In fact, Alceste provides the dreamer-poet with four different excuses from the charges, but none of them comes anywhere near answering the implied questions, and all leave him guilty as charged but plead extenuating circumstances and throw him on the mercy of the court. First—and then again at the conclusion of her defense of Chaucer—Alceste begs the question altogether, simply reminding the God of Love that it is more becoming to a god to exercise mercy than strict justice. Second, she argues, some of the critics of Chaucer's poetry to whom the God of Love had been listening might well have been malicious, envious, or just loose talkers. Then, in the third place, a few of his poems are not too bad, and in others he may have been just too stupid and inept to know what he was doing. Finally (and this is an excuse so feeble that she devotes only a couple of lines to it), Chaucer is a court poet, and maybe someone told him what he had to write. By the time Alceste has finished her argument, we are only about a hundred lines from the end of the Prologue, and the defense has conceded the defendant's guilt completely.

In the discursive introduction, and in the ritual, figurative re-enactment of the themes of that discourse in the vision, Chaucer makes the most direct, complex, and extensive effort anywhere in his poetry to confront and resolve a problem which had occurred as an introductory irritant and a continuing minor theme in every one of his previous works: the nature and functions of art and the justification of the artist.[4] Through the *Book of the Duchess,* the *Parliament of Fowls,* the *House of Fame,* and *Troilus and Criseyde,* Chaucer's problem evolves a sort of recurrent, classical form: art is primarily a matter of adjustment, a reconciliation through language, of *tradition,* which includes artistic forms and conventions, *practical experience,* and *ideal knowledge* (often in the form of dreams and visions). In all these poems except *Troilus and Criseyde,* there is even a common primary structure: a vision, framed by a piece of the poet's personal experience (usually ironically presented) and a part of an old book.

In a way, the structure of the Prologue to the *Legend of Good Women* is a reversion to the experience-books-dream pattern of before *Troilus and Criseyde.* The "book" is here overtly generalized to all tradition, and the "experience" of the daisy-worship may seem at first a bit whimsical, but the early pattern of approach to the vision is clearly here. This time, however, there is the important difference that tradition, act, and ideal are not only the principal structural members of the poem; they are also the principal subjects treated within the structure and ordered by it. So everything about the Prologue leads us to expect that in it Chaucer will try to settle for himself the question of the nature of poetry and how the artist can produce it with skill and certainty. Until the God of Love's charges against Chaucer,

---

4. For a summary of the troublesome problem of dating the Prologue, see the explanatory notes in Robinson. In general, I incline to accept the arguments of J. L. Lowes in "The Prologue to the *Legend of Good Women* as Related to the French Marguerite Poems and to the *Filostrato,*" *PMLA, 19* (1904), 593–683; and in "The Prologue to the *Legend of Good Women* Considered in its Chronological Relations," *PMLA, 20* (1905), 798–864. See also Root's edition of *Troilus,* Introduction, pp. xiv and lxx–lxxx. However, I do not want to make any particular argument concerning the dates.

we had seemed to be moving quite steadily along the lines of orthodox medieval rhetorical-aesthetic theory toward such a settlement, but when the God of Love throws the question back to fundamental matters of operation—that the poet must *know* truth, must himself know *how* to select the *right* traditional means, must manage to do actually what he intended ideally—then everything stalls.

> Ek al the world of autours maystow here,
> Cristene and hethene, trete of swich matere;
> It nedeth nat al day thus for to endite.
> But yit, I seye, what eyleth the to wryte
> The draf of storyes, and forgete the corn?
> By Seynt Venus, of whom that I was born,
> Althogh thow reneyed hast my lay,
> As othere olde foles many a day, . . .   (G. 308–15)

From this point to the end of the poem (about 150 lines) no one has anything to say (except for Chaucer's hastily shushed insistence that his intentions really were good) about how the individual poet can surely select, arrange, and control specific means to produce particular, good poems by general or theoretical standards. There might seem to be at least two clear choices here, and Chaucer comes close to each of them, although finally he takes neither. On one side, we are not at this point in the argument very far from a Sidneyan notion of Imagination—a special kind of near-divine insight into ideal truth granted to the poet along with his technical powers. On the other hand, neither are we very far from an ironic rejection of all the traditional rules, standards, and purposes, and a kind of post-Romantic insistence that the poet can only write what he sees, follow intuitions, and hope for the best. But Chaucer here claims neither of these, nor any other possible resolutions.

What he does is simply to retreat into the system of ironic evasions, of which we have been kept half aware all through the vision, although more remotely and less consciously than we were in the introductory 88 lines. But in the vision, the irony is situational—a fact of the structure of the visionary world—rather than a consequence of any discrepancy between the poet's matter and his attitude toward it. And to the degree that the order of the visionary world is susceptible of various and conflicting but equally possible interpretations, judgments become proportionally uncertain. Chaucer, the creator of the *mythos* of the Prologue, has stalled over the question of just how to accomplish in his poetry what he apparently knows he ought to accomplish; Chaucer the seeker, the dreamer-poet on trial within the vision, finds himself in a world whose overtones so often seem to clash with its appearances that he is never quite sure what the effective standards of judgment are.

This last uncertainty is most obvious in the dreamer-poet's failure to recognize Alceste, his transfigured daisy. She *is* the daisy, and the dreamer-poet carefully notes all the details of her appearance which show it, but he does not recognize the identity, apparently not even after the *balade* of the lovely ladies has reasserted it. She is to be the attractive cause for the good poetry he is yet to write, but he does not know it. She is the figure from ancient legend who unites books, vision, and actuality, but (after all the talk about traditional knowledge in the introduction) he has forgotten the old book back home in his chest, in which he might have looked her up.[5]

5. But in defense of the dreamer as bibliographer, it ought to be noted that modern scholarship has done little better with locating that book. The neo-Ovidian metamorphosis which the God of Love provides for Alceste is, as far as we know, his own or Chaucer's invention. Quite literally, Alceste both is and is not a character out of antiquity surviving in old books.

There is a more fundamental, though less obvious, irony in the character of Alceste, an irony which colors the whole vision world in which she and the God of Love exist. The dreamer-poet nowhere shows overtly any consciousness of it, but the ambiguous hierarchical structure of the dream world, and particularly the choice of language by which Alceste and the God of Love are presented, suggest constantly to the reader that this *paradis d'amour* might, by a different interpretation of "Love," become a Christian heaven. Alceste is not only the intercessor for a sinner whose case requires that justice be tempered with mercy; she also wears the crown which is both daisy and pearl, drawing into the poem a richly suggestive set of ambiguities based on the double meaning of *margarita* (daisy and pearl). Earlier poets, some of whom Chaucer had been cribbing in the introduction to the vision, had fairly well stablized a conventional distinction between the two readings of this hoary pun, its "daisy" aspect suggesting regularly the perfection of the courtly lady, the object of human, sexual love, and its "pearl" aspect suggesting virginal purity, an expression of divine love.[6]

There are several interesting directions in which we might pursue the problem of the double character of Alceste and her visionary milieu, but since I am most concerned here with the aesthetic implications of the poem, I want to emphasize particularly its suggestion of the ultimate difficulty for a poet who considers his art

6. Cf. Lowes, *PMLA*, *19* (1904), 593–683, and the body of commentary, much too large to list here, which has grown up around *The Pearl*. Thomas Usk, a contemporary whose work owes something to Chaucer's, has a good deal to say in his *Testament of Love* about the various meanings and their relationships. See also the remarks on the daisy in D. W. Robertson, "Historical Criticism," in *English Institute Essays*, 1950, ed. Alan S. Downer (New York, 1951).

as an adjunct to morality: Which morality must it serve, and what will be the result for its quality?

It is not enough to say that Chaucer is merely borrowing from the courtly love convention. He is indeed borrowing from it, in order to use one of the fundamental ambiguities implied in its conventional language so that they are part of what Muscatine calls "its inherent fitness to mean." The Prologue even intensifies awareness of the ambiguity, in its manner of presentation of Alceste, particularly. And there had been other medieval writers (notably Andreas Capellanus and Dante) who had equally sensed the problem for the writer in the paradox of feeling consequent upon the ambiguity. Further, Chaucer did choose to build this court of love as a setting for the trial of a poet, and a major element in its interlocking ironies is that several of the particular questions about properly moralistic poetry turn out to be the same in the two contradictory moralities. It is just that the specific answers to them are so disturbingly different. It is trouble enough that the poet, even with his mortal sight cleared by supernatural vision, cannot always recognize the relationship between the actual and the ideal (daisy-Alceste); it is nearly too much when the ideal itself appears as multiple, or containing within itself illusion and diffraction. Even when he may have been sufficiently instructed to comprehend Alceste as the apotheosis of the daisy, a poet can scarcely be expected to manage a set of characteristics which identify her as an ectype of Venus and the Blessed Virgin simultaneously.

The same difficulty (with the same irony) is reflected in the God of Love's indictment of particular poems. The two which seem to have offended him most are the *Romaunt of the Rose* and *Troilus and Criseyde,* and just why those two in particular should have so bothered the God of Love is certainly an interesting question. In the first place, the two poems proceed from moralities so different that it is nearly impossible to see how they could both be heresies against the same law.[7] Even if we assume that the God of Love's charge is directed against some lost Chaucerian translation of the whole poem, rather than only against the fragments we now have, we are still faced with the difficulty that there is a clear shift in moral perspective between the two parts of the *Romaunt*. *Troilus and Criseyde* would obviously offend a courtly God of Love, but again ironically; it would do so precisely because it is clearly and insistently moral. And it measures the morality of the God of Love against the morality of the Christianity which is at once suggested and parodied by the dream world of the Prologue. The whole paralyzing system of ironies is further strengthened by the recollection that it was the God of Love who first put the aesthetic discussion on a moral basis. Even the dreamer-poet's final attempt to excuse himself begs the question:

> But trewely I wende, as in this cas,
> Naught have agilt, ne don to love trespas.
> For-why a trewe man, withoute drede,
> Hath nat to parte with a theves dede;
> Ne a trewe lovere oghte me nat to blame,
> Thogh that I speke a fals lovere som shame.
> They oughte rathere with me for to holde,
> For that I of Criseyde wrot or tolde,
> Or of the Rose; what so myn auctour mente,
> Algate, God wot, it was myn entente
> To forthere trouthe in love and it cheryce . . .
>
> (G. 452–62)

It is precisely what constitutes "trouthe in love" that is at issue, a question complicated further by the col-

7. Robinson's headnote to the *Romaunt of the Rose* points out how difficult it is to make a case for any offense to a courtly God of Love from the surviving fragments of the Middle English translation.

lateral one of the possible discrepancy between intention and effect in poetry.

The line of reasoning begun in the very first lines of
the Prologue has now finally turned back upon itself
—become completely circular. Chaucer had begun with

> A thousand sythes have I herd men telle
> That there is joye in hevene and peyne in helle,
> And I acorde wel that it be so;
> But natheles, this wot I wel also,
> That there ne is non that dwelleth in this contre,
> That eyther hath in helle or hevene ybe,
> Ne may of it non other weyes witen,
> But as he hath herd seyd or founde it writen;
> For by assay there may no man it preve.
> But Goddes forbode, but men shulde leve
> Wel more thyng than men han seyn with ye!   (G. 1–11)

From there, the argument had taken him from perception to interpretation, from actuality to art. Then the
aesthetic question ultimately resolved itself into a moral
one, and in doing so returned to the fundamental problems of human perception: contradictory multiplicity,
illusion, incomplete data, defective will, the discrepancy
between intention and act.

The ending of the Prologue to the *Legend of Good
Women* is almost purely mechanical. The God of Love
grants Chaucer mercy; Alceste sets his penance, which
is to write again and try to do better; the Prologue closes
with the poet, after all no more certain than before,
awake and writing. Books, visions, actions; the poet's
intentions, the technical devices of language, the emotional responses of the readers; how, finally, is the poet
to adjust all these knowingly, truthfully, and artfully?
In any particular instance, how does the poet proceed
safely and surely from theory to practice? These are the
questions which I think provoke the aesthetic discussion

in the Prologue. In a way, it had been a continuing discussion from the *Book of the Duchess* on; here it absorbs
the primary machinery of the poem, forcing Chaucer directly into a critical confrontation with his principles and
accomplishments. Then it relaxes, still unresolved. And
the legends themselves, which follow the brilliant Prologue, are flat, more or less unrelieved failures. As a first
attempt at the framed series of tales, a possible formal
escape from the circularity of the old, compulsive, book-
experience-dream pattern, the *Legend of Good Women*
takes Chaucer exactly nowhere. Neither attempt—the
theoretical one in the Prologue nor the practical one in
the legends themselves—really works. Lacking a complete text of the finished *Canterbury Tales,* I remain
doubtful that Chaucer ever resolved the problem satisfactorily for himself.

What the Prologue to the *Legend of Good Women*
leaves us with is a statement of a complex problem in the
persuasive adjustment of language to truth, and several
suggestions about the mortal limitations which make the
problem even more complicated in practice than it is in
theory. As I have already suggested, it is a problem for
which Chaucer sought various solutions in the structural and stylistic experiments of his various poems, and
many of these will be explored in subsequent chapters.
But it is also a problem which, despite the variety of his
attempts to solve it, remains essentially the same for
Chaucer from the *Book of the Duchess* to the end of his
career. Throughout the range of his work, it is stated or
alluded to in a constant set of terms which seem to me
to indicate clearly that both the basic concepts in the
problem and the means by which Chaucer attempted
to solve it grow directly out of the orthodox rhetorical
aesthetic which descended from a kind of fusion of Cicero
and St. Augustine, through the thirteenth-century school
rhetoricians, to (among others) Dante and Chaucer.

4. The First Structural Stereotype: The *Book of the Duchess*, the *House of Fame*, and the *Parliament of Fowls*

ONE OF THE MAJOR DIFFICULTIES encountered by students of the history of poetic theory is the problem of how to interpret, in their various contexts, terms or statements which may represent only different ways of formulating the same thing, or which may look very much alike but actually proceed from different assumptions and imply different conclusions. To a considerable extent we are involved in both versions of this problem in trying to evaluate the relationships between medieval aesthetic theory and poetic practice. On the one hand, I think we have generally tended to exaggerate the gap between the two by taking the structure and terminology of medieval poetics (particularly the academic expressions thereof) in their narrowest and most arbitrary senses, making them appear to be dealing most of the time with questions either peripheral or irrelevant to what modern theorists are most concerned with in the nature of poetry. And at the same time we quite properly insist that we read Chaucer, for instance, because he is a great poet in terms of our necessarily modern understanding of what poetry is and does. One particularly damaging consequence is that we create a false medieval-modern conflict which we must rationalize around, usually either by insisting that Chaucer was not a medieval poet in terms of the definitions of art offered by his contemporaries, or by an appeal to his contemporary audience as a limiting factor in our understanding of his art, thus by implication denying his poetry to modern sensitivity and relegating him to the status of historical documentation. On the other hand, a study such as this can discover similarities between Chaucer's ideas about poetry and those of the rhetorical theorists which tempt one to explain them in terms of direct influence, but which might just as well occur because both the poet and the theorist had seen through to what we still consider some of the fundamental problems of art.

When Horace speaks of poetry as a way of rearranging fact to increase its profit and delight; or Vincent of Beauvais tells us ". . . the function of the poet, then, is this, that with a certain beauty he converts actual events into other species by his slanting figures";[1] or the school rhetoricians of the thirteenth century write of disposition, amplification, and abbreviation as ways of reworking old material to illuminate truths in it which had become obscure; or Chaucer tells us his poetry attempts to cultivate new corn in old fields; or Pope argues that poetic language dresses Nature to human advantage; or, in our own time, Whitehead defines art as ". . . any selection by which the concrete facts are so arranged as to elicit attention to particular values which are realisable by them";[2]—when these men make such assertions, they are all talking about the same basic problem: the relation of art to truth and belief. Certainly for some of these men the question of the contents of truth, and therefore the criteria for belief, were assumed a priori, so that their

1. See above, Ch. 1, p. 32.
2. *Science and the Modern World* (New York, Macmillan, 1925), p. 280.

technical analyses of art take notably different forms from those we find in other analysts for whom the content of truth and the criteria for belief are either still open questions or have been differently defined.

I think that one of the distinctive features of Chaucer's view of poetry is that very early in his development as a poet he became engrossed with the question of art, truth, and belief largely as he found it stated and analyzed in the aesthetic tradition represented by the school rhetoricians. But he also became aware that while a priori assumptions might do very well for the theorist —even leading to technical analyses of procedures with great practical advantages—the poet in practice simply couldn't make those assumptions. That is, to say that truth is known and defined by extra-poetic means, but that it may be activated among men by poetry is a generalization which doesn't help a poet much in deciding which is the truth which he must (despite his human limitations) perceive and illuminate. And since Chaucer, as has often been pointed out in support of the wrong conclusions, was not a metaphysician or epistemologist, his statement of the problem comes not in a formal rejection of the theory, or even in any organized critique of it. Chaucer found the traditional theories sound and reasonably satisfactory as far as they went. Instead of rejecting or rewriting them, what he did was to invent structures and a style (largely along the lines recommended in the treatises) which would make us see the various truths they might contain, but in simultaneous awareness of the poet's (and all men's) limitations and fallibility. The consequence, as no reader of Chaucer has ever failed to notice, is a distinctly ironic voice. Perhaps part of the reason why the irony (as again almost everybody has observed) has so little bitterness in it, and so often includes the author along with the subject, is that it has its origin in the poet's humility before the un-realizable possibilities of his art. Dante may have claimed with confidence the title of poet even after the proud assertion that there was no more authoritative human voice than that of poetry; Chaucer would claim the title on those terms only as he could hedge it with the defensive qualifications of irony.

There are several ways in which the problems under discussion produce visible effects in Chaucer's poetry, besides providing the principal theme of the Prologue to the *Legend of Good Women* and a recurrent topic for a sizeable scattering of commentary throughout his work. In the remaining chapters I want to examine the over-all structural patterns which he designed and some of his peculiar manipulations of style, to see what additional light they may throw on his poetic art.

With respect to structure, the bulk of Chaucer's work (excluding the short lyrics) can be usefully divided into three groups: 1) combinative structures—*Book of the Duchess, Parliament of Fowls, House of Fame,* Prologue to the *Legend of Good Women*—in which there is some version of the book-experience-dream formula; 2) inclusive single narratives—*Anelida and Arcite* and *Troilus and Criseyde*—in which he retells and redecorates an "old storye," unframed and continuous; and 3) framed collections of tales—*Legend of Good Women* and *Canterbury Tales.* Since the chronology of Chaucer's work is still in pretty much the same precarious state it has always been in, it would be foolhardy and pointless to try to arrange these structural groups so as to suggest any particular direction of development in his poetics.[3]

3. See Paull F. Baum, "Chaucer's 'The House of Fame'," *ELH, 8* (1941), 248–56, and Bertrand H. Bronson, "The Parlement of Foules Revisited," *ELH, 15* (1948), 247–60, for recent, amusing, and pointed critiques of untested traditional assumptions in dating Chaucer's works.

In fact, if there is any reliability at all in even the relative
datings which the last three or four generations of Chaucer scholars have tended to agree upon, then the three
categories quite evidently overlap in enough ways that
the only safe generalization (which I suspect is the right
one anyway) is that almost from the beginning of his
career, Chaucer was experimenting with at least the first
two kinds of structure. There seem to be cogent reasons
for assuming that several of what later became *Canterbury Tales* were produced considerably earlier than
1387–1400, so he must have been experimenting with
conventional straight narrative structures along with the
more unorthodox kind of thing in the *Book of the
Duchess,* the *House of Fame,* the *Parliament of Fowls,*
and the Prologue of the *Legend of Good Women.* If the
Legend of Good Women should after all be significantly
earlier than Lowes and Kittredge argued,[4] or if the
House of Fame be dated relatively early and taken as an
abortive attempt to get a collection of tales under way,[5]
then perhaps all three types were being experimented
with throughout the middle and late years of his career.

But, Chaucer criticism having only recently worked
out of the over-rigid confines of an earlier triperiodic
view, I do *not* want to suggest another to replace it.
Rather, the three structural types should be taken as indicative of three different tentative solutions in Chaucer's poetry to the aesthetic problems which I have been
discussing. The fact that there are unfinished works in
the list both complicates criticism and indicates in itself

4. Marian Lossing, "The Prologue of the Legend of Good Women
and the Lai de Franchise," *SP, 39* (1942), 15–35, and Carleton Brown,
"The Date of Prologue F to the Legend of Good Women," *MLN, 58*
(1943), 274–78, have both argued for earlier datings.

5. As Manly first suggested in *Kittredge Anniversary Papers* (Boston,
1913), 73 ff., and Sypherd denied in "The Completeness of Chaucer's
Hous of Fame," *MLN, 30* (1915), 65–68.

the uncertainty and dissatisfaction with which Chaucer moved from one kind of provisional solution to another. It should also make any critic extremely cautious about asserting that one or the other of these structural types represents Chaucer's final answer.

The most frequently repeated and perhaps the earliest of the three characteristically Chaucerian structural stereotypes is the one he began with in the *Book of the Duchess* and, probably, was still interested in as late as 1394, when he may well have been revising the Prologue to the *Legend of Good Women*. It is also, interestingly enough, the most original of the three types. Despite the closeness of these poems to the French love-vision in one of their three elements, the constant playing with different alignments of all three—old books, experience, and dreams—is nowhere paralleled in the sources.[6] The stereotype is also removed by several degrees of derivation from what is generally stated in the treatises of the academic theorists about setting up a basic structure. However, the kind of structure Chaucer produces in these poems can easily enough be seen as an extention of traditional structural principles. Dante, starting also from rhetorical theory and the practice of the "regular" poets, produced in the *Commedia* a structure which could be generally described in the terms I have been using: old books (especially Vergil), experience, and vision.[7] It may be even more interesting to note that if

6. See Marshall W. Stearns, "Chaucer Mentions a Book," *MLN*, 57 (1942), 28–31: ". . . it seems probable that the mention of a book in love-vision literature can be correctly called a conventional device only after Chaucer. Chaucer's use of it appears highly original and although the opening lines of the *Roman de la Rose* may have suggested it to him, he is responsible for its virtual origin and outstanding use as an integral component of the love-vision" (p. 31).

7. I do not intend the comparison as still another interpretation of Lydgate's "Dante in Inglissh."

most of these poems are relatively early—and all but the *Legend of Good Women* seem nearly certainly to antedate *Troilus,* at least—then the structural type which Chaucer created earliest was the least conventional, and in his later and greatest poem, *Troilus and Criseyde,* he worked with a structural pattern straight out of the textbooks.[8] Even the framed collection, which he seems to have turned to last, is more conventional than the first stereotype, in that there were several roughly analogous collections in contemporary and previous continental literature.[9]

Although I really do not know what to make of it, the four poems in this category (*Book of the Duchess, House of Fame, Parliament of Fowls,* and Prologue to *Legend of Good Women*) have regularly suggested to a variety of critics a variety of interpretations involving special occasions for the poems. Only for the *Book of the Duchess* has the occasion been agreed upon with anything approaching unanimity. But even if they are all occasional poems, and even if we could fix with certainty the occasions for all of them, that would not obviate further interpretation or critical analysis. An occasion is a peg upon which the poem is hung, and it may or may not limit the extent or direction of development which the poet makes of it in his poem. To lapse for the moment

8. Bronson, *In Appreciation of Chaucer's "Parlement of Foules,"* Univ. of Calif. Pubs. in English, *3*, no. 5 (Berkeley, 1935), 193–223, makes essentially the same point about the direction of Chaucer's development, but he holds that it is the Prologue to *LGW* which is the "return to convention." Obviously, I cannot agree about the Prologue, though he is clearly right in calling attention to the fact that "progress" is not always from "convention" to "originality."

9. Claes Schaar, *Some Types of Narrative in Chaucer's Poetry,* Lund Studies in English, 25 (Copenhagen, 1954) works from observation of the organizational style of narrative passages, rather than the structural patterns of whole works, but he reaches similar conclusions about the relative originality of the earlier works.

into thirteenth-century terminology, an occasion[10] may provide the "source" which is then re-emphasized by amplification, abbreviation, and the labor of stylistic illumination, just as an old book may. More succinctly, it is the business of the poet to write elegies, not obituaries. Whatever may have been their separate occasions, all these poems share some important overt themes and some ways of developing those themes. As poems, they are more alike than previous criticism has made them appear,[11] and I am a good deal more interested in their artistic similarities than in the occasions which may lie behind them.

First, of course, they share the tripartite structure I have used to define this category. Closer investigation subsequently will show how each of them works out its own alignment and weighting of the parts.[12] Second, all four are ironic in a special sense which is a direct consequence of their structural peculiarities. Specifically, in all these poems, major ironies result from disparities or contradictions between one structural element and one or both of the others. Without tracing them out into details of structure, Dorothy Bethurum has nicely noted and defined[13] the most important of these, in moral and philosophical terms. Speaking of the *Book of the Duchess* (the remark could apply, in slightly different senses, to the other poems in this category as well), she points out that

10. As Geoffrey of Vinsauf and Jean de Garlande both recognized.

11. These poems have, of course, traditionally been classed together as "love-visions," and Kemp Malone, in *Chapters on Chaucer* (Baltimore, 1951), notes a few other similarities. Charles Muscatine, who treats them very briefly in *Chaucer and the French Tradition* (Berkeley, 1957) calls the three earlier poems in the group "the experimental stage of Chaucer's poetry" (p. 98).

12. See above, Ch. 3, for the analysis of the Prologue to *LGW*.

13. "Chaucer's Point of View as Narrator in the Love Poems," *PMLA*, 74 (1959), 511–20.

the author's experience ". . . constitutes his principal, though not the only, realistic criticism of the dream of love he has described. It is made possible by the position he has taken as narrator."[14] And a little later, speaking of the *House of Fame,* she observes: "Here begins the opposition that goes all the way through the poems under discussion: books versus life, authority versus experience." But I think the opposition varies among all three possibilities, with experience set against dream, and dream against book, as well as book against experience; and in each opposition both members are limited by the contrast. Life, as compacted into the created character of "narrator" or "dreamer," may provide a "realistic criticism of the dream." So may the dream provide an idealistic criticism of life. The book may provide a useful critique of both, or resolve their apparent differences, or itself be shown as limited and unreliable or contradictory.

However, the problem in these four poems is certainly as much aesthetic as it is moral or philosophical. In three of the four (*House of Fame, Parliament of Fowls,* and the Prologue to the *Legend of Good Women*) the motive for the vision is the education and improvement of the poet, and the problems of art are as much evident in the thematic materials as the problems of love are. In fact, only the *Parliament of Fowls* really contains what could accurately and without qualification be called a love-vision, although all four are generally and somewhat carelessly labeled "conventional love-visions."[15] All four conclude with the author involved one way or another in writing. And all, including the *Book of the Duchess* (the only one in which the improvement of the poet is not a declared purpose), begin with some discussion of

14. Ibid., p. 513.
15. Cf. Robinson's explanatory headnotes to the four.

the problem of literature as related to tradition and current experience.

Finally, to conclude this general catalogue of similarities, none of these four is strictly speaking a narrative poem in the sense that *Troilus and Criseyde* is, or *Anelida and Arcite* sets out to be. In none of the four is there any "plot," as we ordinarily understand that term in connection with fiction; the themes are not externalized in a formally interlinked sequence of action and character. All of them mix together a variety of sources, usually of quite different sorts, rather than working from one primary source or model and overlaying it with additional materials, and all of them are nearly impossible to classify generically with any precision.[16]

As a structure, and in its correlation of structure and style to demonstrate a moral theme, the *Book of the Duchess* is the most satisfactory poem in this group. I hasten to add that it reaches a recognizable formal conclusion and a finished demonstration of theme largely by aligning books, dream, and experience in such a way as almost to avoid raising the questions which add much both to the depth and to the inconclusiveness of the other three. Perhaps the *Book of the Duchess* can achieve such unity partly because it is a more strictly occasional poem, and the occasion sets most of the limits, granted a poet good enough to use them.[17] There is very little of

16. Except by the kind of indirection which lets us say, knowing the extra-literary occasion, that *BD* is an elegy; or, having what we assume to be all the legends he composed to follow it, to say that the Prologue to *LGW* introduces a framed collection. But neither of these is a classification really based on the internal structure of the work in question.

17. This is essentially the position taken by B. H. Bronson in "The Book of the Duchess Reopened," *PMLA,* 67 (1952), 863–81; James R. Kreuzer, "The Dreamer in the Book of the Duchess," *PMLA,* 66 (1951), 543–47; and Earle Birney, "The Beginnings of Chaucer's Irony," *PMLA,* 54 (1939), 637–55.

the refraction of artistic and moral perspective which complicates and helps prevent any satisfactory closure in the others.

E. T. Donaldson said in his recent *Chaucer's Poetry*[18] that a rhetoric is, among other things, a kind of defense, a way of protecting one's unarguable intuitions by projecting them into reliable, symmetrical, and apparently practical (i.e. generalizable) patterns. In the *Book of the Duchess,* as Bronson (among others) notes,[19] the organizing principle of the rhetoric—and what makes the defense work—is a series of identifications which the structure blocks out and the style links together:[20] the poet's experience, the fable from the old book, and the content of the dream, particularly the "experience" of the Black Knight. The identification is made partly through the common emotional situation of the Narrator, Alcione, and the Black Knight, but more specifically through repeated implications of their common subjection to the "lawe of kynde." The Narrator is more or less aware of this subjection all along, Alcione learns of it at the instruction of Ceyx, and the Black Knight has temporarily forgotten it and must re-learn it in the course of the dream. Presumably he does, if we allow enough and the right kind of emphasis on his "She ys ded!" at the end of the dialogue.

In the *apostrophe* which opens the poem, the Narrator raises the question of "kynde" at once, pointing out how contrary to it his own situation is:[21]

18. (New York, 1958), p. 941.

19. *PMLA, 67* (1952), 863–81.

20. Note the similarity in method to what Chaucer does with the daisy and Alceste in the Prologue to *LGW.*

21. I should like very much to know the exact significance of "ymaginacioun" in this passage and why and how it works against "kynde," but I am unable to answer either question.

> For sorwful ymagynacioun
> Ys alway hooly in my mynde.
>   And wel ye woot, agaynes kynde
> Hyt were to lyven in thys wyse;
> For nature wolde nat suffyse
> To noon erthly creature
> Nat longe tyme to endure
> Withoute slep and be in sorwe.   (14–21)

Then at line 50 a short *digressio* picks the subject up
again and the poet, who has just explained how far out
of normal adjustment with "kynde" *he* is, reminds us of
the old scholars and poets who were so in accord with
"kynde" that they made poems which men will read as
long as they love the "lawe of kynde." And as he is retelling one of these wonderful old fables, he interrupts
it with another *digressio* to underscore the precision with
which craft has counterfeited kind in it:

> Such sorowe this lady to her tok
> That trewly I, which made this book,
> Had such pittee and such rowthe
> To rede hir sorwe, that, by my trowthe,
> I ferde the worse al the morwe
> Aftir, to thenken on hir sorwe.   (95–100)

Just before the dream itself begins, and with these suggestions already in the background, Ceyx delivers a kind
of summary of the negative implications of the "lawe of
kynde":

> For in your sorwe there lyth no red.
> For certes, swete, I nam but ded;
>
> .   .   .   .   .   .
>
> To lytel while oure blysse lasteth!   (203–11)

What I want to emphasize here is the way in which style, by a variety of schematic and figurative devices— *digressio, apostrophe, sententia,* etc.—amplifies various elements in the structure so as to thread through them a common insinuation, and one which will provide the moral and aesthetic resolution for the poem. In the *Book of the Duchess,* this pattern is relatively uncomplicated by ironic ambiguities, and once the suggestions have been set working in the introductory passages, they are picked up and kept going through the dream, both in the plain style of the Dreamer and in the highly decorated style of the Black Knight. In fact, the next overt reference to Nature comes as the Black Knight is being introduced, and it comes in language closely echoing that with which the Narrator had introduced himself in his opening *apostrophe:*

> . . . for, by my trowthe,
> Hit was gret wonder that Nature
> Myght suffre any creature
> To have such sorwe, and be not ded.   (466–69)

By now the choice of language is not only working to keep us aware of the "lawe of kynde," but it is beginning also to link together Narrator and Knight—life and dream.

In the twenty-five lines or so following the Knight's complaint, the Dreamer gives us a detailed analysis of the Knight's departure from the natural order, concluding with

> For he had wel nygh lost hys mynde,
> Thogh Pan, that men clepe god of kynde,
> Were for hys sorwes never so wroth.   (511–13)[22]

22. Note also how the validity of the "lawe of kynde" is here again generalized through time (as it had been in lines 52 ff.) by the choice of the ancient personification.

And then, in the Knight's long speech immediately following—one of the most densely and elaborately figured
passages in Chaucer's poetry, thick with *repetitio, translatio, abusio,* oxymoron, an extended *allegoria,* etc.—he
anatomizes his own disorder in language which constantly measures it in terms of its perversion or inversion of
"kynde." The Dreamer, again, at line 715 summarizes
and underscores in plain terms what the Knight has been
elaborating in very elegant ones:

> Have som pitee on your nature
> That formed yow to creature.

The linking of Knight and Narrator continues, too. At
line 803 the Black Knight describes his callow days before Love reformed him with the phrase "Al were to me
ylyche good"; Chaucer had said of himself in his eight-
year sickness, "Al is ylyche good to me."

But even in this poem, where books, experience, and
vision are harmonized by stylistic insinuations which
refer them all to a common and viable moral reality,
there are several suggestions of a tension pulling against
the unity so nearly dominant in the poem. These, as I
said a little earlier, are not developed into principal
themes as they are in the other three poems of this group,
but they do foreshadow the development in the others
and require some comment here.[23]

Although stylistic echoes like those I have just been
noting do work to identify common elements in the
situations of Narrator, Alcione, and Knight, some peculiarities of structure and language work at the same time
to isolate, diminish, and make less comprehensible the
experience of the Narrator—a narrator who this time
does not appear as a poet until the very end of the poem.

23. Some of my argument at this point has been anticipated by Birney,
in "The Beginnings" (see above, n. 17).

The presentation of his melancholy is ironic to a degree nearly impossible to specify; we are no more sure about how seriously to take it than we are about its cause. Perhaps it is a love-sickness, but the grounds for saying so are rather slight. Perhaps it is a very serious matter, despite the tone of "That wil not be mot nede be left," but how much does the narrator really need the profound and austere solace offered by the awareness of mortality under natural law? And what is the tense of the opening lines? Do they apply to the time at which the poet is writing (i.e. after the vision—the time of the last line of the poem) or are they intended to indicate a state existing before the night's sleep during which the vision occurred? After all, he did get relief from his sleeplessness, as he remarks at line 221, though it came not from the "only physician" mentioned in line 39, but from the old book.[24]

Probably more striking than any of these, however, is the comic interlude of the Narrator's prayer to the God of Sleep which separates the old story from the beginning of the vision. In none of the other poems in the group, however differently they may align book, experience, and dream, is old fable so blocked off from the rest of the poem by such a comic intrusion of experience. And one nearly inevitable result (reinforced by the parody-rhetoric of the Narrator's prayer) is that we see his "experience" as after all different from that of Ceyx and Alcione, or the Black Knight. Even under the "lawe of kynde" there are differences troublesome enough that we do not know whether they are of degree or of kind. Like Alcione's serious prayer, the Narrator's burlesque one got results, and it saved him from the death which had threatened him in the introduction. (Alcione's prayer, however, had ultimately released her into death.)

24. Or perhaps from Morpheus, or "som wight elles, I ne roghte who."

Whether that correspondence implies that the Narrator's melancholia had been a clown's affliction I think we simply cannot tell from the poem. Just before moving into the particulars of his reading and dreaming, the Narrator had dismissed further discussion of the matter:

> but that is don.
> Passe we over untill eft;
> That wil not be mot nede be left;
> Our first mater is good to kepe.   (40–43)[25]

But "until eft" is a marvellously indefinite phrase. The ending of the poem brings us back through the dream to the bed and book and then on down to the immediate present with the poet putting the last period to his manuscript, thus presumably joining the "other poets" who honor the "lawe of kynde." Of what consolation, if any, has been his, we hear no more. All we can say at the end is that there is, even *sub specie aeternitatis,* more than enough variety in experience and response to make wisdom difficult and painful.

In all the later versions of the book-experience-vision stereotype, irony and tension are to develop a good deal more sharply out of the apparent discrepancy or irreconcilability of the three. In the *Parliament of Fowls,* the *House of Fame,* and (most noticeably) the Prologue to the *Legend of Good Women,* ironic contradictions develop even within the vision itself, as they do not in the *Book of the Duchess.* And as the three principal elements in the stereotype structure drift apart and begin to work more openly against each other, the theme of the artist's

---

25. A nicely ironic *occupatio;* so far there hasn't been any other matter in the poem. Our first matter *was* the narrator's trouble, and to keep to it could now only mean to go on to an explanation or full revelation of it.

problem becomes much more basically and overtly involved. But in the *Book of the Duchess* Chaucer does not strike his familiar pose of the struggling but inept poet of Love, which he knows only from books. The problem of the poet is phrased at the opening of this poem not as a problem but as a laudatory generalization which does not, at the time, include the Narrator. At the end of the poem, he simply says, "All right, I've put it into poetry," quietly joining those he had earlier praised without calling any attention to his abilities or inabilities to belong among them.

Although there are in it the uncertainties I have mentioned, the *Book of the Duchess,* on its limited and perhaps too generalized terms, does assert a useful identity of book, dream, and life,[26] an identity knowable and revealable through art—even though the benefit to the artist may remain an unsettled question. Except for those latent ironies—and they are very important—the *Book of the Duchess* might have been written directly from Jean de Garlande's structural formulae.[27] Its beginning (morally speaking) is in a proverb, and in a way the whole poem is a demonstration of Ceyx's short last speech to Alcione. The proverb is amplified by skillfully working together a pastiche of borrowed material, re-

26. Cf. Muscatine, p. 98: "It is the least accomplished technically and the narrowest in scope, but it is in a sense the most finished. It is the most homogeneous in style and the clearest in meaning."

27. Benjamin S. Harrison, "Medieval Rhetoric in the Book of the Duchesse," *PMLA, 49* (1934), 428–42, raises the same specious argument which Naunin had raised earlier: that where Chaucer's style seems closer to his French sources, there the "influence" of the school rhetoric can be discounted. I do *not* contend that Chaucer wrote BD as a way of working the exercises set by the manuals. But there is really no way to separate influences as precisely as Naunin and Harrison assert; one influence does not invalidate a similar one; and, finally, the argument is reversible: perhaps if Chaucer's taste hadn't been formed by the orthodox theories, he never would have liked the French poems.

decorated rather formally by fairly elaborate figuration, all strung together principally on the thematic thread of the "lawe of kynde." But, as will be even much more effectively evident later in *Troilus and Criseyde,* Chaucer must reveal a truly human morality, so that the "worldes blysse" that lasts so little while must be seen as real bliss, within its limits desireable and worth desiring,[28] and its loss a real loss which requires a hard-won reconciliation. Otherwise both morality and art are cheapened and made false to actuality, as well as logically unnecessary. Consequently, the decorative elaboration of style in this poem amplifies by throwing suggestions principally in two directions[29]: a dominant emphasizing the beauty of the transitory, and an absolutely essential minor, reminding us both that the transitory is not always so lovely and that there is a larger and more stable pattern into which the transitory fits.[30]

The *House of Fame* takes the problems latent in the unresolved ironies of the Narrator's situation in the *Book of the Duchess,* and those buried in the formulation about old poets and the "lawe of kynde," and makes them the central motif of the poem, insofar as it has one. Consequently, the not fully developed irony of the poet's personal situation vis-à-vis the situation in his poem becomes a deliberately double point of view, maintaining unresolvable ambiguities all through the poem. In Book III these are translated into the very structure of the

28. Cf. Alexander J. Denomy, "Courtly Love and Courtliness," *Speculum, 28* (1953), 44–63.

29. Sometimes simultaneously, as when the undercurrent of Nature images and references runs through the Knight's elaborate description of his beloved.

30. Dorothy Bethurum, "Chaucer's Point of View," phrases it: "The heart of Chaucer's position as narrator is to set off the contrast between books and experience, between the stable world of learning and the fragile world of love" (p. 520).

allegory. In Book II they remain matters of viewpoint, reflected principally in the dialogue and in stylistic exaggeration. In Book I, where the poet is alone, they must be managed as they are in the Prologue to the *Legend of Good Women,* by a style and a juxtaposition of topics. In one way, that means of handling ambiguity carries right through the poem, in its over-formal, overblown rhetorical paraphernalia of proems, invocations, etc., which suggest pretensions to high art at the same time that the parodic tendencies of the style and the content of the poem deny them.[31]

In the *House of Fame's* version of this structural stereotype, the salient characteristic of the alignment of books, dreams, and experience (aside from the fact that they so patently fail to corroborate each other) is the absence of that careful blocking of each into its own structural area which characterizes the structure of the *Book of the Duchess.* The dream is this time very nearly a complete framing device. The old book—the retelling of the Aeneas-Dido story—comes within it, in Book I, and the poet's experience is, in Book II, introduced within the dream by the attribution of it to the dreamer as a life outside the dream but relevant to its character and purposes. The Proem, however, and the Invocation to Book I do come outside the dream, and they raise questions about books and dreams which send us into this particu-

31. Robert J. Allen, "A Recurring Motif in Chaucer's 'Hous of Fame'," *JEGP*, 55 (1956), 393–405, is the only critic, to my knowledge, who defines the problem of the poet as a "motif" in the poem, although Miss Bethurum recognizes its presence: "The implication is, I think, that the tidings of love he is to hear will furnish more material for his poems, for certainly mere tidings of how other people fare would not be the reward a lover looked for" (Bethurum, p. 514). It will become apparent, however, that I consider the "poetic problem" rather more than a "recurring motif" in *HF,* and that I do not agree with Professor Allen about the contrasting attitudes toward experience in the scholar and the literary artist.

lar dream (which contains much about old books) in a very carefully prepared frame of mind.

In a manner akin to that of the discussion of books and experience which opens the Prologue to the *Legend of Good Women,* Chaucer opens with a Proem discussing dreams in terms of the variety of opinions about them available in the old books. These opinions are so at variance ". . . that oure flessh ne hath no myght / To understonde hyt aryght, / For hyt is warned to derkly" (49–51). Whether this is the fault of the books or the dreams there is no way to say, but the net effect is that each makes us distrust the other, and this just as we are about to hear of a wonderful dream in which the poet is to be told that a vision will correct him where books had led him wrong and experience had yielded him nothing at all. Furthermore, all this ought to result in some improvement in Geffrey's poetry, as we learn from the Eagle, first in the long speech from line 605 to line 699,[32] again as the Eagle leaves him at the end of Book II ("And God of heven sende the grace / Some good to lernen in this place"), and finally in another long speech near the end of the poem (lines 2000–26), concluding with the reminder that Jove

> ". . . yaf expres commaundement,
> To which I am obedient
> To further the with al my myght,
> And wisse and teche the aryght
> Where thou maist most tidynges here,
> Shaltow here anoon many oon lere."[33]

32. It seems to me that the statement of the poem is simply contrary to Sypherd's assertion that ". . . the purpose of the journey, which is the purpose of the poem, is not to provide Chaucer with new poetic material." See "The Completeness of Chaucer's Hous of Fame," *MLN, 30* (1915), 67.

33. This passage does not seem to me properly punctuated in Robinson's text. There almost certainly needs to be heavier punctuation than a comma after "here," or quite possibly a stop after "aryght."

The conclusion of the Invocation (lines 81–110) gives still another twist to the knot of uncertainties tied up in the Proem. The reader is dragged into the problem too, so the poet's problem is now not only what to believe, how to find out, and how to put it into verse, but also what the audience will make of it. And this time, contrary to his usual attitude, Chaucer charges his readers directly with the responsibility for understanding him, and in the curse delivered upon those who do not understand, gives negative recognition to the possibility that poetry may fail not through its own fault, but through that of its readers. He evidently had less faith in the infallibility of his audience than do some modern critics, who would make it the standard of critical judgment.[34] Altogether, by the time we reach the first line of the vision story proper, learned tradition, visionary revelation, individual perception, and the *concensus gentium* have all been cast into doubt, though nothing has been denied outright. After that start, it is little wonder that Geffrey comments, only about 250 lines from where the poem breaks off, that so far he hasn't learned anything he didn't know before he started, except for the mere mechanics of the house of Fame:

> "For certeynly, he that me made
> To comen hyder, seyde me,
> Y shulde bothe here and se,
> In this place, wonder thynges;
> But these be no suche tydynges
> As I mene of." "Noo?" quod he.
> And I answered, "Noo, parde!
> For wel y wiste ever yit,

34. Cf., among others, A. C. Baugh's remark, ". . . I do not care to look too far below the surface of Chaucer's poetry to discern a meaning that few in the audience for which he wrote would have grasped," in "Fifty Years of Chaucer Scholarship," *Speculum*, 26 (1951), 665.

Sith that first y hadde wit,
That somme folk han desired fame
Diversly, and loos, and name." (1890–1900)[35]

The organization of materials within the three-part structure is also indication of the concern with books, dreams, and experience, although the baffling result in this poem is that as structural materials they seem to have almost no connection with each other. Technically, the vision spans all three parts. Actually, most of Book I is the retelling of an old story, and while the story is going on, we lose almost all awareness of the dream. True, at line 314 he insists that he dreamed the whole thing; but digressions on the difficulty of writing poetry (245–52), moral apostrophes to the reader (265–92), and the long digression proving the moral by collecting book authorities (283–426) certainly counter that insistence by establishing a clear and direct poet-to-reader relationship, very much of the sort that will subsequently characterize *Troilus and Criseyde*. It would be all but impossible to guess that Book I had been part of a longer poem, if the manuscript had happened to come down to us separately and with the beginning and ending destroyed. But the real point is that stylistically as well as structurally, Book I (excluding the Proem and Invocation) has a completely separate existence; it does not suggest anything which follows, and critics have been able to correlate its "sentence" with the rest of the poem only by abstracting to so great a degree as to vitiate comparison.

---

35. This passage by itself, even discounting all arguments from the structure of the poem, seems to me to invalidate claims that *HF* has an over-all unity in some continuous "education" of the poet or "progressively universalizing impulse." See particularly David M. Bevington, "The Obtuse Narrator in Chaucer's *House of Fame*," *Speculum, 36* (1961), 288–98; and Paul G. Ruggiers, "The Unity of Chaucer's *House of Fame*," *SP, 50* (1953), 16–29.

After all the interpretations and arguments are in, the same assertion remains true of Book II: it also has its own self-contained existence, with the exception that its ending leaves a logical (though not necessarily poetic) link to Book III. The Eagle has brought Geffrey to Fame's house, but Geffrey hasn't yet told us about what happened there. This is the Book which contains all we are to get of "experience" in this poem. Although this time we are unmistakably in the dream all the while, the humor depends largely on a style which presents the extraordinary in very commonplace colors; and either directly or by implication the constant topic of conversation is Geffrey's experience outside this dream. It is summarized, criticized, corrected, and various offers are made to supplement it; it is, in fact, what had brought on the vision. But Book I had not even mentioned it, and Book III scarcely does. Again, Book II has a style all its own, which it shares with neither of the others, although much of its over-celebrated humor[36] derives from parodying by one means or another the rhetorically decorated styles of the other two. The mode of operation of that humorous style is foreshadowed in the opening of Book II: a short but almost pretentiously high-serious Proem introduces a Book which within thirty lines has dropped into simple farce and tired jokes about a nagging wife and a swelling waistline.

Yet Book II does clearly define some issues, so that it is possible (most critics have agreed about the *House of Fame* to this extent) to say fairly easily what it is about, and to see that its "statement" quite closely parallels that of the Proem to Book I. The problem is, as the Eagle

36. "Over-celebrated" because here and elsewhere in his works, Chaucer's great skill with humorous dialogue has drawn so much critical attention that it has made us much too slow to see other, more important things in his art.

makes clear, one of reliable sources of knowledge to make the poetic services which Geffrey had been offering to the God of Love more rewarding to all concerned. Equally clearly, in this case neither books nor experience had done the job (at least in the opinion of Jove and the Eagle), so the vision now had to take over. But as the Proem to Book I had left us able finally to trust neither book nor dream, so again does Book II, adding a dimension to the uncertainty by suggesting the extent to which experience shares their limitations.

A good deal of earlier criticism to the contrary notwithstanding, there simply cannot be any question here of a "turning from books to life as the model for art." First, as much of the satiric wit of Book II is at pains to point out, one is always too close to life to see it either broadly or very clearly; thus even the Eagle takes whatever help Aristotle can give him, and Jove's gift to Geffrey was not (as it might appropriately have been) an affair with the lady next door, but a visionary expedition to another world. Second, and I think more important and more noticeable, what the Eagle promises Geffrey as aid and comfort is a completely indigestible mass of "tydynges"—information.[37] If the Eagle's "demonstration" is correct, then what Geffrey will find for his profit and delight at the house of Fame will be everything that any-

---

37. Again, it seems that rather careless reading has led to and supported some untenable theories about the nature of *HF*. The "tydynges" Geffrey is to get are, from their first mention in line 644 to their last in line 2143, unmistakably plural; and especially in Book II. 672–99 and Book III. 1960–76, long passages pile up *frequentatio* and *polysyndeton* specifically to exaggerate the plurality (and unmanageability?) of the "tydynges." Certainly no interpretation—occasional or otherwise—which insists on a single final piece of news can be made to square with the rest of the poem, although probably the opposite extreme of arguing a series of tales to complete it is defensible only through lack of evidence to the contrary.

one has ever said. And all this will be not only without
any sorting of true from false, or useful from useless, but
rather with the prior assurance that the nature of the
place will guarantee that no such sorting can occur.

> ". . . The grete soun,"
> Quod he, "that rumbleth up and doun
> In Fames Hous, full of tydynges,
> Bothe of feir speche and chidynges,
> And of fals and soth compouned.
> Herke wel; hyt is not rouned.
> Herestow not the grete swogh?"   (1025–31)

This is surely an *embarras de richesses* for a poet who
has been accused of lack of knowledge of life, and it just
as surely undercuts the stiff and tiresome allegory of
Book III, as well as theories which maintain that Geffrey's
voyage with the Eagle taught him a proto-naturalistic
theory of art.

In Book III, finally, we reach the otherworldly destina-
tion and the whole Book is devoted to its description. As
Book I had concentrated largely on an old book and
Book II on Geffrey's experience, Book III devotes its stylistic energies to the elaboration of the banal marvels of
this dreamland. It is a good example of Chaucer's ability
to produce exactly the kind of poetry which some critics
believe the rhetorical poetic produced inevitably: exaggerated elaboration of the obvious without any illumination. If the Eagle were the narrator of Book III, we might
take the whole thing as a rather overextended parody.
But he is not, and the style—elaborate but not certainly
overelaborated—gives us no clear warrant to take it as
such anyway. What we do know is what Book II led us to
expect and Geffrey himself remarks (lines 1890–1900),
that the pageantry of the House of Fame was neither very

new nor particularly useful to him.[38] Whatever ending may have been intended or written and then canceled could not change that impression. The House of Rumor is after all only a kind of de-allegorization of Eolus' clarions, and even less likely (if that is possible) than the House of Fame to provide him "tydynges" which can be of any use.

The *House of Fame* was nearly impossible to end, or perhaps any ending would be as good or bad as any other, because the poem is not about any particular tidings, and it has already said what it has to say about tidings in general. I wonder, in fact, if an important reason for the high incidence of unfinished work among Chaucer's poems might not be that, in accord with the aesthetic tradition behind him, he sought in his poetry to make his statement by formal arrangement rather than in a particular substance or by abstract declaration. This approach to his art left him with a particularly acute version of two classical problems of the poet: a formal arrangement has to be an arrangement of something, so that the substance itself may come to make demands (such as narrative completeness) which the poet wasn't originally much interested in; and the formal arrangement may just not work out, as it clearly did not with the relation of most of Book I to the rest of the *House of Fame*. Further, when the end is to raise questions, and the means chosen are contrast and irony, the problems of reaching a "conclusion" are greatly complicated. In the *Parliament of Fowls*, Chaucer brings off a splendid illusion of

38. Cf. Baum, "Chaucer's 'The House of Fame'," p. 255: "While we are not to suppose that Chaucer had planned a complete hoax and ended deliberately in the middle of a sentence, still there can have been little to add . . . In such a state of uproar and tumult, men trampled under foot and climbing over one another, no item of serious news could be expected. The whole tenor of the second and third books is against such a possibility."

termination with the purely technical device of the roundel of the birds, and it is a little surprising that he did not experiment more with that kind of illusion. But the *Parliament of Fowls* is also, like most of the rest of his poetry, work in which the problems of art and the truths it is to contain occur simultaneously and almost inseparably. For instance, Love can (usually) be explored, questioned, analyzed through a medium (poetry) which is necessary to the process, but which itself shares the limitations and uncertainties it is trying to explore in the "subject."

The *House of Fame*, however, has no such "subject." It is certainly not a discussion of Love, nor of Fame, although it contains an example of one and a description of the other. All it has is the manner—the attempt to twist around the arrangement of books, dreams, and experience so as to produce some ironies which could illuminate the problem of art, knowledge, and illusion. After a start in Book I which no one has yet explained satisfactorily, the poem returns to the ironies of the Proem and Invocation and develops them to a point of paralysis by the end of Book II—a paralysis of exactly balanced uncertainties about books, dreams, and life which is in itself the principal "meaning" of the poem as it stands. Book III translates those ironies into the overt, cumbersome, and mathematically precise allegory of the palace of Fame, and as soon as they are separately embodied in so rationalistic a set of conventions, they are no longer instructive ironies at all, but only jejune platitudes which do not even seem to apply to the kind of artistic problem Book II had left us with. I think Book III is an attempt to illuminate the problems by reclothing them in a different set of amplificatory figures; but the Book is repetitious, in the end, rather than recapitulatory, because, as Chaucer himself realizes late in Book III, the new figures do not amplify anything. Even within Book III, the repetition of part of the mechanics of Fame, in the slightly altered figure of the House of Rumor, shows the same futile struggle toward a different image, one which will turn the ironic balance a bit so we can see it differently and more completely. Perhaps this is the point at which Chaucer really learned his distrust of formal allegory.

The *Parliament of Fowls* returns us to what is apparently a much clearer and more finished statement, and certainly its structure is a firmer and sharper alignment of books, experience, and dream. Perhaps it is an indirect result of the switch to the rhyme royal stanza, but for whatever reason the opening machinery is both compressed and intensified figuratively. The first four stanzas are a complex and profound statement of the problem of the poet which can be matched elsewhere in Chaucer's poetry only in the Prologue to the *Legend of Good Women;* the old book is neatly reduced to eight stanzas, and carefully linked, formally at least, to the introductory stanzas and to the vision which follows; the roundel and return to waking reality conclude the vision with a technical and psychological symmetry which no other poem in this group displays—not even the *Book of the Duchess.* And, perhaps most comforting to readers and critics, the poem indisputably has as its subjects poetry and love, although there has been disagreement about the relative importance of the former and the meaning of the latter.

Yet every careful reader of the poem knows that such a general description of it is misleading if not downright false, even though it is scrupulously accurate. Everywhere one looks in the *Parliament of Fowls,* its precise formalities contain elements divided against themselves. In the opening stanzas on love and literature, not only is there the uncertain relationship between them, but each is further complicated by the apparent discrepancy between experience and tradition. Even though the old book is this time one about a dream, and the principal character from the old book becomes Chaucer's guide for his dream, the only substantive or affective harmonies between book and dream are so general as to appear almost fortuitous. Neither Bennett's erudition nor Lumiansky's ingenuity can really make them seem primary to the poem.[39] Scipio's dream, which Chaucer read in the old book, seems at first glance to offer instruction about the salvation of the followers of true felicity and the damnation of "brekers of the lawe" and "likerous folk," but lines 81–84 make it clear that in the end they will all reach heaven anyway. And though Africanus does show up to guide Chaucer in his dream, it was Venus who caused him to have the dream. At least so he says in line 115; between lines 99 and 108, he had been uncertain, thinking perhaps it had been a natural consequence of his reading.

And the vision itself is equally self-negating. The inscription on the gateway to the enchanted garden (a parody of Dante, but Chaucer's single gate leads both to

39. J. A. W. Bennett, *The Parlement of Foules: an Interpretation* (Oxford, 1957), and R. M. Lumiansky, "Chaucer's *Parlement of Foules:* A Philosophical Interpretation," *RES, 24* (1948), 81–89, both see the poem as an attempt to study the relation of true to false felicity. At the same time, both seem partly to anticipate the argument I am developing here about the primacy of essentially aesthetic problems in the materials and structure of *PF*. Bennett writes (p. 23): "This is precisely what Chaucer attempts, however modestly, in the *Parlement of Foules;* the complex experience being that of the poet himself when he ponders the problems and paradoxes of love, and in particular the relation of personal love to the common weal and to the laws set in the universe by Nature, vicar of God." Lumiansky, similarly, maintains (p. 83) that "the unifying theme . . . I take to be *Chaucer's unsuccessful search for a way* of reconciling true and false felicity" (italics mine).

heaven and to hell) sets the pattern at the very beginning. On one leaf of the gate is painted, "Thorgh me men gon into that blysful place / Of hertes hele and dedly woundes cure," etc., and on the other, "Thorgh me men gon . . . / Unto the mortal strokes of the spere," etc. The garden itself is divided into two areas: first, the over-rich, neo-classical, barely animate temple of Venus, glazed and painted and populated with a curious mixture of alle-gorical personages from the *Roman de la Rose* and figures from classical poetry.[40] Then, outdoors, the open-air "hill of flowers" and surrounding amphitheater where the Goddess Nature (here also mainly a love deity) holds *her* court. And Nature's servants, too, are divided against themselves: the aristocrats, for whom love is an ideal at-traction, and the commoners, for whom it is (again) an irreconcilable variety of things ranging from sentimental self-deception to cheerfully mindless fornication.[41]

In the end, in any of these pairings, the net effect is that each makes the other look inadequate, if not silly. Perhaps that is itself enough (as Bronson's *Apprecia-tion* seems to argue), when it is as gracefully and deftly done as it is in the *Parliament,* but it is not what the Chaucer who spoke at the beginning of the poem was setting out for, nor is it exactly what Africanus (echoing the Eagle of the *House of Fame*) had promised:

> "But natheles, although that thow be dul,
> Yit that thow canst not do, yit mayst thow se.

40. It is no doubt true that, compared with its original in the *Teseida,* the description here reduces the voluptuousness and sensuality of the scene. But within this poem, the contrast is not with Boccaccio, but with the other part of the garden where the debate of the birds occurs.

41. Cf. Bronson, *In Appreciation,* p. 212: "Moreover, and this is a point of the utmost importance, the whole interest of the debate lies in the contrasting attitudes to which the various birds give expression, and not at all in the problematical merits of the three suitors."

> For many a man that may nat stonde a pul,
> It liketh hym at the wrastlyng for to be,
> And demeth yit wher he do bet or he.
> And if thow haddest connyng for t'endite,
> I shal the shewe mater of to wryte." (162–68)

Nor did it seem enough to the poet who speaks in the final stanza. Although his guide at the beginning of the dream had promised him he would learn things about love which would enable him to write better poetry, Chaucer the dreamer is no more able than we readers or the birds to reconcile or make categorical sense out of the clutter of disparate perspectives the vision offers him. The lovely roundel with which he hushes the inconclusive debating is so pleasing a technical tour de force that a dazzled reader feels almost ungrateful if he notices that it doesn't conclude the poem at all—that it leaves all its basic questions about love and art unanswered. But then, Chaucer, when he woke up, noticed the same thing, and ends his poem with an almost apologetic stanza (which is also to some unspecifiable degree ironic):

> And with the shoutyng, whan the song was do
> That foules maden at here flyght awey,
> I wok, and othere bokes tok me to,
> To reede upon, and yit I rede alwey.
> I hope, ywis, to rede so som day
> That I shal mete som thyng for to fare
> The bet, and thus to rede I nyl nat spare. (693–99)

We do not always do Chaucer's poems any great service when we try too hard to harmonize the various gospels they may assert. It is too easy that way to oversimplify

almost out of existence their principal poetic implications. Particularly, we may deny to Chaucer one of the
poet's most effective resources: playing the forms of his
poetry against its substance, for a complexity of statement not otherwise attainable. The possibilities are
particularly rich when form or substance or both are
highly conventionalized, as Sidney and Donne were
later to realize and exploit nicely for their different purposes with the sonnet. A kind of miniature of what I am
talking about occurs in the roundel at the end of the
Parliament of Fowls, when the birds in Nature's own
garden borrow the literary artificialities of French lyric
(Chaucer pauses to point it out) for their praise of Nature. How harmonious their natural chirpings are we
have been overhearing for the preceding 300 lines, but
"hir usaunce" must be observed, and it is the declared
business of art to produce order where life (or dream)
does not. By defining love in a *sententia* which Chaucer
knew well was most commonly employed in defining art,
and by talking about both love and literature in terms of
their problematical relations to old books and experience, the first four stanzas had sent us into the poem concerned about the ways in which the orders of art correspond to those of life. What follows is a poem with a
formal order unusually tight, symmetrical, and precise,
suggesting a unity or harmony of its contents which is
simply not in them. No one has ever demonstrated that
there is any thread of stylistic allusion and identification
running through to connect experience, book, and
dream, as in the *Book of the Duchess.* Bennett's brilliant
analysis of the stylistic modulations from section to section in the poem argues quite the opposite. And even the
most unquestioningly cheerful embracement of the doctrine of plenitude cannot explain away the contradictory

variety within that overcrowded uniformity.[42] The highly stylized art which here clothes the contradictions ac-
centuates rather than diminishes them, and the grace of
conclusion is possible only by the deception that an artful
order (the roundel) implies the same concord and resolution in the singers as in the song.

In the *Book of the Duchess,* formal stability accords
with a relatively overt harmony of content, and the im-
position of a unifying style upon a carefully blocked and
separated structure produces dimension—depth—much
more than it produces paradox or dissonance. The *House
of Fame,* as it stands, offers no real subject and a variety
of contents, though it is fairly clearly framed in terms of
the question of art and knowledge. Although the stretching of the dream frame to include both book and experience looks like an attempt at formal stability, the poem
still splits into three distinct styles, two of which (the
ironic of Book II and the allegorical of Book III) overlap
to no visible purpose and one of which (the rhetorical-
narrative of Book I) stands insistently apart and aloof
from the other two. As a result there is nearly nothing to
use as a fixed point of reference in trying to determine
what the form of the work might have been an attempt
to realize. But in the *Parliament of Fowls,* Chaucer nearly matches the subtlety and complexity of the Prologue
to the *Legend of Good Women* in turning the form and
the substance of a poem into a mutual critique, and consequently making of the whole an essay in poetics as
well as a poem about its subject. A content of paradox

42. Bennett, *Parlement,* makes this point perfectly clearly (". . . this
is a poem of paradoxes and antitheses"), but later curiously argues that
"to accept Nature is to reject dualism"; yet surely even in those parts
of the garden ruled over by Nature, there are both dualism and irreduc-
ible pluralism—dualism of ideal and "practical" love, and pluralism in
the varied notions of the practitioners of each.

and contradiction is distributed through a highly stable, almost ritualized form (perhaps for the moment chronology and sources can be ignored in order to concentrate on the fact that Chaucer re-used this pattern in four major works). The charming formalities themselves constitute a criticism of the intractability of the content at the same time as the content keeps us always on the verge of awareness that the artifice is mainly illusion.

And yet in all four—*Book of the Duchess, House of Fame, Parliament of Fowls,* and Prologue to *Legend of Good Women*—the search for the key of remembrance continues. Even though each time a sense of the reasons for its ultimate failure is built into the structure and style, four times Chaucer rearranged his original stereotype, and four times introduced his readers to it by reminding them that it was the ancient obligation of the poet to illuminate the truth with delight.

Measured against the traditional rhetorical poetic described in Chapter 1, the great originality of these poems is in their attempt to exploit the possibilities of *dispositio*—over-all structural arrangement—in ways more complex and meaningful than anything the manuals suggest in their perfunctory treatments of it. Even in the *Book of the Duchess,* the skeletal structure provides considerably more than a coordinating frame for affective verbal elaboration (*elocutio*). And the structural irony which plays so large a part in the effectiveness of most of them derives regularly from the invocation of our sense of paradox and contradiction in the claims of art to reorder knowledge and feeling. On the other hand, none of these works approaches the depth and consistent focus of unifying stylistic artifice of *Troilus and Criseyde.* That may well be one reason why they so often seem to most of us contradictory rather than paradoxical, fragmentary rather than complex.

Perhaps, taken all together, the greatest accomplishment of the poems in the combinative group is that they come as close as they do to making great poetry out of their own inability to move beyond the thirteenth-century aesthetic, of which Chaucer clearly sensed the strengths as well as the limitations and failures.

5. The Last Experiment: The *Canterbury Tales*

INFREQUENTLY, but with some persistence, the theory that the *House of Fame* (or sometimes the *Parliament of Fowls*) may have been intended to introduce a collection of tales comes up again for discussion or passing comment. Obviously, there is no way of proving the contention and, true or false, it adds little or nothing to our understanding of the poems as we have them. But it is an interesting idea all the same, because it is an indication, however indirect, of a response to the problem of various and apparently irreconcilable values and perspectives in Chaucer's earlier poems. To a few critics, at least, Chaucer's difficulty in making those values and perspectives cohere in a single demonstration has suggested the possibility that a variety of different narratives within a single frame might provide the reconciling structure which he was never quite able to achieve with the variously ironic adjustments of the books-dreams-experience stereotype. Whether or not Chaucer himself consciously saw the problem in those terms, he has left us two clear attempts at framing a collection of tales, one of them introduced by an extended review of his continuing problems in poetics, and it will be useful here to see the *Canterbury Tales* and the *Legend of Good*

Women as different but related experiments in a different kind of solution for those problems.

Since both collections as we have them are incomplete, there are very immediate practical limits to how far the critic can go in assessing their structures. There are, however, some interesting differences between the two which are worth comment. Readers of the *Legend of Good Women* have almost universally noted that it is not, strictly speaking, a framed collection, but rather a group of stories with a prologue and a common theme. And as Lumiansky has observed,[1] if the theme had not been announced in the Prologue, it would be easy to make a wrong guess at it from reading the legends by themselves. There is no linking machinery—no formal device for interrelating the tales or making them seem to qualify each other. The Prologue does not have anything formally or schematically to do with the series of tales. It could be followed by almost any collection of narratives in almost any order, as the General Prologue to the *Canterbury Tales* certainly could not. Even if the manuscripts of the legends were badly scrambled, we should scarcely know it, or at least nothing in the Prologue or in the individual legends would suggest that it mattered. If one enjoys speculative psychoanalysis at six centuries' remove, that radical incoherence may be a better reason for Chaucer's abandoning the project than his putative boredom with a theme which in fact his poetry never abandons from first to last.

The *Canterbury Tales,* though in a way less complete, is at the same time far more coherent. At least it lets us see enough of a form to give us the illusion that we can infer the rest of it, even though its central principle of organization is irrecoverable or never clearly existed. Al-

1. "Chaucer and the Idea of the Unfaithful Man," *MLN, 62* (1947), 560–62.

though we know the theme of the *Legend of Good Women,* nobody really cares; the legends do not amplify it, in the thirteenth-century sense of giving a larger and clearer or more effective development. But although we do not and cannot ever know clearly the "theme" of the *Canterbury Tales,* it is virtually impossible to read them without trying to formulate one (or some), and seeing pieces of structure in some clusters of tales which seem to be thematically or stylistically connected. In fact, most of the speculation in the past century about the order and arrangement of tales has not been textual criticism, or based on any external evidence concerning the manuscripts,[2] but is instead a kind of masked pursuit of a definitive structure and so a confused sort of interpretative criticism.

What all this seems to point to is the conclusion that the ruins we have of the *Canterbury Tales* do belong to a structure. Their frame is a "disposition" in the medieval sense; an arrangement which suggests values or ideas that can be developed by the way in which the basic structure is amplified. But the now commonplace dilemma of Chaucer criticism remains: the amplification in this structure was to have proceeded by two different sets of means—one in the frame narrative, and the other in the separate tales—and there is apparently simply no way to determine clearly what was to have been the final relation between the two.

Besides the traditional scholarly debating topics—dramatic propriety, missing links, order of tellers and tales, etc.—there is a further matter which constantly affects critical discussion of the *Canterbury Tales,* although the discussants do not usually seem conscious of it. I mean the general and fairly wide discrepancy in

2. As Robert A. Pratt points out in "The Order of the Canterbury Tales," *PMLA, 66* (1951), 1141–67.

quality between the frame narrative and the group of
tales. The frame, or all that we have of it in the General
Prologue and the links (about 3400 lines in all), is a
truly impressive stylistic achievement. One has no hesit-
ation in agreeing with all the critics since Dryden that
it is one of the great things in English poetry. One might
be forgiven, also, for noting at the same time that it is
not a poem, but only an incomplete part of a poem. However, my point is that when one gets away from the frame
narrative, the *Canterbury Tales* contain a fair amount
of relatively pedestrian narrative poetry, a little that is
downright bad, and a handful of tales—the Nun's Priest's,
the Miller's, the Reeve's, the Merchant's, perhaps the
Knight's and Pardoner's—which are first-rate. Inevitably,
different readers will quarrel over the evaluation of particular tales and perhaps specific value judgments are
ultimately untenable in the present state of critical
knowledge. But it is not so much each particular evaluation that I am concerned about as it is the fairly certain
generalization that when we look carefully and honestly
at the tales themselves, apart from tellers and framing
action, only about a third (or less) of them seem to most
of us really superior poetry.

Of this apparent discrepancy there are several notable
consequences in the tradition of Chaucer criticism, most
of them dependent on the peculiarity that all of us seem
to have felt it, but few have declared it directly or openly.
The most important consequence, I think, is that we have
had nearly no criticism of the *Canterbury Tales* in toto
as they actually exist. Almost all of us have somehow
wanted to excuse Chaucer from that bulk of quite ordinary verse in what is supposed to be his greatest and most
mature work. Kittredge and Manly especially (though
in different ways), and many others as well, have built
or defended theories of the intended structure and pur-

pose of the whole on the basis of the frame and the handful of superior tales, and said little about the rest, but talked as though the same judgments would apply to all. To still others, the proper response has seemed to be the construction of theories of successive revisions, with much of what remains in the texts labeled "early" and "unrevised" work.[3] The result is similar; the poorer stuff is moved out of the way as not yet assimilated into the new structural design, and the new structural design is defined on the basis of a fraction of what we have of the work. Again, many have given careful consideration to the less inspired tales, one by one, in comparison to their sources, in order to demonstrate that, for example, although few readers would willingly give up the *Parliament of Fowls* in exchange for the Man of Law's tale, still the latter is a considerable improvement over Nicholas Trivet. The frequently repeated appeal to the taste of the times is deceptive too. Contemporary taste never explains the quality of a poem, and what it can account for is equally present in the Nun's Priest's tale and in the Manciple's, for instance, and we are still left with the obvious difference.

It seems to me that what is required, in discussing the structure of the *Canterbury Tales* and its relation to Chaucer's poetics, is simply to admit the range of quality in the contents and then studiously ignore it altogether. For the purpose of defining a structure—or speculating about an incomplete one—all the elements observable in it must (at least as a prior assumption) be taken to be functional. No critic is very apt to argue (at least not since Dr. Johnson on the metaphysicals) that because he does not like some of the metaphors in a poem, they

3. Perhaps the circularity of such argument needs asserting again: we date the poorer tales earlier because they are poorer, and then argue that they are poorer because they were written earlier.

therefore do not function in it, or that its structure should be defined by extrapolation from the good metaphors. And the individual tales in the *Canterbury Tales* are, within their framing structure, like the metaphors in a short poem; they are amplificatory devices, although of course very complicated and extended ones. It is rather too bad that one very limited way in which the amplification may sometimes work has so nearly preempted all the critical discussion of this kind, but Kittredge *redivivus* in Lumiansky[4] should teach us something about the possibilities for using subordinated narrative, even though we must insist at the same time that the tellers themselves are figures in a larger design, and there are several cases where the narrative cannot very well serve to amplify the character of the teller.[5] Once more, I think the attempt to extend any single functional mode into an inclusive structural principle will inevitably lead us wrong. The evidence from the earlier poems as analyzed in preceding chapters, and the very troublesome variety of the contents themselves should lead us to suppose a multiple, complex, and probably ironically overlaid structure in the finished work. But as the *House of Fame* should certainly demonstrate, without the finished work we simply have no way of defining just how and in what directions the structure will operate.

Recent studies by Arthur W. Hoffman[6] and Ralph F. Baldwin[7] have, I think, presented much more nearly adequate views of the thematic and structural complexity which is to be found in the *Canterbury Tales*. Baldwin,

4. *Of Sondry Folk: the Dramatic Principle in the Canterbury Tales* (Austin, 1955).

5. Cf. Kemp Malone, *Chapters on Chaucer*, Ch. 10 and 11.

6. "Chaucer's Prologue to Pilgrimage: the Two Voices," *ELH*, *21* (1954), 1–16.

7. *The Unity of the Canterbury Tales*, *Anglistica*, *5* (Copenhagen, 1955).

particularly, has done much of what needed to be done
to indicate what can be seen of the Chaucerian poetic
in the *Canterbury Tales*. Yet while I generally agree with
the conclusions presented by both men, there is one kind
of limitation in their studies which needs comment in
connection with what I have just been arguing. Both
base their analysis largely on the General Prologue,
which is fair enough, since both remain well aware that
it is only one part of the poem, and we should expect to
find in an introductory part especially useful evidence
of the nature of the poem to follow. Moreover, both
studies demonstrate convincingly that a general line of
thematic relationships and general means of developing
them are indicated in the General Prologue. But all
through the earlier works, Chaucer had been quite sure
and clear about the *general* purposes of poetry, and had
concurred in the traditional theories of how language
should be made to work for those purposes. Yet repeatedly in the earlier works an introductory announcement of the indisputable generalities had led into a system of paradoxes and contradictions which inevitably
altered the question, making it focus on the particular
choices (both in knowledge and in art) that the individual poet has to make in producing actually efficacious
poems. His first try at a framed collection is prefaced by
a long and difficult discussion of exactly such questions
about how to assure a workable correlation of agencies
and purposes, but the Prologue does not solve the problems, and the collection of legends is an uncompleted
failure. The General Prologue to the *Canterbury Tales*
is of course a very different thing, and its relationship
to the frame narrative and tales is clearly of a different
sort (and much tighter) than that in the *Legend of Good
Women*. Nevertheless I think that the nature and man-
er of the discussion in the earlier poems, and the kind of

fundamental aesthetic problem that emerges in them, should lead us to expect that the apparent certainties of the General Prologue might well have developed into paradoxes in the finished work.

There are evidences, also, in what we have of the *Canterbury Tales* themselves, that ironic complications may be setting in, in the complex but nonetheless clear moral demonstration which Hoffman and Baldwin have defined in the General Prologue. For one thing, there are the several passages scattered through the frame story and the tales[8] which raise again the same questions about poetry and the same troublesome variety of opinions about how to make it work which we have become familiar with in the earlier poems. Since more of these occur in the frame than in the tales, I doubt that there can be any question of their being unrevised remnants of early work. Then too, E. T. Donaldson's perceptive study of Chaucer's roles in the frame as pilgrim and poet[9] makes it unmistakably clear that there is latent in the *Canterbury Tales* the same ironic divergence of perspectives, inevitably defining a problem in the relation of art to knowledge, which Chaucer had been working with in the poems of the combinative group. It is also very probable that we have something to learn in this connection from the proponents of the "marriage group" theory, even though we cannot accept their conclusions in detail. When one assembles such a group of tales with fairly closely related themes (even though the assemblage be the work of the critic rather than the poet), it does become clear that an apparently controlled variety of perspectives runs through them. And unless we are willing to settle for the disappointing oversimplification of the Franklin's tale, the perspectives remain ironically

8. See above, Ch. 2.
9. "Chaucer the Pilgrim," *PMLA*, *69* (1954), 928–36.

divergent, just as do those of the dreamer-poet or poet-pilgrim. Finally, with a poet as sensitive to conventional forms, and as skillful with them as Chaucer is, it may not be an over-refinement of analysis to suggest that the formal literary parodies in Sir Thopas and the Nun's Priest's tale (both of them of forms he elsewhere uses seriously and straight) are still another version of the problem of perspective as a limitation in making choices, artistic as well as moral.

I spoke a little earlier of the separate tales as amplificatory devices, working in the total structure somewhat as the more purely verbal schemes and figures do in shorter, less complicated structures. And that way of looking at them may suggest a different kind of analysis that can profitably be made of the group of tales which has survived. There are some things to be found out about a poet's work by studying the kinds and structures of imagery he employs, as long as we remain carefully aware that such study of images necessarily considers them in the context of a set of categories established by the analyst rather than in the structural contexts the poet set for them, and as long as we really do consider the images and not simply the things they refer to. In the same way, it is interesting to survey the whole collection of Canterbury tales, completely apart from tellers or frame, as a mass of amplifying material—all that we have to work with—and try to see just what kinds of things Chaucer had brought together for his poem. We know very well that the tales as raw material may be quite different from what they could become in the finished structure, but what they are as raw material is *something;* and although there has been piecemeal comment of the sort I suggest, no one has ever, to my knowledge, set down a complete tabulation and classification of that sort. The actual statistics are of no profound importance in themselves, but to tabulate them may hold our attention to some things which it is easy to forget when struggling to comprehend Chaucer's last great experiment.

Of the 19,435 lines in the *Canterbury Tales* as Robinson prints them, I count 15,964 devoted to the stories themselves and 3471 to the General Prologue and all the surviving linking material.[10] Of these, I have set aside as unclassifiable the 58 lines of the Cook's tale. The 23 tales which make up the remaining 15,906 lines provide a virtually complete sampler of conventional forms for the shorter narrative in the late middle ages, the Canon's Yeoman's autobiography being apparently the only "original" in the group. The nature of the project the God of Love set for Chaucer prevents any such formal experimentation in the *Legend of Good Women,* but except for *Anelida and Arcite* and *Troilus,* we do not find any of the forms employed in the *Canterbury Tales* used anywhere else in his earlier work. And in both *Anelida and Arcite* and *Troilus,* the romance form is altered almost beyond recognition, as it is not in any of the *Canterbury Tales.* Chaucer must either have swept together into the *Canterbury Tales* all his essays in the conventional shorter narrative types, or not begun working in them until fairly late. At any rate, the tales are a far more perfect cross section of fourteenth-century literature than the frame is of fourteenth-century society.

Partly in irritation with colleagues who insist on talking as though all the *Canterbury Tales* are like the Miller's and the Reeve's, and partly to underscore some matters of proportion which even professional Chaucerians

10. It is not important that these counts be precise to the line, so I have simply counted as Robinson numbers the lines, without worrying over variant MS readings, canceled or restored links, or parts of links, etc.; the small differences which might result would not affect the kind of proportional comparisons I am making.

occasionally seem to lose track of, I have divided my classification of the tales by conventional form into two groups, "serious" and "humorous," which I mean here in their most general and ordinary senses, as descriptive of the immediate effect of the work.[11] The figures following each title indicate the number of lines in the tale. The fifteen tales which are definitely not humorous classify as follows:

Romances:
  Knight's Tale (2250)
  Wife of Bath's Tale (408)
  Squire's Tale (664)
  Franklin's Tale (896)
Saint's Legends:[12]
  Man of Law's Tale (1029)
  Clerk's Tale (1092)
  Physician's Tale (286)
  Second Nun's Tale (434)
Miracles:
  Prioress's Tale (203)
Sermons:
  Pardoner's Tale (441)[13]
  Parson's Tale (1006)
Fables:
  Manciple's Tale (258)

11. It may need to be said again that these classifications are made considering the tales individually and completely apart from tellers and the frame. However, it would be very difficult for the context to make a serious tale humorous; ironic or satiric, perhaps, but hardly a complete reversal of its effect.

12. In only one of these is the protagonist literally a saint, but in form and effect, as well as in the characters of the protagonists, they are so alike that the distinction is doctrinal rather than literary.

13. This tale might possibly be classified as an exemplum; it is one case where it is difficult to separate tale from prologue precisely.

Anomalies:
>Melibee (922)
>Monk's tragedies (776)
>Canon's Yeoman's autobiography (762)

There are two tales, the Friar's (344 lines) and the Merchant's (1174 lines), which are not humorous, although they are obviously satiric and make use of grim or bitter humor to achieve their effects. Although neither is in any way an atypical medieval tale, and analogues for all or parts of both have been pointed out,[14] neither fits any of the conventional formal categories listed above, and it is hard to assign to either a generic label other than "satire," which is after all not a formal distinction.

The six remaining tales, all humorous, fall into two groups, although the second group requires double classification. First, there are the four fabliaux:

>Miller's Tale (668)
>Reeve's Tale (404)
>Summoner's Tale (586)
>Shipman's Tale (434)

The other two, Sir Thopas (206½ lines) and the Nun's Priest's tale (626 lines) are parodies, the first of one kind of romance; the second is more properly a combination of parody and burlesque, but as far as the form is concerned, it produces its mock-heroic effect by a juxtaposition of a sort of courtly romance and beast-fable.

The two things most obvious from this tabulation are that there is more than four times as much "serious" poetry in the tales as there is "humorous,"[15] and that three forms are used repeatedly—the romance, the saint's legend, and the fabliau each occuring four times. Since

14. See Robinson's notes.
15. 12,981 lines against 2925.

no other form except the sermon is repeated among the
ten or eleven represented, there would seem to be special
significance in this blocking, and one is immediately
tempted to assert an expanded version of the old "marriage group" theory. Three kinds of love—divine, courtly, and animal—provide half the tales we have left (12
out of 23), and well over half the total bulk of story material (9188 lines out of 15,906).[16] Each kind of love is
presented in its conventionally appropriate narrative
form, we have four versions of each, and within each the
intensity of concentration is nearly complete. In these
tales, courtly love does not meet divine love or animal
love within any one story, though obviously they all
meet within the frame.[17] And this investigation of the
characters of love raises to equal importance the divine,
which the earlier poetry (with the exception of *Troilus
and Criseyde*) had scarcely approached at all.

Within this apparent symmetry of arrangement, the
great variation in the lengths of the twelve tales produces
a proportional weighting of the three groups which one
might argue is evaluative, or at least indicative of an
order of interest. The result is something not unlike
what might be predicted on the basis of Chaucer's pre-
Canterbury poetry: courtly love is the center of interest,
occupying him for 4254 lines, including the longest and
most elaborate tale of the whole series.[18] Divine love and

16. These estimates could be swelled a bit; certainly the Prioress's
miracle and the Merchant's satire, and perhaps the Nun's Priest's mock-
heroic courtly romance, might be added to the "matere of Love."

17. The Nun's Priest's tale, which for the moment I am not considering, is a major exception to this statement. However, it is about
the only exception to be found anywhere in the tales, whether of love
or some other theme. Taken individually the Canterbury tales are re-
markably homogeneous in style.

18. The Knight's, with 2250; it is almost exactly twice as long as the
next longest tale, the Clerk's.

animal lust receive considerably less space; the former, 2844 lines and the latter, 2093.[19]

But there are obviously several things wrong with the assertion of so neat a pattern in the tales, even though there is clearly something in the phenomena I have been noting. First, the tales of the Prioress, Merchant, and Nun's Priest would have to be counted in if we are considering the tales as a broad investigation of love. In fact, counting them in does not greatly affect the kind of proportional balance described above, but it does blur the sharpness of the formal as well as the thematic categories, and thus (as with many other problems in the *Canterbury Tales*) makes us unwilling to trust the completeness or exactness of our observation of what looked like a clearly emergent pattern. Furthermore, to make the balances categorically, as I did, is deceptive. Only two of the fabliaux, the Miller's tale and the Reeve's, really have much to do with the lower order of love, and it is not the exclusive or primary motif in the Reeve's tale. The Summoner's and Shipman's tales involve it only quite indirectly, and we are left with only two tales, totaling a few more than a thousand lines, devoted principally or in considerable part to it. Finally, there is the difficulty that the eight remaining tales are nearly impossible to relate to this pattern,[20] or to form into any other groups or patterns. Undoubtedly, other tales were to have been added, and they might well have produced other patterns or altered present ones. But in looking only at the material we have, I think we can speak only

19. By stretching the stated distinctions a bit and adding the Prioress's tale, one could produce an interestingly neat (and highly deceptive) series: ca. 4000 lines for courtly love, 3000 for divine, and 2000 for animal.

20. Unless we adopt the dubious expedient of arguing that because they are moral, or have morals, they belong with the tales of divine love.

of tentative groupings with certain kinds of potential for development, but which always blur out into uncertainties at the edges, and which always leave a remainder of unaccountable pieces.

Before we leave these three principal blocks of tales, however, there are a few more or less formal matters to be noted. It is no doubt true that one reason for Chaucer's concentration on the romance, the saint's legend, and the fabliau is that they are the major and the most common forms in the narrative tradition upon which he was drawing. These three narrative types are also interestingly related to each other. The romance and the saint's legend, of course, are in structure practically indistinguishable, the differentiating factor traditionally being in the kind of protagonist and (more important to resultant effect) the kind of elaborative language. Ordinarily the fabliau is relatively unelaborated verbally, has also its own kind of hero, and is structurally noticeably different from the other two types in the absence of the episodic elaboration which characterizes them. So, besides offering him the conventional associations with different levels of emotional experience, these common traditional forms offered Chaucer also a range of related but different ways of using a structure of actions, from the dominance of a single uninterrupted action in the fabliau to the nearly complete submergence of action in the narrowly focussed sentimental rhetoric of the saint's legend. Interestingly, also, Chaucer narrows the range of difference in these twelve tales. His fabliaux are notably more stylistically elaborated, and his romances and saint's legends less episodic, than their conventional models.[21]

21. The Man of Law's tale and the Squire's tale, however, do still show fairly clearly their ancestry of rambling and inconsequent narrative.

Within each of the three groups, Chaucer experiments variously with the possibilities of the form. Each of the four romances belongs to a different sub-class of the genre; the saint's legends fall into three sub-groups, with the Man of Law's and the Clerk's tales repeating essentially the same kind, and the Physician's and Second Nun's each moving in a different direction; the Miller's and Reeve's tales give us one type of fabliau, and the Summoner's and Shipman's tales another. Running through all these, and several of the tales in other categories as well, is a kind of continuous experiment with the relation of stylistic elaboration to the basic narrative structure underlying it. The Pardoner's tale, once it gets clear of its introductory machinery, reduces its morality almost completely to action, with nearly no verbal elaboration of the narrative, either for description or commentary or characterization. The Summoner's and Shipman's tales, although less severely concentrated, share this insistence on the course and pattern of events.[22] The Prioress's tale, at the other extreme, becomes almost pure lyric, with the action scarcely narrated at all but only referred to in order to establish points of reference for emotional elaboration. The Second Nun's tale is nearest to it among the four saint's legends, but all four of them deal heavily in such potentially sentimental elaborative devices as *apostrophe* or *exclamatio,* and the focussing of single emotions by the repeated use of restricted groups of highly charged adjectives (*determinatio*). Between these extremes stand the romances, with their complex balancing of action and stylistic elaboration, or the similar but still very different versions of the same thing in the Merchant's tale or the Nun's Priest's.

Chaucer's old aesthetic preoccupations look very dif-

22. See the tabulations of figures and percentages of elaboration in Naunin and Manly.

ferent, certainly, when they are spread this way through a series of not very clearly connected single narrative experiments, but I think they are with us still. The Philistine heresy of the ignorant plain speaker takes a new form in the unelaborated insistence of narrative line in the Pardoner's tale, although it is raised to a level of art which the Eagle and the cuckoo and the duck never dreamed of, by the concentration of plot precision to a point at which it becomes figurative demonstration. The dead-center aesthetic orthodoxy of the God of Love in the Prologue to the *Legend of Good Women* receives five-fold obeisance in the one-dimensional elaboration of morality into sentimentality by the Man of Law, the Clerk, the Physician, the Second Nun, and the Prioress. And I think even the ironic dubiety of the introductions to the *Parliament of Fowls* or the *House of Fame* has its counterpart here in such procedures as the verbal elaboration, in the Knight's tale, of an already elaborate episodic action, so that the whole thing, stopping just barely short of parody, turns into a nearly frozen and inconclusive ritual.[23] Certainly the Nun's Priest's tale reorganizes and revitalizes almost exactly the same set of paradoxes out of which Chaucer had built the flawed and partial structures of the *Parliament of Fowls* and the *House of Fame*. But what ultimate complication—or resolution—of these inescapable insolubles Chaucer might have achieved by their juxtaposition within the frame and their relation to it, it remains impossible to guess.

However, there is one line of Chaucer's continuing poetic experiment which I should like to look at a little more closely, partly because it seems (especially in the

23. Cf. the excellent but rather differing discussions by Muscatine, p. 175–90, and Dale Underwood, "First of the Canterbury Tales," *ELH*, 26 (1959), 455–69.

light of late nineteenth-century views of his poetry) so
"un-Chaucerian," but even more because it shows him
continuing to try to make something of the most narrowly literalistic version of rhetorical orthodoxy: poetry is
the sentimentalization of abstract morality.[24] In the five
tales of the "sentimental experiment"—those of the Man
of Law, the Clerk, the Physician, the Second Nun, and
the Prioress—it is almost as though he is, in a typically
detached and dispassionate manner, working toward a
medieval version of *poésie pure*—a moral statement
which will be immediately apprehensible emotionally
and nearly incomprehensible by any rational or intellectual faculty. That is, in fact, very nearly what the
Clerk tells us at the end of his tale of Griselde:

> This storie is seyd, nat for that wyves sholde
> Folwen Grisilde as in humylitee,
> For it were inportable, though they wolde;
> But for that every wight, in his degree,
> Sholde be constant in adversitee
> As was Grisilde; therfore Petrak writeth
> This storie, which with heigh stile he enditeth.
>
> .   .   .   .   .   .
>
> And [God] suffreth us, as for oure excercise,
> With sharpe scourges of adversitee
> Ful ofte to be bete in sondry wise;
> Nat for to knowe oure wyl, for certes he,
> Er we were born, knew al oure freletee;
> And for oure beste is al his governaunce.
> Lat us thanne lyve in vertuous suffraunce.
>
> (IV. 1142–62)

24. I say "continuing" because these tales remain in the last collection
which Chaucer put together; I have no more idea than anyone else does
when he first actually wrote them down.

And this pushing toward the extreme limits of a style or form occurs not only in these five notably sentimental tales. It is little different, though at the other end of the scale, from the reduction of action to an almost diagrammatic demonstration of theme without any stylistic emotionalization in tales like the Pardoner's and Summoner's. Muscatine puts it: "When Chaucer writes at either end of the scale of values, indeed, his style becomes correspondingly extreme."[25] But it may be as well at either end of a scale of relative weightings of disposition and amplification that Chaucer chooses to reduce procedures to extremity.

There are several shared characteristics, besides the relatively highly rhetorical styles and direct emotionalism, which help to associate these five tales in a group. Four of them are in rime royal stanzas (the Physician's tale, in couplets, being the odd one in this case), and Chaucer does not use that stanza anywhere else in the *Canterbury Tales.* Four of them (this time the Prioress's tale is the exception) have heroines cut very much from the same pattern, despite the fact that Cecilia's formal sainthood separates her somewhat from the others.[26] Muscatine to the contrary notwithstanding, I do not see in these five tales any real deployment of the realistic and artificial counter-conventions which Chaucer elsewhere uses to gain a depth and complexity that none of these tales approaches. Even the kinds of artifice—the

---

25. *Chaucer and the French Tradition,* p. 173.

26. Cf. Muscatine, p. 192: "[The rime royal stanza] . . . is of course not inherently expressive, but in the *Canterbury Tales* it is always an implement of seriousness." It would seem, more precisely, that in *CT* it is always an implement of a particularly concentrated artifice of emotion. Muscatine also anticipates me in feeling some connection among several of the heroines in this group: "Griselda, indeed, shares some specific traits with Constance of the *Man of Law's Tale,* and the virgin-heroine of the *Physician's Tale*" (p. 193).

devices of style—in them are noticeably limited in range
compared with the Knight's tale, say, or the Nun's
Priest's. As I noted above, *apostrophe, exclamatio,* and
determinatio are the most common devices in all five,
although the limitation of range is not constant throughout the group; the Man of Law and the Clerk employ a
wider range of schemes and figures than do the Physician,
the Second Nun, and the Prioress.[27]

There are some differences in the disposition of the
base narrative in these tales, too, which make one devout-
ly wish for an established chronology for the group. But
that is so far out of the question that one must rather
be very careful to emphasize that a logical ordering of
them for critical purposes is *not* intended to have any
implications concerning their relative dates, even though
it would be nice to suppose that the Man of Law's tale
is the earliest and the Prioress's the latest. Chronological
questions aside, however, the point I am suggesting is
that the Man of Law's tale is the most "narrative" of the
five, spending a high proportion of its thousand lines in
recounting a series of not particularly consequent epi-
sodes. (It always surprises me to check the line numbers
and realize that the Man of Law's tale is actually not
twice as long as the Clerk's, but a hundred lines shorter.)
The Clerk's tale greatly reduces this plurality of episode,
at the same time increasing the amount of stylistic decoration, but still devotes a good part of its space to the
narration of action. In the Physician's and Second Nun's
tales, the movement of the narrative is less important to
the final effect, and in the Prioress's tale, the story is in
effect frozen into a kind of basic situation and the major
effort is in the rhetorical elaboration of its emotional implications.

27. Cf. again the tabulations in Naunin.

Bernard I. Duffey has already examined the Man of Law's tale[28] and compared it with its original in Trivet's *Chronicle,* with results which support in detail my argument here,[29] although his further conclusion that Chaucer could not have been serious in the effort seems to me a gratuitous application of the intentional fallacy. Muscatine's treatment of the Clerk's tale is also relevant.[30] But I should like to discuss at greater length the patterning of the style in the Prioress's tale, because in it, Chaucer seems to me to have accomplished what he was working toward in this whole group of tales. Of course that does not necessarily make it better poetry in general, but it does make it particularly relevant to a discussion of Chaucer's poetics.

The Prioress's tale, like the Second Nun's and the Man of Law's, opens with an invocational *apostrophe* (the Prioress's is double—to God and to Mary), and also, like the Clerk's, ends with an *apostrophe.* The textbooks called this the "artificial," as opposed to the "natural" order, and the Prioress's tale is the only one of the group which doubles the artifice by both beginning with it and ending with it. In accord with what has already been said about the reduction of the purely narrative aspects of the tale, it contains none of what the manuals list as "structural" figures, except the *apostrophe,* sometimes considered a form of *digressio,* and even then it ought to be pointed out that these digressions do not elaborate

28. "Intention and Art in the Man of Law's Tale," *ELH, 14* (1947), 183. Germaine Dempster, in *Dramatic Irony in Chaucer* (Palo Alto, 1932), also anticipated this conclusion, in her undeveloped assertion that the MLT is "more lyric and rhetorical than narrative."

29. "[Constance] exists, like so many other devices of the story, as a means toward certain definite ends of emotional impression" (p. 186). And the tale is "a basically mechanical, though skillful, implement for exciting the reader's superficial emotions" (p. 187).

30. *Chaucer and the French Tradition,* pp. 190–97.

the action, or even describe or analyze the feelings of the characters in it, but are regularly direct solicitations of a specified response from the reader. Not counting the opening invocation, which is not really a part of the tale proper, there are five such appeals to the reader scattered through the 203 lines,[31] and they account for a little more than ten per cent of its content—24 lines in all.

Although there is an occasional *comparatio* or *sententia* scattered through,[32] the real labor of style in this tale, apart from the *apostrophes* noted, is concentrated in three repeated and very similar devices: *circumlocutio, epithetum,* and *determinatio.* These devices can (and do) frequently overlap, and it is particularly difficult always to distinguish the first two sharply, as in "This newe Rachel" for the boy's mother, at line 627. Perhaps it makes little difference; the principle is the same in both, and very important to this kind of poetry: the substitution of a highly connotative phrase or word for a primarily denotative one. Fairly clear examples of *circumlocutio* occur in "Oure blisful Lady, Cristes mooder deere" (510); "Oure firste foo" (558); "O cursed folk of Herodes al newe" (574); "O martir, sowded to virginitee" (579).[33] *Epithetum* occurs in "This innocent" (566), "This cursed Jew" (570), and "his mooder, honour of mankynde" (619). The tendency to black-and-white contrasts in these examples is not simply a function of my selections, but is characteristic of the whole machinery of elaboration in the poem.

Determinatio—the controlled application of selected limiting adjectives—is the device which most efficiently distributes these flat but insistent emotional contrasts

31. Lines 513–15, 574–78, 579–85, 607–08, and 684–90.
32. *Comparatio* at lines 484–86, 674, and 676; *sententia* at 512, 576, and 632.
33. Also in lines 581, 609, and 656.

throughout the tale, and it carries essentially the same effects right across from apostrophaic elaboration to narration. Also, being the kind of device it is, it can operate within other kinds of figures, and what happens in the Prioress's tale is that the whole stylistic texture is permeated with a coloration of opposed but not at all equally balanced sentiments. Chaucer uses a limiting adjective with a substantive[34] about seventy times in the tale, and the principal groupings of repeated or very similar adjectives are as follows: the group "litel," "smale," "yonge" provides seventeen of the adjectival constructions, about one-fourth of the total; the opposed group, "grete," "chief," "large" gives five; similarly, a large but semantically tightly knit group, "tendre," "sweet," "blissful," "free," "sely," "innocent," "meek," "kinde," "pitous," "deere," "cleere," "merciable" is used for sixteen constructions (nearly another quarter of the total), as against ten uses from the group "cursed," "foul," "hateful," "yvel," "sinful," "unstable."

To conclude, the Prioress's tale is the summation of an effort, running through five of the twenty-three tales, to write a purely affective narrative in which irony, characterization, and complexity of action all give way to a very rigidly controlled stylistic artifice.

Seen from the direction from which I have been looking in this chapter, the *Canterbury Tales* is a collection of experiments in separating the individual elements of the poetic problems in the earlier poetry, and working them out in single narratives (and groups of narratives) in a range of conventional types. I think the major overall problem in the *Canterbury Tales* is a structural one, as it had been in the early poems, but in several cases Chaucer has isolated and "perfected" a style (as I have

---

34. Except for "salte" in "salte teeris" and "pale" in "pale face," these adjectives are all quite non-specific and highly loaded emotionally.

been showing in the "sentimental experiment") to answer one or another of the challenges which his poetic convictions set for him. And quite apart from the universally acclaimed development and mastery of the semi-dramatic "realism" of the frame, there are several stylistic developments in the tales which are strikingly different from the earlier work, even though they are fairly clearly experiments growing out of problems defined in it. The starkly schematic action of the Pardoner's tale, the narrow and insistent verbal artifice of the Prioress's, or the self-destructive irony of the Merchant's, are all extreme stylistic developments which, if they do not always show Chaucer's poetry at its best, nevertheless show it at its most determinedly experimental, in the individual modes of the complex and paradoxical poetic which he had begun to worry out in the *Book of the Duchess.*

6. *Troilus and Criseyde,* a Historical View

I

As FAR AS WE CAN JUDGE from what survives of his
work, Chaucer seems twice in his career to have put aside
his experimentation with structures which would in-
corporate the old books in some new sort of frame, and
set himself to the remaking of a single, extensive, unframed narrative.[1] The first attempt at this most poetically orthodox of procedures produced one of his least
interesting (and, again, incomplete) failures, *Anelida
and Arcite.* The second produced his most complex and
most finished poem—and his greatest: *Troilus and
Criseyde.* It is not very hard to see what went wrong with
Anelida and Arcite and, probably, why it was left unfinished. In the attempt to elaborate the narrative so as
to realize its emotional potential, Chaucer had turned
the poem into a lyric almost before he got the action
under way, and Anelida's long "compleynt," in its extreme prosodic and imagistic elaborateness, both par-
alyzes the movement of narration and pretty well gives
away all at once the emotional impact that the whole

---

1. Obviously, such a statement must be qualified by the recognition
that some, or even much, of the short narrative in the *CT* may have
been earlier work.

narrative might have been expected to develop.[2] On the other hand, it is extremely hard to delineate all of what went right with *Troilus and Criseyde,* as it is with any complicated and good literary work. But particularly in the past thirty years, critics have made it increasingly clearer that the very conventionality of much of its content and procedure is one major element in its artistic success. From Karl Young to E. T. Donaldson and Charles Muscatine, the most distinguished and perceptive critics have contributed to disembarrass us of the older notions (still not altogether extinct) that the poem's excellence lies somehow in its almost being something it is not: proto-Shakespearean tragedy or proto-Richardsonian novel, or what you will. In short, the great gain in relatively recent criticism has been that it has looked for the excellence of *Troilus and Criseyde* in its poetry —in its own distinct and unique way of happening. At the same time, we have also been learning a good deal more about the possibilities for a poem's achieving its uniqueness out of its sublimation of common conventions, and have thus nearly laid the ghost of the old Wordsworthian misconception of the conflict between tradition and originality.

My principal aim in this chapter is to extend the consideration of the poem's transformation of conventional elements to include the means—the choices and procedures, insofar as we can infer them from the structure of the poetry—by which the transformations are accomplished. Earlier chapters should have indicated already the extent to which I feel that the poetics, the principles of choice and procedure, in *Troilus and Criseyde* are

2. Although he states it in different terms, I think this is essentially what Pratt felt about the poem too, after his study of Chaucer's various uses of its source; see his "Chaucer's Use of the *Teseida,*" *PMLA,* 62 (1947), 598–621.

STRUCTURAL DISPOSITION 173

more academically orthodox than they are anywhere else in Chaucer's work, although I mean by that neither that Geoffrey of Vinsauf is the ultimate author of the poem, nor that its poetic is different in kind from what we have been examining. I think there is considerable interest and importance in the fact that the kind of criticism practiced in the rhetorical manuals will yield a more satisfactory analysis of *Troilus and Criseyde* than of any other major Chaucerian piece;[3] and there is something to be learned from the observation that, generically speaking, the conventionality of *Troilus and Criseyde* lies principally in its conformity to one type of stylistically elaborate, morally tendentious, and emotionally moving narrative defined theoretically in the textbooks. Despite its affinities with all of them, it is not a romance or love-vision or legend or complaint, or any of what might be called the practical genres which the French tradition offered as developed structural types. And as C. S. Lewis has pointed out,[4] though to partly wrong conclusions, it is certainly not the kind of extended *allegoria* of its author's amatory nightmares that Boccaccio's *Filostrato* is. Dante's words can be made into as accurate a historical definition as we are likely to have of *Troilus and Criseyde:* it is an exercise of the eloquent and courtly vulgar tongue (though not entirely in the high style); it is a piece of rhetoric set to music, to move the hearts of men.

Since the most recent full-length study of *Troilus and Criseyde* raises once more the old objection that the "influence" of rhetorical theory on Chaucer is questionable

3. This is not to say that such a rhetorical analysis will give a wholly satisfactory criticism; only that it will define many of the problems which a satisfactory criticism must take into account.

4. "What Did Chaucer Really Do to *Il Filostrato?*" *Essays and Studies,* *17* (1932), 56.

or of little use to the critic because inseparable from other "influences,"[5] perhaps I should say again, emphatically, that it matters very little what specific combination of agencies helped establish and reinforce Chaucer's sense of the primary problems and procedures of art. As Miss Hamilton pointed out several years ago,[6] it is not altogether surprising that a man might learn the same thing in two or three different places; and even that arid old academic, Gervais de Melkley, conceded that although there is a natural genius which produces good poetry spontaneously, the safest way is by practicing composition and *reading good poetry*.[7] This is about as close to an overt statement of Horatian classicism as can be found among the rhetorical treatises, but all agree that their attempts to codify the principles of composition must be supplemented by careful reading of the best models and by practice in composing.[8] Such statements are very important in helping to define the proper uses, for a modern critic, of the *schemata* and analyses available in the treatises. The rhetoricians themselves had at least some awareness that no system of theoretical formulations could by itself either explain or produce poetry. We know that by the time he wrote *Troilus and Criseyde*, Chaucer had devoted a good many years and three or four major poems to the same artistic problems which

5. Sanford B. Meech, *Design in Chaucer's Troilus* (Syracuse, 1959). See esp. Preface, vii: "I shall draw also upon the scholarship devoted to general literary influences, neglecting, however, one very considerable branch of it, that devoted to the presumed effect upon Chaucer of rhetorical theory. I eschew treatment of this effect, not because I question its presence in the *Troilus*, but because, after diligent attempts, I have found myself utterly unable to separate it from other influences."

6. See above, Ch. 1, n. 14.

7. *Ars versificaria*, Introd.; text in Faral, p. 328 ff. (See Ch. 1, n. 7.)

8. See the discussion in Faral, Ch. 4, of the sources of rhetorical doctrine. Alcuin, Geoffrey of Vinsauf, and John of Salisbury are quoted on the three ways of perfecting a style.

are basic to rhetorical theory. We know that he studied most carefully those stylistic artificers in the other vernaculars who were pushing the purely verbal implications of rhetorical theory to the most precious extremes. We know that he read and weighed critically[9] the treatises themselves. The most practical inference for the modern investigator, it seems to me, is that Chaucer's *Troilus and Criseyde* represents one manifestation of some fundamental poetic attitudes which, although they are more than a century out of date and beginning to disintegrate by Chaucer's time, are fortunately preserved for us in another and more explicit (though less adequate) manifestation in the thirteenth-century treatises.

E. T. Donaldson's essay on *Troilus and Criseyde*[10] speaks of the paradox in the narrator's attitude toward the stuff of his story, the superimposed images of the action as completed, ended, far past and known, and as live current experience, in process, immediate and emotionally exigent. Because Donaldson's critical stance is, as usual, *ad hoc* and rests (overtly, at least) on no theoretical associations, medieval or modern, his commentary provides a particularly useful answer to curious theoretical "defenses" like those of C. S. Lewis,[11] who seems to feel that at best the medieval poetic was a disordered garden of disparate and artificial flowers, although the flowers were pretty and medieval gardeners thought they could smell them. For the double vision which Donaldson describes is exactly the aim of poetry in the rhetorical definition: the double validation of truth by finding it in the past and making it live in the present. It is also a double vision which Chaucer, elsewhere in his work,

9. I take his parodying of some aspects of them and his serious quotation of others to indicate conscious exercise of judgment.
10. In his *Chaucer's Poetry*, pp. 965–80.
11. See above, n. 4.

speaks of having enjoyed himself while reading good
poetry.[12] If, for a while, we talk about selection, amplification, and abbreviation as ways of reconstructing an old
story so that a fitting style can distribute through it the
particular decorative emphasis which will reactivate it,
we are not necessarily talking about things visible only
through a singularly astigmatic medieval eye.

First, there is the matter of what sort of rough structure Chaucer obtained by tossing aside all but 2750 lines
of the *Filostrato*'s 5704, compressing those into 2580, and
then adding some 5660 more lines, either of his own or
(more often) borrowed from Boccaccio or someone else.[13]
In the preface to *Il Filostrato*, addressed to his own ab-
sent lady, Boccaccio reveals why he chose to tell this tale
and how,[14] and throughout the poem, including the invocation and the final *commiato,* he continues to weave
into and around the narrative a ground of expressive and
evaluative language which makes of the whole a sustained

12. Cf. the comments on the story of Ceyx and Alcione in *BD*, or of
Tereus in *LGW*.

13. See Meech, *Design*, for a detailed account of exactly what, where,
and how Chaucer altered *Il Filostrato*.

14. "E il modo fu questo, di dovere in persona di alcuno passionato,
siccome io era e sono, cantando narrare i miei martirii. Meco adunque
con sollecita cura cominciai a rivolgere l'antiche storie, per trovare cui
potessi verisimilmente fare scudo del mio segreto e amoroso dolore. Nè
altro più atto nella mente mi venne a tal bisogno, che il valoroso giovane
Troilo, figliuolo di Priamo nobilissimo re di Troia, alla cui vita, in
quanto per amore e per la lontananza della sua donna fu doloroso, se
fede alcuna alle antiche storie se può dare, poichè Criseida da lui som-
mamente amata fu al suo padre Calcas renduta, è stata la mia similissima
dopo la vostra partita" (pp. 124–26). "Nelle quali [i.e. rime] se avviene
che leggiate, quante volte Troilo piangere e dolersi della partita di
Criseida troverete, tante apertamente potrete comprendere e conoscere
le mie medesime voci, le lagrime, i sospiri e l'angosce; e quante volte le
bellezze, i costumi, e qualunque altra cosa laudevole in donna, di Criseida
scritto troverete, di voi essere parlato potrete intendere" (p. 128). Quoted
from *The Filostrato of Giovanni Boccaccio,* ed. N. E. Griffin and A. B.
Myrick (Philadelphia, 1929).

personal lyric. Chaucer intrudes upon the action of his poem for exactly opposite reasons: to remain constantly between the reader and the action, objectifying it for him and eliciting from him an attitude toward it. Boccaccio's conception of his subject is as a more or less allegorical device upon which he can impose as ultimate substance his own emotions. Chaucer—and here is a key to the whole difference between the two poems—re-emphasizes an old narrative in order to point out in it particular aspects of the truths it may exemplify, and he begins by separating himself sharply and completely from the action and all the characters in it.

> To the clepe I, thow goddesse of torment,
> Thow cruwel Furie, sorwynge evere yn peyne,
> Help me, that am the sorwful instrument,
> That helpeth loveres, as I kan, to pleyne.
> For wel sit it, the sothe for to seyne,
> A woful wight to han a drery feere,
> And to a sorwful tale, a sory chere.
>
> For I, that God of Loves servantz serve,
> Ne dar to Love, for myn unliklynesse,
> Preyen for speed, al sholde I therfore sterve,
> So fer am I from his help in derknesse.
> But natheles, if this may don gladnesse
> To any lovere, and his cause availle,
> Have he my thonk, and myn be this travaille.
>
> (I. 8–21)

To free the narrative for such an approach to it, he first stripped Boccaccio's poem of all material irrelevant to his own purposes—all its machinery of personal identification and expression—and then amplified the remaining narrative in such a way as to produce a new poem.

If I may rephrase, regroup, and somewhat amend the

results of textual comparisons made by a succession of scholars from Rossetti to Meech, Chaucer's *abbreviatio* left the base narrative little altered save in the proportion of rising action to falling. His *amplificationes* are worked into and around the narrative, without substantially altering its course, in six principal areas of elaboration:[15]

1. The largest single block of change and addition is in Books II and III, in the elaborate preparations for the consummation. This includes not only the machinations of Pandarus, but a large amount of explanation and analysis of the growth and development of love.

2. Next in size is the space devoted to the elaboration of the character of Pandarus.

3. The character of Criseyde is not only expanded, but radically altered by Chaucer. We also see more of her following the separation of the lovers, and Chaucer relates more fully her affair with Diomede.

4. The hymn to Love, the predestination soliloquy, and the translation of Troilus to the eighth sphere are perhaps spliced in later.[16] These are about the only tamperings with Boccaccio's presentation of Troilus.

5. A series of songs, *apostrophe,* and invocations is interspersed at strategic points. Included in this group should also be the proems, many of which Chaucer adds or revises, and the *envoi* and moral "epilogue."

6. Threaded through the poem, usually in very short units, but adding up to a considerable bulk, are Chaucer's remarks in his own person. These take various forms, most often that of direct address to the reader[17] and of

15. None of these is exclusively or even principally filled up with freshly invented material, but rather with concatenations of other borrowings.

16. See above, Ch. 3, n. 1.

17. These remarks, by the way, are almost never so phrased as to imply unequivocally a physically present listening audience.

personal commentary upon the characters or the action.[18]

These groups, considered in terms of their effect on the whole structure of the poem, turn Boccaccio's two-level work into a multiplex one which may appear variously stratified as the angle of view changes (as it has from Legouis' day,[19] for instance, to our own), but I should like to consider it here as composed of four major agencies of effect: action, characterization, lyric interpolation, and authorial commentary.

The foundation for the whole structure is, of course, the action which, getting under way at stanza 40 of Book I, is then divided fairly naturally into the five books in which Chaucer chose to arrange it. The first sets forth the complete initial situation, with Troilus in love and Pandarus prepared to aid him; Book II contains the machinations preparatory to the climax; Book III, opening with the first meeting of the lovers and closing with Troilus's hymn to Love, completely contains the happy relations of Troilus and Criseyde; Book IV motivates and accomplishes their separation; and Book V relates Criseyde's desertion and betrayal and Troilus's death. But for Chaucer as for his thirteenth-century preceptors, the

18. Henry Lüdeke, *Die Funktionen des Erzählers in Chaucers epischer Dichtung* (Halle, 1928), studies carefully the personal intrusions of the poet as compared to the practice of his contemporaries, and concludes that in general, "[Chaucer] ist in weit höherem Grade als bei anderen Dichtern der Mittler zwischen Dichter und Hörer" (p. 133). With respect to *T&C* in particular, however, he concludes that certain qualitative distinctions must be made between it and the source poem. "Der kühl räsonnierenden Teilnahme des Erzählers steht die leidenschaftlich Warme zur Seite, die die Gefühlsmässige Wirkung des Dargestellten auf den Darsteller selbst mitteilt" (p. 10). Concerning the problem stated in his title, he generalizes about *T&C:* "Im *Troilus* hat Chaucer die Rolle des Erzählers voll entwickelt" (p. 12).

19. Émile Legouis, *Geoffrey Chaucer,* in *Les grands écrivains étrangers* (Paris, 1910), judged the structure incoherent and the poem a "glorious failure."

action of a narrative poem is all potential,[20] and ultimately is only what the realization of a style can make of
it. The rhetoricians scarcely discuss the plotting of an
action; Chaucer hardly ever bothers to invent one, and
in *Troilus and Criseyde* he did not even try to rearrange
much the one he had borrowed.

Most of the rhetorical theorists upon whose work this
study is based treat the problem of characterization in
two places: under *descriptio*, which is consistently listed
under amplification, and occasionally as a kind of *digressio;* and, in more general terms, under the levels of style.
The two kinds of discussion are actually closely related,
in that together they indicate an almost completely static
concept of characterization and a method of presenting
character in more or less set pieces. The *descriptio*
formulae are presented in detail by all the rhetoricians.
They are based, with little modification, upon Cicero's
list of the "places of invention" for character,[21] and the
"places" *(loci),* such as name, course of life, habits and
mannerisms, emotional qualities, etc., do not of themselves either limit very severely or direct very specifically
the process of characterization. But the fact of their
being lumped together under a single aspect of technique
reflects just as it reinforces the medieval habit of blocked
characterization. What defines even more effectively the
tendency to stylized, set characterization is the way in
which the distinction of levels of style takes on personal
and social connotations. What Dante rehabilitates into
a subtle principle of stylistic modulation is in the academic theorists largely a decorum of type psychology.
Geoffrey of Vinsauf, in his *Documentum de modo et*

20. That is, except for his rare experiments like that in the Pardoner's
tale, discussed in the preceding chapter.
21. *De inventione,* I, 24–25.

arte dictandi et versificandi, says in definition of the levels of style:

> Et tales recipiunt appellationes styli ratione personarum vel rerum de quibus fit tractatus. Quando enim de generalibus [MS faulty here; *generalibus* should read *grandibus*] personis vel rebus tractatur, tunc est stylus grandiloquus; quando de humilibus, humilis; quando de mediocribus, mediocris. (II. 145)

Jean de Garlande equates the three levels of style to the three states of human life: pastoral—low style; agricultural—middle style; upper classes and nobility—high style.[22]

These two groups of ideas about character, together with the ancient rhetorical concept of the function of style in eliciting praise or blame, combine to produce not only static characterization, but characterization by types and characterization slanted in terms of the author's evaluation of his characters.[23] Fixity and fitness—character established and unchanging, given typical significance through the selection of attributes consistent with the status of the character in the action: these are the controlling ideas in the presentation of character for the

22. See Faral, p. 87. Faral's statement is probably too strong, but it indicates the relationship under discussion here: "Pour l'école du XIIe et du XIIIe siècle, [affaire de style est devenue] affaire de dignité sociale: c'est la qualité des personnes, et non plus celle de l'élocution, qui fournit le principe de la classification" (p. 88).

23. Faral, p. 79: "Les caractères qu'il faut attribuer à un prélat, explique Matthieu de Vendôme [I. 64], sont la force de la foi, l'amour de la vertu, la pureté de la religion, la grâce de la piété; à un prince, c'est la rigueur de sa justice; à une femme, c'est la beauté, c'est-à-dire l'élégance des formes unie à l'agrément du teint. . . . Ainsi se constituent des figures conventionnelles d'où sont exclus les traits variés et imprévus de la réalité." Only the last inference needs to be questioned. It is scarcely a necessary conclusion that because a character is typical he is "unreal"; and the standard of *réalité* begs the question of function.

rhetoricians, as they evidently were for many medieval poets as well.

Chaucer's skill with dialogue, and a range of other technical skills, produces at times so strong an illusion of reality around the central characters of *Troilus and Criseyde* that it is quite possible to forget the typicality and representativeness of the characters. It is also worth noting that a fair share of the illusion of reality comes not from the actual processes of characterization, but from the affective immediacy of the moral and emotional problems within which the existences of the characters are defined. And a good deal of the actual characterization comes in set pieces—in blocks of exposition by the narrator, or in the kind of near-soliloquy which Muscatine aptly labels "non-representational monologue."[24]

Arthur Mizener[25] and, more recently, Muscatine have commented revealingly and at length on the elements in the patterns of characterization which remove it from the realistic and motivational-psychological categories in which earlier criticism had sought to define it. Muscatine and Meech[26] have also had valuable things to say about the use of conventional styles to differentiate characters for representative purposes—a point to which I shall return a little further on. But to sum up the general effect of Chaucer's realignment of his source in the area of characterization, the two most striking results are a great increase in attention to characters and a simultaneous broadening and intensification of their representativeness, their typicality. Such changes as the alteration of the age and personality of Pandarus, and the careful removal of the reader from any direct contact with the

24. *Chaucer and the French Tradition*, pp. 133 ff.
25. "Character and Action in the Case of Criseyde," *PMLA, 54* (1939), 65–79.
26. *Design*, Ch. 3.

feelings of Criseyde are part of the preparation for the kind of ironic, self-criticizing configurations of character and action which Chaucer had repeatedly struggled with in the different forms of his earlier poetry. Troilus, Criseyde, and Pandarus are all three presented solely in terms of the love affair which is the poem's chief immediate concern, although the care with which the terms are distinguished and distributed among the characters forces us to see the love under a variety of conventional aspects. Chaucer is still, even in this structurally most orthodox of his poems, using *dispositio* as a direct agency of meaning with a finesse and precision which the manuals scarcely seem to have foreseen as a poetic possibility. I think that is still another connection with the structurally less orthodox poetry of the earlier experiments. Each character is given a set of constant characteristics[27] with respect to that love, and in no case are we given any information—especially concerning motivation—that does not contribute to the elucidation of the nature of that love. What we have in the three characters is a series of types, superbly realized and vitalized, which, taken together as an element in the structure of the poem, give Chaucer an area in which to develop an effectively complex presentation of courtly love, and prepare for a commentary upon it.

The first two areas of rearrangement, taken together, provide a full expository treatment of the doctrine of courtly love, through embodiment in characters and through an action which mounts to the highest exaltation

27. True of Criseyde too. The old debate over her "flaw," as Mizener pointed out, is largely the consequence of trying to arrange mathematically precise correspondences between a set of actions and a set of characteristics. As far as the poem itself is concerned, we get one set of characteristics for Criseyde and no subsequent revision or alteration of them. We get two sets of actions for her, and they are contradictory, but neither is inconsistent with the general characteristics.

which that love can provide, and then proceeds to destroy it. It is in the third and fourth of Chaucer's principal amplificatory areas that the evaluations implicit in the structure (as revised by the first two kinds of rearrangement) are realized. These amplifications constitute a much smaller total bulk than those already discussed, but they bear most important clues to the total meaning of the poem. In fact, the operation of these evaluative elaborations in connection with the more purely substantive strata is an excellent demonstration of the different meaning acquired by the term "didactic" when it is used to describe the process of conceiving of a poetic structure in terms of an evaluation implicit in the whole structure of the poetry and not merely written over it or appended to it. It seems to me that this is the maximum artistic potential of rhetorical theory, taken at its best and as a whole system, and given a competent poet who can really feel his art in those terms.

In *Troilus and Criseyde,* it is the system of lyric and *apostrophe,* set within the structure of the narrative proper, which provides the openings through which Chaucer may move outward from the action into a larger evaluation. This third structural area is delimited by the terminal points of the first and second *cantici Troili* (Book I. 400–34 and Book v. 638–58). It is organized in ten major sections, with perhaps a few short interjections to be included also. These major lyric departures from the line of action are all set pieces, at least a stanza in length;[28] each comes at an important point in the action, but only one (Antigone's love song) can be said to have any bearing at all on the course of the action; none come in conversational exchanges—that is, none are ordinary speeches of the characters, picked out of the action to

28. Actually, only two (Troilus's second *aubade* and his plaint to the empty palace) are less than 20 lines long.

support the argument here. The ten clear-cut examples
of this structure of lyric elaboration are:

I. 400–34: first *canticus Troili*
II. 827–75: Antigone's song
III. 1422–42: Criseyde's *aubade*
III. 1450–70: Troilus's answering *aubade*
III. 1702–8: Troilus's second *aubade*
III. 1744–71: Troilus's hymn to Love
IV. 958–1082: Troilus's predestination soliloquy
V. 218–45: Troilus's plaint, "Wher is myn owene
lady, lief and deere"
V. 540–53: Troilus's plaint to the empty palace
V. 638–58: second *canticus Troili*

These ten important lyric amplifications are all excellent examples of a device to which all the rhetoricians
devote large amounts of space in their catalogues of the
means of amplification. Geoffrey of Vinsauf gives more
attention to *apostrophe*[29] than to any of the other seven
standard figures of structural amplification which he discusses. Although Geoffrey considers as *apostrophe* interjections both by the author and by the characters in the
poem, his treatment indicates that a clearly lyric quality,
partly measured by the concentration of tropes, is a characteristic of the device in either case. Faral notes that
the *apostrophe* frequently constitutes a lyric form by itself; the complaint, for example, is only an *apostrophe*
dislocated from its circumstances, and Geoffrey recognizes it as such by citing one as an example of the device.
Even the separable, lyric character of Chaucer's inset

29. As Chaucer somewhat disrespectfully notes in the Nun's Priest's
tale (3338–54). See Faral's whole section on "Amplification." The ancients define *apostrophe* as any exclamation (direct) inserted to strength-
en the expression. The medieval rhetoricians, however, all seem to have
considered it a form of amplification.

apostrophe passages is recognized in the rhetorical manuals. The fact that they are good lyrics and structurally functional, even if frequently adapted from another source, seems to me to constitute no argument that they are not the same sort of thing as those elaborative decorations which Geoffrey of Vinsauf described.

Taken as a group, apart from their individual contexts, these ten lyrics constitute a kind of distillation of the emotional progress of the poem, held together by a thread of thematic imagery in much the manner of a very condensed sonnet sequence. A little later, when we move from *dispositio* to *elocutio,* we shall examine that imagery more closely, but it concerns *dispositio* to show how these ten lyrics are significantly spaced through the poem. They interrupt the action at each major turn of events, and four of them are interspersed in the almost continuously lyric high plane in the action from the consummation scene through to the end of Book III. The first *canticus Troili* comes at the beginning of the rising action, as Troilus chooses to love Criseyde. Antigone's song, in Book II, immediately precedes (and helps to precipitate) Criseyde's decision to accept his love. The three *aubades* mark the ends of the two completely happy meetings which are presented in detail. Troilus's hymn to Love concludes the joyful third book, and immediately precedes the announcement of Calchas's decision to recall his daughter. The predestination soliloquy follows Troilus's first interview with Criseyde after the announcement of the exchange. The two plaints of Troilus punctuate the waiting period following the separation. The second *canticus Troili* immediately precedes the exchange of letters which makes it evident that the separation is permanent. In the light of all the debate there has been over problems of characterization in the poem, it is interesting to note that of these most graphically emotional projections in the poem, Criseyde is given only one, the first of the two *aubades* which conclude the consummation scene. One is given to Antigone, and the other eight are all spoken by Troilus.

With respect to the combined elements of character and action, the series of lyrics plots out the curve of emotional tension through the poem, but it is the manner in which they concentrate the emotional significance of the action which makes them most a part of the evaluative machinery, and which leads us out of the action for its own sake toward the final level of commentary: Chaucer's digressive interjections as author-interpreter.

Lüdeke's figures,[30] compiled under the Germanic illusion of the possibility of mathematical precision in such matters, undoubtedly overspecify the location and effect of authorial commentary, but they are useful and indicative in general of some things which he did not associate with them. Counting only the expressions in the first person, he found that they constitute 2.47 per cent of the total lines in Book I, 3.36 per cent in Book II, 4.34 per cent in Book III, 1.18 per cent in Book IV, and 3.9 per cent in Book V. First, it is apparent that the pattern of dispersal throughout the poem corresponds closely to that of the lyric interpolations, starting at a fairly low frequency, increasing through the second book to a high in Book III, and then dropping sharply to a low in Book IV, but rising again to a proportionally high frequency in the last book. All together, about 290 lines of *Troilus and Criseyde* are given over to first-person address by the author, as compared to about 250 lines in the ten lyric apostrophes.

Chaucer, having chosen a subject and a substance, and having rearranged them in such a way as to imply the

30. See above, n. 18.

nature of his personal commentary, proceeds in this outer shell of the structure to underscore the elements of the complex truth which the substance exemplifies. It is under the amplificatory figure *digressio* that the rhetoricians treat this aspect of composition,[31] and the manner in which the figure is treated, at least in some of the manuals, is significant once again in the case against defining rhetorical theory as primarily an overrationalized system of devices to help the poet avoid his responsibilities to structure. Geoffrey of Vinsauf makes no mention of narrative digression (i.e. moving off on tangential lines of action), but he does classify two modes of authorial interruption. First, he says, the author may depart out of the subject through comparisons or similar devices. Second, he may intersperse comment which anticipates a course of events to be taken up again later. It is properly the business of the subsequent discussion of style to investigate precisely the variety of effects of these digressions, but there is also some structural significance in the observation that they may be divided almost exactly at the end of Book III; nearly all before that point (except the opening stanzas of Book I) are of Geoffrey of Vinsauf's first category, and nearly all thereafter are of the second.

II

In the distribution of the various efforts which make up the total process of poetic composition, *elocutio* (style) bore the double burden of preserving the dignity and beauty fitting to the subject and of carrying through the poem the particular emphases for which the processes of selection, amplification, and abbreviation had prepared

31. Some of Chaucer's commentary could be properly classed as *apostrophe*—the proems and invocations, for example, as well as some inset exclamation in the course of events.

a structure. Hence the apparently disproportionately large amounts of space devoted to the ornaments of style in the manuals,[32] and the vague and confusing double standard of classification.

The ancient distinction of three levels of style is retained by the medieval theorists, but in a much altered sense. The tendency of this principle of stylistic classification to change into a principle of characterization has already been noted; the rhetorical manuals consistently define the three levels in terms of a general standard of decorum, but rarely invoke them as a principle for classifying kinds of figures. A second distinction in levels of style is made on the basis of the nature of the figures themselves. This is the underlying distinction in terms of which the many lists of figures are arranged. There does seem to be a rough correspondence, however, between these two kinds of stylistic distinctions, for the "difficult ornament" is occasionally spoken of as particularly pertinent to the high style, and the "simple ornament" to the middle.[33] The low style was apparently below the level of figurative elaboration.

The distinction between the two kinds of ornament is ultimately one between the kind of image which operates by a transfer or association of meaning and the kind which operates primarily by the patterned arrangement of words. Within the class of simple ornament, a further twofold division is observed. This division repeats, at a lower level, the same kind of distinction made between

32. Matthieu de Vendome gives two of the four parts of his treatise to the ornaments; Geoffrey of Vinsauf, about half the *Documentum* and 1200 lines of the *Poetria;* Jean de Garlande, two of the seven chapters of his *Poetria.*

33. The varying terms, used more or less interchangeably, for the kinds of ornament indicate the sense of correspondence: for difficult ornament, *egregia verbi locare, modus gravis, difficultas ornata,* etc.; for simple ornament, *sermo levis, ornata facilitas, via plana,* etc.

the difficult and simple ornament. Figures of words—
primarily grammatical or phonetic arrangements—are
differentiated from figures of thought such as rhetorical
balance, parenthesis, repeated modifiers, etc. I think it is
possible that what we have in this schematization is an indirect, perhaps not fully conscious, recognition of a problem which medieval poetic theory never faces up to directly: the implication in the notion of decorum that there
must be a hierarchy of beauty and worth inherent in language, apart from the content it is made to convey. If decorum is to have any reasonable meaning at all, it must depend on the adjustment of two different hierarchical orders, idea and language, so that they correspond precisely.
Medieval aesthetic theorists, like their colleagues in other
fields, speak much of the regular structure of creation
and the ideas embodied in it, and they clearly commit
poetry to the observation of those structures. But they
make no discourse at all of what it is in language which
makes it apt and appropriate for decorous deployment.
In a sense Euphuism and late eighteenth-century "poetic
diction" are both relatively extreme examples of a conscious working out of such implications in the idea of
decorum, and of translating them into prescripts and
practice based largely on a hierarchy of vocabulary. The
thirteenth-century rhetoricians are closer, in their way,
to an adequate hypothesis of the relationship between
art and idea, in that theirs is at least a hierarchy of formal complexity in the figurative constructs possible with
language. They carry out the hypothesis with a dogged
inner logic, and no outer rationale, so that its real bearing on an adequate theory of linguistic decorum is, as I
said, confused and uncertain. I discuss the point here
mainly to indicate that in what has often been made to
seem a uselessly artificial schematization of figurative
language there may be concealed a response to very im-

portant aesthetic problems, and poets with the highly developed formal sensitivities of Dante or Chaucer are very likely to have sensed them as problems of their own.

In *Troilus and Criseyde,* we do not often find Chaucer at his most stylistically elaborate[34] (*Anelida and Arcite,* the earlier attempt at the independent narrative, is a good deal more dense, figuratively), and he deals rather sparingly in any of the difficult ornament. But, especially in the light of what I have argued earlier about the transfer to the vernaculars of Latin stylistic precepts, what we should expect is that the figurative elaboration we do find in the poem should effectively realize the thematic implications of Chaucer's structural rearrangement of *Il Filostrato.* The decoration should provide the affective[35] substance which in a sense "fills up" the areas of amplification, although that way of putting it overemphasizes the purely quantitative aspects of the term "amplification." That is, the various areas of structural alteration I have marked out will be bound together by a style which can control implication, and move from one level of it to another. The bare narrative contains, as Chaucer handles it, the suggestion of a certain kind of love.[36] The presentation of character expands and de-

34. I have checked Naunin's catalogue carefully against the text and added to it all additional figures that I have observed. Most of these Naunin had either not listed, or listed as doubtful because they are so common in all poetry that he did not feel it justifiable to count them as rhetorical. I have included them (most of them are tropes) on the grounds that a theory of style does not have to invent the figures it includes, and that it would be a poor theory indeed if it did not include the most commonly used figures.

35. In the medieval rhetorical concept of poetry, "affective" must involve judgment reached through emotional conviction, not simply emotional response.

36. The same narrative in Boccaccio's poem does not suggest the same kind of love, and Boccaccio's story moves in a very different direction. The story by itself is not *necessarily* a courtly love story, nor is any story *per se.*

fines the idea of that kind of love and contains the suggestion of its emotional qualities, which are distilled into the most stylistically elaborate of the structural layers, the interposed lyrics. These, in the terms and structures of their imagery, both present the most moving statement possible of that love and suggest the limitations or confusion in values which the running authorial commentary helps point up for us. In fact, it is in that relatively small group of the rhetoricians' figures which Chaucer uses most freely that the binding force is most concentrated. Although the rhetorical manuals may not offer us satisfactory explanations of how or why these figures operate effectively, Chaucer's poetry demonstrates that they do.[37]

The most obvious manner in which figurative language can function in any narrative is by producing the suggestions or associations which are generally described as "atmospheric." In *Troilus and Criseyde,* the atmosphere so produced is specific and conventional; it is the atmosphere of that unique medieval literary world in which the only people are perfect lovers or their enemies

---

37. The figures of *digressio, sententia, comparatio, exclamatio, translatio, frequentatio, repetitio,* and *traductio* are the most frequently employed in *T&C.* Together they account for nearly three-quarters of the figures Naunin found in the poem. I have used Naunin's catalogue for all such tabulations, although it is a bit difficult to gather from it information of this kind about particular poems; he catalogues by device rather than by poem. It should also be noted here that Naunin's method of listing these figures is somewhat misleading (see above, n. 34). He catalogues *digressio* under "figures especially pertaining to structure," but does not note that *exclamatio* might also be a structural figure. Neither does his method of listing indicate that some figurative patterns might be composed of two or three different figures at the same time. A proverb, for example, is sometimes stated as a comparison, and in a verbal pattern involving repetition or some other such scheme of arrangement. This can make a considerable difference, if the figures are to be considered in terms of their effects.

and the only events the joys and sorrows of courteous
love.[38]

> And so bifel, whan comen was the tyme
> Of Aperil, whan clothed is the mede
> With newe grene, of lusty Veer the pryme,
> And swote smellen floures white and rede,
> In sondry wises shewed, as I rede,
> The folk of Troie hire observaunces olde,
> Palladiones feste for to holde.
>
> And to the temple, in al hir beste wise,
> In general ther wente many a wight,
> To herknen of Palladion the servyse;
> And namely, so many a lusty knyght,
> So many a lady fressh and mayden bright,
> Ful wel arayed, both meste, mene, and leste,
> Ye, bothe for the seson and the feste.
>
> Among thise othere folk was Criseyda,
> In widewes habit blak; but natheles,
> Right as oure firste lettre is now an A,
> In beaute first so stood she, makeles.
> Hire goodly lokyng gladed al the prees.
> Nas nevere yet seyn thyng to ben preysed derre,
> Nor under cloude blak so bright a sterre
>
> As was Criseyde, as folk seyde everichone
> That hir behelden in hir blake wede.   (I. 155–77)

The first four lines are a short *descriptio*, of the most
conventional character in both manner and substance.

---

38. I have not found much justification in the poem for Karl Young's
statement that Chaucer was trying to "transport the reader—or audience
—away from contemporary reality to a distant and romantic Troy"
which was to be reconstructed by means of ancient, archaic, "Trojan"
detail. See his "Chaucer's *Troilus and Criseyde* as Romance," *PMLA, 53*
(1938), 38–63.

The beginning of the narrative sequence here (although
it does not happen to be the beginning of the poem) is
precisely the kind of beginning recommended by Geoffrey of Vinsauf in the *Poetria* under the figure *descriptio;*
and it is almost invariably through some such descriptive gateway that the world of courtly love is entered.
When we pass through it here, we are prepared to recognize the persons we meet in the next few lines. The two
contrived comparisons through which Criseyde is introduced into the scene do not describe her; they suggest the
conventional qualities associated with such a character
in such a story.

Through the first three books, the suggestions struck
off by the figurative elaboration in the purely narrative
sections continue to be of this kind, and are produced
by similar means.[39] The *descriptio* of spring, spring flowers, etc., is sufficiently recurrent to provide a kind of
theme image for those three books. A more elaborate
version of it opens Book II, this time with a small *allegoria* worked in:

> In May, that moder is of monthes glade,
> That fresshe floures, blew and white and rede,
> Ben quike agayn, that wynter dede made,
> And ful of bawme is fletyng every mede;
> Whan Phebus doth his bryghte bemes sprede,
> Right in the white Bole, it so bitidde,
> As I shal synge, on Mayes day the thrydde, (II. 50–56)

In Books IV and V, the effects of such elaboration are
different in quality, as the thematic development requires. The same use of *descriptio,* again of a thoroughly
conventional nature even in the manner of the contrast,
occurs early in Book IV. The effect—the atmospheric

---

39. Similar examples occur in II. 820–26; II. 918–24; and III. 351–55.

suggestion—has been reversed, but the way in which the
figure operates to bind the bare account of events to the
theme as it is developing at other structural levels remains the same.

> And as in wynter leves ben biraft,
> Ech after other, til the tree be bare,
> So that ther nys but bark and braunche ilaft,
> Lith Troilus, byraft of ech welfare,
> Ibounden in the blake bark of care,
> Disposed wood out of his wit to breyde,
> So sore hym sat the chaungynge of Criseyde.
>
> (IV. 225–31)

And to complete the parallel with the stanzas from Book
I quoted above, the *comparatio* in the following stanzas
(applied to the character who appears in the atmosphere
established by the preceding *descriptio*) gives a foreshadowing suggestion about Troilus:

> He rist hym up, and every dore he shette
> And wyndow ek, and tho this sorwful man
> Upon his beddes syde adown hym sette,
> Ful lik a ded ymage, pale and wan;   (IV. 232–35)

Of course it is of little significance to interpretation
simply to note that the images in these cases are perfectly
conventional ones,[40] or that we can find labels for them
in the rhetorical manuals. What makes them effective
as poetry is that they serve to give a set of qualitative
suggestions to the narrative, and those suggestions are
what make it possible for the poem, in other superimposed areas of suggestion, to evolve a theme out of the
events of narrative. It requires no knowledge of rhetor-

---

40. Although it might be held that they are able to function as they
do *because* they have conventional associations.

ical theory to observe this; the effects are both obvious to the sensitive reader and describable, *as effects,* in many different sets of terms, some more and some less adequate. But if we are interested in the particular instrumentality by which a given work of art achieves a construction capable of producing such effects, then we are bound to consider the particulars of technique. And it is the particulars of technique which are time-bound.[41]

At the level of the simple narrative, the figurative decoration elaborates a conventionally established story in order to establish in it a particular combination of qualities. It is not of primary importance whether we find few or many figures; the question of "rhetorical influence"—of whether Chaucer's poetry is put together in the same manner as that ideal poetry which the rhetoricians were attempting to describe—must be answered by determining whether the figures we do find operate as the rhetorical theorists believed the ornaments of style could and should operate.

41. Henry W. Sams, in "The Dual Time-Scheme in Chaucer's *Troilus,*" *MLN, 56* (1941), 94–100, anticipated my description of the effects of these devices, without being concerned with the nature or derivation of the devices. The special virtue of his discussion is that it indicates the extent to which such elaborative figuration helps to direct the horizontal movement of the narrative as well as to connect it vertically with thematic development: "There are in the poem two concentric and contradictory time schemes; one of them is based upon the formal dating of the books, the other upon a proportionately spaced series of seasonal images" (p. 94). "This divergence of seasons, ever narrowing, is maintained into the second book, undisturbed by the conventional dating on 'Mayes day the thryd.' The background is constantly that of flowers, meads, and the season of love, but the climate of the story is not so. Gradually the imagery of the story converges toward that of the setting; the limit can only be, of course, at the climax of the plot" (p. 97). Then, after quoting the passage from Book IV cited above, Sams concludes: "Thus the imaginary time scheme is reinforced at the very point where the formal time scheme collapses; and a hiatus of three years does not disturb the unity of the plan" (p. 99).

Neither the doctrine of *descriptio* of persons, nor that of levels of character corresponding to levels of style is very directly helpful in tracing out the details of Chaucer's management of style to give evaluative coloration to his characters, although together they do provide some general insight into the habit of representative and typical characterization. At the point in the action where Criseyde is in process of changing lovers, Chaucer pauses long enough to give us conventional textbook descriptions of Diomede, Criseyde, and Troilus, but this is about as much evidence as the poem gives of the use of that kind of *descriptio* in characterization. These are gallery portraits, much abbreviated, of the sort which might justify the older estimate of the nature of rhetorical influence upon Chaucer, if they were all we had to go on. But I think one of the most interesting stylistic developments in *Troilus and Criseyde* is a kind of extension and clear realization of the vague practical implications in the loose theory of adjusting levels of style to kinds of characters. In this case, of course, there is no real question of distinction in the social hierarchy; rather, it is in the aspect of love shown in the character. I refer to the consistent use of the more complicated elaborative figures in the elaboration of the character of Troilus, both in his speeches and in what we are told about him, and to the domination in the presentation of Pandarus of *sententia,* a figure of a much plainer order and one which is often not a trope at all.[42]

42. Since I first made these observations and worked out the supporting evidence in my doctoral dissertation some years ago, Meech (Ch. 3) and Muscatine (Ch. 5), presumably working quite independently of each other and certainly of me, have arrived at and published nearly identical conclusions. I welcome the corroboration, and thus only summarize the matter here, although I offer a somewhat different analysis of the style of characterizing Criseyde; it is not, however, in essential disagreement with theirs.

The first speech we hear directly from Troilus, the first
canticus Troili, is a long *apostrophe,* opening with:

> "If no love is, O God, what fele I so?
> And if love is, what thing and which is he?
> If love be good, from whennes cometh my woo?
> If it be wikke, a wonder thynketh me,
> When every torment and adversite
> That cometh of hym, may to me savory thinke,
> For ay thurst I, the more that ich it drynke."
>
> (I. 400–06)

Not only is it *apostrophe,* but the opening lines are elaborated by two figures of words: the *repetitio* of "if"
clauses, and *contentio,* the balancing of these clauses
against each other in paired oppositions. The stanza concludes with two lines of conventional metaphor *(translatio).* This is the language Troilus speaks throughout
the poem. The language the narrator uses about him
regularly lacks the *translatio* and *contentio* which help
to figure forth Troilus's idealism and his inner struggle
with it. It tends instead to a slightly elevated dignity
(when it is not ironic), achieved through the more superficial patterning of the schemes: *repetitio, determinatio,*
etc., or an occasional brief and mild *exclamatio.*

> But Troilus lay tho no lenger down,
> But up anon upon his stede bay,
> And in the feld he pleyde the leoun;
> Wo was that Grek that with hym mette a-day!
> And in the town his manere tho forth ay
> Soo goodly was, and gat hym so in grace,
> That ecch hym loved that loked on his face.
>
> (I. 1072–78)

Pandarus, in his speech promising assistance to Troilus
(I. 624–44), manages to pack ten *sententiae* into twenty-

one lines. This concentration of sententiousness is of
course an exaggeration for comic effect, but in all other
respects, including the pedantic banter, this is the characteristic tone of Pandarus.

Criseyde is handled in a still different and more complex manner. Her speech, when she is in the presence of
other characters, is consistently unelaborated dialogue,
straightforward and wonderfully natural. In the passages
where she speaks alone, the quality is not the same; in
structure (and sometimes in idea) these speeches tend to
parallel similar ones by Troilus, but with much less
elaborate figuration than his. Her debate with herself,
after she has learned of Troilus's love, takes her through
the same dialectical gymnastics as we have observed in
the first *canticus Troili,* but the figurative elaboration
does not appear until the narrative is resumed immediately following.

> "What shal I doon? To what fyn lyve I thus?
> Shal I nat love, in cas if that me leste?
> What, par dieux! I am naught religious.
> And though that I myn herte sette at reste
> Upon this knyght, that is the worthieste,
> And kepe alwey myn honour and my name,
> By alle right, it may do me no shame."

> But right as when the sonne shyneth brighte
> In March, that chaungeth ofte tyme his face,
> And that a cloude is put with wynd to flighte,
> Which oversprat the sonne as for a space,
> A cloudy thought gan thorugh hire soule pace,
> That overspradde hire brighte thoughtes alle,
> So that for feere almost she gan to falle.   (II. 757–70)

The emotional repercussions which are realized in the
imagery of Troilus's speeches are in the case of Criseyde

externalized and picked up in the evocative *comparatio*
of the following narrative. This, too, is a repeated pattern. Even the decision and its impact upon her (which,
again, occur together in the feudal metaphor of the last
stanza of Troilus's *canticus*) are split apart and externalized. Antigone's song replaces the direct choice made by
Troilus, and the beautiful metaphor of the narrative
following catches the concomitant emotions:

> A nyghtyngale, upon a cedir grene,
> Under the chambre wal ther as she ley,
> Ful loude song ayein the moone shene,
> Peraunter, in his briddes wise, a lay
> Of love, that made hire herte fressh and gay.
> That herkned she so longe in good entente,
> Til at the laste the dede slep hire hente.
>
> And as she slep, anonright tho hire mette
> How that an egle, fethered whit as bon,
> Under hire brest his longe clawes sette,
> And out hire herte he rente, and that anon,
> And dide his herte into hire brest to gon,
> Of which she nought agroos, ne nothyng smerte;
> And forth he fleigh, with herte left for herte.
>
> (II. 918–31)

The pattern of development is repeated in the later betrayal. Criseyde's last speech to Diomede in the decisive
interview ends thus:

> "I say nat therfore that I wol yow love,
> N'y say nat nay; but in conclusioun,
> I mene wel, by God that sit above!"
> And therwithal she caste hire eyen down,
> And gan to sike, and seyde, "O Troie town,
> Yet bidde I God, in quiete and in reste
> I may yow sen, or do myn herte breste." (v. 1002–08)

And after Diomede has left, the emotional possibilities, not figuratively elaborated in Criseyde's as yet unexpressed decision, are picked up in the oblique but nonetheless insistent suggestions of the astronomical metaphor, so that the love star's following the sunset before pale moonrise in effect expresses Criseyde's decision before she has consciously made it.

> The brighte Venus folwede and ay taughte
> The wey ther brode Phebus down alighte;
> And Cynthea hire char-hors overraughte
> To whirle out of the Leoun, if she myghte;
> And Signifer his candels sheweth brighte,
> Whan that Criseyde unto hire bedde wente
> Inwith hire fadres faire brighte tente,   (v. 1016–22)

It is perhaps another aspect of the same thing that of the inset lyrics which concentrate the emotional significance of the love story, Criseyde speaks only one.

Insofar as the states of feeling which are the center of focus in the poem are developed within the characters themselves, it is in Troilus, and not in Criseyde, that we observe that development. With Criseyde, we are always moved outside her at critical moments. Troilus, through the figurative elaboration of his speeches, as well as through the lyric inserts, remains the spokesman for the deepest personal experience of courtly love. I do not believe that Criseyde is a more complex character, or a less typical one than Troilus. Her typical aspects, as far as the courtly ideal is concerned, are less emphasized in the presentation, because it is in Troilus that such typical aspects are being fully developed, and Criseyde has her own kind of representativeness to serve.[43]

It is in the lyric interruptions of the action that the

43. Cf. Muscatine, pp. 153–65.

heaviest concentrations of figurative elaboration by difficult ornament—meaningful image—are to be found,
and regarding the function of these lyrics in the whole
structure, I am most interested in the ways in which the
terms of their images serve to define a particular aspect
of the experience of courtly love. The constant suggestion
of these images is double: of conscious subjection of the
individual will to love, and of an order of natural harmony larger and more remote than individual will or
human love. In the eight of these lyrics which are assigned to Troilus, the figure *contentio* repeatedly dominates to align the two sets of suggestions (as they had been
so differently aligned for similar effect in the earlier
poems) in nearly paralyzing ironies.[44] Troilus, after two
stanzas of stormy metaphor in the first *canticus,* cuts
through the knot of contradictions implied in his own
imagery with an act of will which defends itself not with
logic but with the rhetoric of Christian dedication and
the feudal contract.

> And to the God of Love thus seyde he
> With pitous vois, "O lord, now youres is
> My spirit, which that oughte youres be.
> Yow thanke I, lord, that han me brought to this.
> But wheither goddesse or womman, iwis,
> She be, I not, which that ye do me serve;
> But as hire man I wol ay lyve and sterve.
>
> "Ye stonden in hir eighen myghtily,
> As in a place unto youre vertu digne;
> Wherfore, lord, if my service or I
> May liken yow, so beth to me benigne;
> For myn estat roial I here resigne

44. Similarly, Troilus's inability to act in the narrative is another
projection of the dilemma of ideals which dualism imposes upon mankind.

> Into hire hond, and with ful humble chere
> Bicome hir man, as to my lady dere." (I. 421–34)

The second *canticus* is a reprise of the imagery in the first, but this time (whether Troilus knows it or not, the issue is decided) not arranged in a *contentio*.

> "O sterre, of which I lost have al the light,
> With herte soor wel oughte I to biwaille,
> That evere derk in torment, nyght by nyght,
> Toward my deth with wynd in steere I saille;
> For which the tenthe nyght, if that I faille
> The gydyng of thi bemes bright an houre,
> My ship and me Caribdis wol devoure." (v. 638–44)

Antigone's song (II. 827–75) continues the Christian and feudal metaphor. The natural imagery of Troilus's open-ing *contentio* in the first *canticus* has here receded into the *descriptio* which introduces the song, but the paradox of human love as free bondage, as both willed and neces-sitated, is beginning to move into focus in Antigone's formulations of the metaphors.

> "O Love, to whom I have and shal
> Ben humble subgit, trewe in myn entente,
> As I best kan, to yow, lord, yeve ich al,
> For everemo, myn hertes lust to rente." (II. 827–30)

> "And whoso seith that for to love is vice,
> Or thraldom, though he feele in it destresse,
> He outher is envyous, or right nyce,
> Or is unmyghty, for his shrewednesse,
> To loven . . ." (II. 855–59)

Troilus's predestination soliloquy in Book IV addresses itself directly and openly to this question, dissolving the *contentio* into an expanded dialectic which is almost bare of tropes (save for the long *comparatio*, lines 1023–36),

although it is highly schematized. And as the first *canticus*
had evaded the oppositions by an act of will, this soliloquy evades them by an exaggerated declaration of necessity.

> "For som men seyn, if God seth al biforn,
> Ne God may nat deceyved ben, parde,
> Than moot it fallen, theigh men hadde it sworn,
> That purveiance hath seyn before to be.
> Wherfore I sey, that from eterne if he
> Hath wist byforn oure thought ek as oure dede,
> We han no fre chois, as thise clerkes rede."
>
> (IV. 974–80)

As we move toward the center of the poem, the imagery
in the lyrics tends to combine into very complex formulations the microcosmic and macrocosmic associations,
the sexual and the Boethian implications of the natural
images, and the willed thraldom paradox of the courtly
feudal metaphor. Troilus's hymn to Love, the central
lyric in the group, offers the most complete and fully
developed example, with the greatest concentration of
tropes and schemes anywhere in the poem:

> "Love, that of erthe and se hath governaunce,
> Love, that his hestes hath in hevenes hye,
> Love, that with an holsom alliaunce
> Halt peples joyned, as hym lest hem gye,
> Love, that knetteth lawe of compaignie,
> And couples doth in vertu for to dwelle,
> Bynd this acord, that I have told and telle.
>
> "That that the world with feith, which that is stable,
> Diverseth so his stowndes concordynge,
> That elementz that ben so discordable
> Holden a bond perpetuely durynge,
> That Phebus mote his rosy day forth brynge,

And that the mone hath lordshipe over the nyghtes,—
Al this doth Love, ay heried be his myghtes!"

(III. 1744–57)

"So wolde God, that auctour is of kynde,
That with his bond Love of his vertu liste
To cerclen hertes alle, and faste bynde,
That from his bond no wight the wey out wiste;
And hertes colde, hem wolde I that he twiste
To make hem love, and that hem liste ay rewe
On hertes sore, and kepe hem that ben trewe!"

(III. 1765–71)

The figures as well as the concept come from Boethius, and I cannot avoid the conclusion that the substitution is significant.[45] However much a Neoplatonist one holds Troilus to be,[46] the Boethian harmonic scale of creation still demands the perception that the love between man and woman is *not* the principle that controls the universe, nor is mankind constrained to the former as to the latter. But the parallelism imposed upon the imagery by the schematization of this lyric eliminates hierarchical distinction while attempting to retain the order and power:

"That that the se, that gredy is to flowen,
Constreyneth to a certeyn ende so

45. In this, as in my general understanding of this lyric and its pivotal position in the poem, I am essentially in agreement with D. W. Robertson, Jr., "Chaucerian Tragedy," *ELH, 19* (1952); see esp. p. 24: ". . . the religious imagery of Book III is used to show the corruption of Troilus' higher reason, as he substitutes the 'grace' of Criseyde for providence." That is too harsh and one-sided a statement—there are counter-values in the imagery—but it indicates what standard of moral measurement is accumulating as Chaucer's elaborations accrue

46. Cf. E. E. Slaughter, "Love and Grace in Chaucer's *Troilus,*" *Essays in Honor of Walter Clyde Curry* (Nashville, 1954). This study does not contradict Robertson's (see n. 45, above) but is a useful and necessary complement to it.

> His flodes that so fiersly they ne growen
> To drenchen erthe and al for evere mo;
> And if that Love aught lete his bridel go,
> Al that now loveth asondre sholde lepe,
> And lost were al that Love halt now to-hepe."
>
>   (III. 1758–64)

Of course Troilus has no conscious recourse to the
gamut of categorical alternatives made possible to the
readers of the poem by the intervention, between them
and the old books, of historical Christianity. Neither has
any other character in the poem except the narrator. One
of the most damaging reflexes of an insistently dramatic
reading of the poem is that one drifts almost impercep-
tibly into the position of demanding that the total moral
potential within which the poem occurs be available
within the perception of each character whose development brings him under the judgments implied in the
realization of the moral potential. If Troilus can speak
in Boethian metaphors, then he can surely perceive his
overcommitment to the love of Criseyde, even though
he should scarcely be required to respond to Robertson's
catechism on higher reason, grace, and providence. Still,
it seems to me that both Robertson and most of his an-
tagonists have erred in trying to locate the commanding
moral perspective in *Troilus and Criseyde* within one
of its characters, usually in Troilus or (less often) in the
narrator. My argument so far is meant to contribute to
the demonstration that, being a great poem, *Troilus and
Criseyde* defines a complex and humane morality by the
alignment of a variety of agencies and parts. Consequently, because characterization is also only one of the parts,
it should not disturb us very much that Troilus helps to
define, by living under its evaluations, a morality he
could not logically have anticipated. And I think that the

ambiguity which Donaldson has noted in the narrator's attitudes[47] functions partly to assist the reader's awareness of the variety and ironic divergence of the separate, limited, individual agencies such as his own poetic style, or the "characters" of the literary and traditional personages his poem depicts. When the narrator can manage to maintain the detached objectivity of his pose as historian, seeing the characters of the poem typically *sub specie aeternitatis,* his aphoristic judgments parallel those being accumulated in the whole evaluative apparatus of the poem. But when he succumbs, so to speak, to the effectiveness of his own style and sees them momentarily living and complete within their inevitable (and therefore unconscious) historical and human limits, the current of his own sympathies immediately begins to flow counter to the main moral drift of the poem. I think one thing we must see in the style of such a passage as the one just quoted from Book III is that Troilus speaks a language not so much required by the state of his own motives and awareness as by the momentary tactical situation in the poem's whole moral strategy. What is required here—and it is a nearly impossibly difficult requirement—is that while maintaining a decorum sufficient to protect the integrity of his own "trouthe in love," Troilus must speak a language which figures forth the principle of measurement by which integrity and truth and love are ultimately to be defined. At the same time we share with the narrator the paradoxical knowledge that Troilus cannot possibly be expected to understand all of what his speech is designed to make clear to us: the ordered hierarchy of love in the universe which both we and Troilus inhabit, whatever may be the gap in time and the accumulation of accidents of circumstance separating us from him.

47. See above, p. 175 and n. 10.

That we are not dealing in Troilus's hymn to Love
with a Dantean progression from human to divine love[48]
is proven by the quality of the imagery in the lyrics following the lovers' separation—after the lesser Love has
let his bridle go and the microcosm of Troilus has leapt
asunder.

> "O sterre, of which I lost have al the light,
> With herte soor wel oughte I to biwaille,
> That evere derk in torment, nyght by nyght,
> Toward my deth with wynd in steere I saille;
> For which the tenthe nyght, if that I faille
> The gydyng of thi bemes bright an houre,
> My ship and me Caribdis wol devoure." (v. 638–44)

Finally, although stating it as a scheme makes it seem
too mechanically pat, there is nevertheless an impressive-
ly systematic balance of emotional elements worked out
in the themes and imagery of these ten lyrics. Taking the
hymn to Love as the center, and working from the two
sides of its emotional and narrative watershed, the two
cantici share the same imagery to precisely opposite effect, Antigone's song offers one focus of the problem of
freedom and bondage for which the predestination soliloquy offers another and more evasive one, and the

---

48. I have found nothing at all in the poem on which to base the
argument that Troilus "earns" his translation at the end. Granted his
integrity, his truth in love, still that is necessarily a virtue defined by
the limited historical humanity of the circumstances which gave rise
to it. As the pattern of those circumstances shifts with the turning
wheel of Fortune in Bks. IV and V, even the Truth we had so sympathetically admired comes more and more to look uncomfortably like blindness. And it seems particularly difficult to argue that Troilus could earn
a vision of the instability and mis-direction of what look to mortals like
virtues, simply by the diligent practice of what the vision shows him to
be one of the most treacherous and deceptive of them.

three *aubades* and the two complaints give us nearly a textbook example of sophistic rhetoric turned into lyric —the same theme developed to contradictory effects.

If *Troilus and Criseyde* consisted only of the elements I have discussed so far, it might be possible to read it as a kind of personal tragedy of Troilus, destroyed by the fortune to which he subjected himself in choosing to love Criseyde. It is Chaucer himself—or the voice speaking directly to us in the digressions—who prevents us from missing the pressure of implication in his amplifications, and reading it so. Chaucer, that is, with the unwitting assistance of Pandarus; for it is a large part of the function of Pandarus to point up by contrast the exaggeration of Troilus's commitment to love,[49] and to introduce through his own sententious speeches the notion of the control Fortune exercises over the material world of which human love is a part. In fact, in the triangulation of Troilus-Pandarus-Narrator around the enigmatic Criseyde and the doomed but irresistible love, we have another version, now firmly controlled by a limiting narrative, of the mutually evaluative ironic juxtapositions which provided the main lines of structural distribution in the earlier poems. The relationships between Pandarus and the Eagle of the *House of Fame,* or between the "realistic" dialogue of *Troilus and Criseyde* and that of the *Parliament of Fowls,* have been generally recognized; little or nothing has been said of the juxtaposition of ideality and practicality to demonstrate the limited reliability of either, which is a fundamental characteristic of all three poems alike.

In the first dialogue between Troilus and Pandarus, the latter explains:

49. Just as Troilus's idealism measures the shallowness and narrowness of Pandarus's commitment to practicality and platitude.

> ". . . than blamestow Fortune
> For thow art wroth; ye, now at erst I see.
> Woost thow nat wel that Fortune is comune
> To everi manere wight in some degree?
> And yet thow hast this comfort, lo, parde,
> That, as hire joies moten overgon,
> So mote hire sorwes passen everechon.
>
> "For if hire whiel stynte any thyng to torne,
> Than cessed she Fortune anon to be."   (I. 841–49)

The *sententia* involving the conventional metaphor of
the wheel of fortune is strange consolation; it promises
eventual disaster just as surely as it promises eventual
consolation. If Troilus had listened better, he would not
have needed to tax his understanding later with the problem of predestination. And the same kind of unwitting
foreshadowing is evident again at the high point in the
course of Troilus's love. Having helped him to success,
Pandarus speaks words of advice on how to maintain it:

> "For of fortunes sharpe adversitee
> The worste kynde of infortune is this,
> A man to han ben in prosperitee,
> And it remembren, whan it passed is."
>
>   (III. 1625–28)

In the last two books, the continual *sententiae* of Pandarus still serve to remind us of the relationships between
man, woman, and Fortune which the poem illustrates.
The difference now is that Pandarus blithely reverses
their significance. When he is still trying to sustain hope
in his shattered friend, he can say:

> "Thenk ek Fortune, as wel thiselven woost,
> Helpeth hardy man to his enprise,
> And weyveth wrecches for hire cowardise."
>
>   (IV. 600–02)

When, later, hope has grown very dim indeed, the same
proverb is turned to still another meaning:

> "Hastow nat lyved many a yer byforn
> Withouten hire, and ferd ful wel at ese?
> Artow for hire and for noon other born?
> Hath Kynde the wrought al only hire to plese?
> Lat be, and thynk right thus in thi disese:
> That, in the dees right as ther fallen chaunces,
> Right so in love ther come and gon plesaunces."
>
> (IV. 1093–99)

The Pandaric proverbs are as "slyding of corage" as ever
Criseyde was.

But Pandarus is not the spokesman for Chaucer in the
poem. He is quite unaware himself of the genuine moral
significance his proverbs carry in the situations in which
he utters them. In that sense, Lewis is right when he
says that Pandarus's "sentence and doctryne" are only
half humorous.[50] I should add, however, that they do not
have serious significance just because of their proverbial
content. As with so many other elements in the poem,
their conventional nature causes them to function in a
structure designed to activate that nature poetically.
Moreover, there is still the narrator, speaking in the first
person, often picking up the suggestions in Pandarus's
proverbs, and making explicit or implicit commentary
in a realm of values of which no character in the poem
is aware, but which is constantly implicit in the figuration of the inset lyrics.

When the narrator's personal commentary is operating
most effectively, it usually manages to pick up a tone of
voice—some implicit quality in the narrative—and realize it openly in the comment. A subtly neat example

50. See above, n. 4.

comes just after Antigone's song in Book II, as Chaucer notes the effect of the song upon Criseyde. The smile lurking in the four-line summary of Criseyde's state of mind becomes an open joke in the following two lines, even though the immediate subject has changed. Two stanzas further on, in line 917, the smiling tone is recalled fleetingly in a direct address to the reader, but this time it has become almost a knowing smirk. The result is that what might have been a sentimentally romantic moment is kept from quite becoming that, though neither is it turned into a burlesque of itself.

> But every word which that she of hire herde,
> She gan to prenten in hire herte faste,
> And ay gan love hire lasse for t'agaste
> Than it dide erst, and synken in hire herte,
> That she wex somwhat able to converte.
>
> The dayes honour, and the hevenes yë,
> The nyghtes foo—al this clepe I the sonne—
> Gan westren faste, and downward for to wrye,
> As he that hadde his dayes cours yronne;
> And white thynges wexen dymme and donne
> For lak of lyght, and sterres for t'apere,
> That she and alle hire folk in went yfeere.
>
> So whan it liked hire to go to reste,
> And voided weren thei that voiden oughte,
> She seyde that to slepen wel hire leste.
> Hire wommen soone til hire bed hire broughte.
> Whan al was hust, than lay she stille and thoughte
> Of al this thing; the manere and the wise
> Reherce it nedeth nought, for ye ben wise.
>
> (II. 899–917)

The same sort of effect, with deeper implications, is produced by the many interruptions which, sometimes ironically, sometimes directly, sometimes humorously, call our attention to the control Fortune exercises over the careers of those who devote themselves to the love of this world. An example, in the form of *apostrophe,* which combines the ironic, the humorous, and the serious qualities, occurs in Book III just before the sudden rain prevents Criseyde from leaving Pandarus's dinner party. The *apostrophe* is humorous in its exaggeration (and we remember also that Pandarus had waited until a very cloudy evening before inviting Criseyde); it is at the same time ironic and serious, for the lovers are about to consummate a relationship which places them wholly at the disposition of Fortune,[51] and neither understands this. Chaucer comments:

> But O Fortune, executrice of wyrdes,
> O influences of thise hevenes hye!
> Soth is, that under God ye ben oure hierdes,
> Though to us bestes ben the causes wrie.
>
> (III. 617–20)

Just how "wrie" are the causes to us mortals is to become evident, first indirectly (and almost lost in the exuberance) in the hymn in which Troilus proclaims his love to be of the same order as that eternal principle which moves the sun and other stars, and later directly in his tortured tilting with divine foreknowledge.

But to return to the climactic scenes in Book III, all through them the same glancing asides keep us looking critically at Troilus and his love, rather than sharing his experience of it, constantly conscious of ourselves as judicious audience. When Troilus is brought into the room where Criseyde awaits him, Chaucer reminds us of our

51. According to the explanation of the workings of providence offered by Boethius in Bk. v of the *Consolatio,* in the passage which Chaucer extracted to make up Troilus's predestination soliloquy.

dubious situation as we peer over his shoulder into the
bedchamber:

> This Troilus, whan he hire wordes herde,
> Have ye no care, hym liste nought to slepe;
> For it thought hym no strokes of a yerde
> To heere or seen Criseyde, his lady, wepe;
>
> (III. 1065–68)

And a little later, after Pandarus has borne the candle
to the chimney, and the lovers are abed:

> Yet lasse thyng than othes may suffise
> In many a cas; for every wyght, I gesse,
> That loveth wel, meneth but gentilesse.
>
> (III. 1146–48)

> He seyde hire, whan she was at swich a feste,
> She myght on hym han loked at the leste,—
> Noot I nought what, al deere ynough a rysshe,
> As he that nedes most a cause fisshe.   (III. 1159–62)

> Of hire delit, or joies oon the leeste,
> Were impossible to my wit to seye;
> But juggeth ye that han ben at the feste
> Of swich gladnesse, if that hem liste pleye!
> I kan namore . . .   (III. 1310–14)

Along with this sort of thing there are, of course, less
humorous digressions, many of them calling our attention back to the fact that we are not watching a drama
of thwarted love, but the elaboration of an old story from
an old book.[52]

The rhetoricians spoke of two varieties of *digressio*,
the first "out of the subject," and the second to anticipate
events or ideas. The majority of the digressions cited so

---

52. See especially I. 141–47; II. 47–49; and III. 1324–27.

far are of the first sort. With the *apostrophe* opening
Book IV, the quality of the digressive commentary
changes, and throughout Books IV and V it is of the an-
ticipatory sort. In most of these cases it is serious and
clarified reassertion of the Pandaric proverbs.[53]

> But al to litel, weylaway the whyle,
> Lasteth swich joie, ythonked be Fortune,
> That semeth trewest whan she wol bygyle,
> And kan to fooles so hire song entune,
> That she hem hent and blent, traitour comune!
> And whan a wight is from hire whiel ythrowe,
> Than laugheth she, and maketh hym the mowe.
>
> From Troilus she gan hire brighte face
> Awey to writhe, and tok of hym non heede,
> But caste hym clene out of his lady grace,
> And on hire whiel she sette up Diomede;   (IV. 1–11)

Later, when Cassandra has penetrated the portent of
Troilus's ominous dream, we are again reminded, this
time in one of the more ubiquitous of medieval exegeti-
cal metaphors:

> Fortune, which that permutacioun
> Of thynges hath, as it is hire comitted
> Thorugh purveyaunce and disposicioun
> Of heighe Jove, as regnes shal be flitted
> Fro folk in folk, or when they shal be smytted,
> Gan pulle awey the fetheres brighte of Troie
> Fro day to day, til they ben bare of joie. (V. 1541–47)

---

53. The *apostrophe* opening Bk. I anticipates in this way and in these
terms the course of the poem. After that we do not hear that tone of
voice again until the opening of Bk. IV. In that *apostrophe,* as elsewhere
in the authorial interjections, the statement is elaborated by additional
figurative devices, notably *allegoria* and *translatio.*

This greater figurative elaboration is characteristic of the much more markedly apostrophaic digressions of Books IV and V, as the commentary grows more serious.

The last of these digressions preceding the moral apparatus at the very end of the poem bridges the gap (if there is one) in tone between them and it:

> Gret was the sorwe and pleynte of Troilus;
> But forth hire cours Fortune ay gan to holde.
> Criseyde loveth the sone of Tideüs,
> And Troilus moot wepe in cares colde.
> Swich is this world, whoso it kan byholde:
> In ech estat is litel hertes reste.
> God leve us for to take it for the beste!   (v. 1744–50)

And the *apostrophe* which constitutes the "epilogue" turns the implication of the comment inserted in the action into direct moral statement outside the context of the narrative. It has its own dignity and measured cadence, achieved largely through a concentration of immediately recognizable rhetorical figure, not all of it imported along with the substance from Dante. The texture of image and verbal elaboration is of the same sort as is evident in the preparatory commentary excerpted above from the last two books.

Thus in the labor of style, Chaucer amplified the truth which gave the poem its new principle of disposition.

7. *Troilus and Criseyde*, a Critical View

Ars est celare artem may have been a truism for Horace or Pope, but for others, like Yeats, Spenser, or Chaucer, it is only one possible point of view, and a point of view which may as easily lead to unreal oversimplifications of art and experience as to grace or efficiency in inter-relating them. In the long and distinguished tradition of poetry more or less directly about men in their relations to history and Heaven, the artist recurs with strik-ing frequency as a type of the uncertain human struggle to read out of time a significant illusion which may some-how acquaint us with the timeless. It is by no means a specifically Christian preoccupation, nor even necessarily a religious one, unless we mean by "religious" any at-tempt to create an order out of experience. It is, how-ever, a preoccupation which reflects a constant fear that epistemology may turn out to be only aesthetics, at the same time as it expresses a conviction that at least some illusions have special realities of their own, even when we know they were expressly made up for that purpose. And when all, or any significant part, of the energy of a poem is directed toward the consideration of those real illusions which we seem to need in order to keep hold of the past, or of moral reality, or whatever, we are very likely to find art so unconcealed as to demand the reader's continuous and paradoxical consciousness of it as a proc-ess symbolic of its own content.

In a way I am simply rephrasing the major problem of the early parts of Sidney's *Defense of Poesy*. Although Sidney's discussion of the maker who is also a seer, whose illusions are truer than some realities, does not lead him very far toward the definition of a poetry which would express its own defense by forcing the reader's consciousness of its processes, his sonnet sequence (like those of Spenser and Shakespeare, but more overtly) is an attempt at that kind of poetry, as its first and fifteenth sonnets make clear. And we are all accustomed to recognizing in the *Tempest,* or *Lycidas,* or the *Ode on a Grecian Urn,* or the *Four Quartets* a range of versions of this elevation of the poem's own processes into its thematic and symbolic systems. With the exception of Dante's, we have not often seen the same possibility in medieval poetry, perhaps partly because we have been a little too ready to extend Dante's apparent certainty about the triangulation of morality, art, and cognition to all medieval poets and aestheticians. But Dante's very certainty is nearer to the heresy of humanism than it is to the neo-Augustinian orthodoxy of the academic rhetoricians, and their attempt to confine poetry to the useful illusions, by obligating it to a traditional past and a transcendent hierarchy of value, is itself a kind of measure of distrust of the individual poet's certainties. In fact, it might be expected to suggest to at least some poets (if they hadn't thought of it already) the paradoxical artistic self-consciousness I have been talking about. At any rate, whatever its inception, I think the kind of demand made upon the reader's consciousness by the problematic nature of the poem's own art is a major characteristic of Chaucer's poetry. It is one of the reasons for his frequent allusions to technical poetics, and is inseparably connected with his view of art and history as formulated in his phrase "the key of remembrance." The past (and with it, most of knowledge) is lost without a creative act of will—but the will and its creation are human, and so inherently error-prone; and memory is not actually the past, but our useful illusion of it—yet who is sure that his *is* the useful illusion?

Of all of Chaucer's works, I think *Troilus and Criseyde* most demands a recognition of these things for an adequate critical view of it, because it most completely converts them into the topography of its poetry—its being as well as its meaning. True, in the *House of Fame* or the *Parliament of Fowls* or the Prologue to the *Legend of Good Women* these essential aesthetic problems are more overt *topoi,* and the paradoxes and ironies which they embrace are far more literalistically translated into the structural components as well as the surface statement. But at the same time as the failure of these poems is a measure of Chaucer's sense of the complexity and intractability of the problems, their success—their power to convince and move us still—is largely dependent on their ability to involve us sympathetically in their inability to clarify the processes of poetry enough to do much more than reflect ironically back upon themselves. Of course, to make the point I am forced to an over-limited statement. These poems do not, any more than any others, exist without subjects, and poetry is not quite the sole subject of any one of them. Hence the various ironic impasses reached (in the incomplete and complete poems alike) are impasses in the pursuit of intelligence of love, just as they are in the fabrication of the art which will activate the intelligence.

Troilus and Criseyde was Chaucer's first major departure from the experience-books-dreams structure, but traces of the earlier structural habits remain, even in it —most prominently the ancient story. The poet's personal experience has been diminished and redistributed,

to emerge as the narrator's running ironic commentary
on a story in the action of which he does not participate
(as he had in the various "dreamer" roles in the *Book of
the Duchess,* the *House of Fame,* and the *Parliament of
Fowls*). In fact, the vision, which had established the
mode of the narrator's participation in the earlier poems,
has now gone altogether. The permanent truths against
which the ironies of this poem's action work themselves
out are visible only obliquely through the structures of
character and event, and through the associations struck
off by the occasional lyric inserts. Root's interpretation
of the revision of the last three books would seem to
argue that Chaucer went back to the poem to re-emphasize its more evaluative passages. It is certainly in an attempt to get nearer the visionary world that he produced
one of the poem's most debated pieces of business, the
"translation" of Troilus to a vantage point in the eighth
sphere, after the end of the action. But in *Troilus and
Criseyde,* as the now general recognition of its "maturity"
and "control" implies, the narrator's role as developer
of our consciousness of limitation in the processes of
poetry does not produce a circular and self-defeating
irony. It is a way of validating the moral generalizations
which the poem serves by including the poet and ourselves and the poem within the humanity which they
are to measure.

Dryden long ago defended the artifices of the stage
against the rigid prescripts of neo-classical rationalism
with the profound observation that since we know all
art is illusion, no art can succeed unless we are at least
partly conscious parties to the maintenance of the illusion. Thus the best art contrives to create in its audience
a sense of participating in its illusions, without destroying the simultaneous awareness of a detachment sufficient for perception and enjoyment. So if the poet strikes

the balance exactly, he can keep our consciousness of his artifices just sufficiently focussed to prevent empathy from becoming sentimentality and usurping judgment, and at the same time hold us in the poem enough to prevent detachment's becoming moral arrogance and encouraging unjustified conclusions. Exactly so Chaucer, by keeping The Poem—its sources, history, techniques, inspiration, management, and inherent limitations— always just within our field of perception, gives us a reference point for the correlation of the various perspectives in *Troilus and Criseyde*. It is this more than anything else which so differentiates the work from psychological novel, and makes it impossible to define as drama. And the poem as a reference point becomes, for a variety of reasons, a reminder of the limitedness and partiality not of its ultimate moral principles but of any particular man's application of them. In that sense, what it establishes first of all between the poet and his audience is a very special commitment to humanity.

But the poem, that is its techniques and procedures, has some things to do in the way of controlling its materials, besides realizing the community of perception and limitation in its author, characters, and audience. One primary relevance of the study of poetics to criticism lies in the extent to which awareness of the nature of the means may condition response to the ends they serve, and in *Troilus and Criseyde* one of the important ends which must be attained through our consciousness of the artifices which accomplish it is the characterization —long centered upon for interpretative discussions of the poem. In fact, there are at least two different ways in which our knowing collusion with the poet in his artifices prepares us to recognize his characters. The first is less interesting for this discussion and has been more frequently noted by other critics; I mean simply the use of

established conventional styles in presenting characters.
We know and are expected to know what these styles
"mean" as soon as we encounter the particular uses of
them in the poem, and because we know them as techniques, we avoid the error of mistaking a classification
for an identification—of thinking we know *what* people
these are rather than what *kind* they are. That is, we
avoid the error unless we are incorrigibly naturalistic
critics. Characterization by conventional styles does, however, raise a sticky question in historical criticism and
threatens to return full appreciation of *Troilus and
Criseyde* abruptly to the limited fourteenth-century
audience from whose confining grasp modern criticism
is supposedly trying to extricate it. But to some extent
these conventions are self-defining within the poem, and
in any event we must see as we read that the machinery
of presentation of character simply does not give us the
data for a naturalistic reconstruction of "personalities."
Most importantly, the narrator himself warns us openly
that his characters speak by the book, that their first
existence (at least as far as he, the non-lover, is concerned)
was literary, that his re-creation of them is still one degree further denatured, and that a considerable part of
whatever "reality" they attain will have to be projected
onto them from the sentiments of the audience:

> But soth is, though I kan nat tellen al,
> As kan myn auctour, of his excellence,
> Yet have I seyd, and God toforn, and shal
> In every thyng, al holy his sentence;
> And if that ich, at Loves reverence,
> Have any word in eched for the beste,
> Doth therwithal right as youreselven leste.
>
> For myne wordes, heere and every part,
> I speke hem alle under correccioun

> Of yow that felyng han in loves art,
> And putte it al in youre discrecioun
> To encresse or maken dymynucioun
> Of my langage, and that I yow biseche.
>
> (III. 1324–36)

The narrator's opening dissociation of himself from love
and lovers casts a kind of general qualification over the
whole poem, and is the first of many reminders in it that
its language is to be one of literary stylization.

Still, —why? Even within the limits of their separate
conventionalities, the characters of this poem are occasionally given a deportment adequately realistic to indicate that their stylization is a result of choice rather
than incompetence and to make us wonder, as collabora-
tors in the illusion, why the author so insists on its separation from actuality. The answer, again, is that it is a way
of using what we thought to be our superiority as detached readers to maneuver us into a position to see far
more than we could be made to see if we were simply
deceived into total empathy. The fixity and stylization
of character are quite evidently artificializing qualities,
and by allowing, or forcing, the audience to share his
awareness of the fact, Chaucer commits it simultaneously
to the concession that these people—Troilus, Pandarus,
and Criseyde—are basically representative (just as by
similar means he leads us to see that they are partly
representative of *us*) and that their conventional fixity
will allow them to work out the logic of their positions
without the chance inconsistencies and non sequiturs of
actual existence. But what the audience does not realize
it is committing itself to, as it smiles with Chaucer over
the charm of this pageant of illusion in the first three
books, is that as the catastrophe closes in, the set literary
postures of these typical characters will also come to

typify the fatal individuations of human character. They
are, as the conventions had demanded, only what they
are. They have no adaptive resources or flexibility of
choice left after the decisions which set them into mo-
tion at the beginning of the fable. And it is in the nature
of those initial decisions about love that they are irrevo-
cable, granted the limits of human possibility. So the
same characters who had decorated so harmoniously and
handsomely that enchanted long spring morning in the
rose garden, without changing any at all, suddenly betray each other, fail each other and themselves. Because
they cannot change, they must allow the changing circumstances to redefine integrity as insistent blindness
(Troilus), worldly wisdom as foolishly adaptive evasion
of issues (Pandarus), and confident, eager attractiveness
as self-deceiving meretriciousness (Criseyde).

Almost to the very end, our old friend and cooperating
magician, the half-clown of a narrator-scholar-poet who
knew better all the time, is still making excuses for the
lot, particularly for Criseyde, partly on grounds that they
are literary types so we shouldn't feel too badly and partly
on grounds that, like us, they did the best they could
with what they had. But because the Chaucer who invented all three illusions—of the narrator and of the immediate audience and of the poem that lies between them
—has seen to it that his actual audience is aware of how
much of itself is in these illusions, we are able at last to
see that both sets of definitions are true, and that each by
itself is false.

We should also see, because we are kept aware of the
poem itself, that the correlation between the truth and
falsity of these impressions of the characters is a function
of their placement in an artistic structure which—as
arbitrarily as all created illusions—fixes them and then
measures them against different eventualities. We shall

not explain the ironic ambiguity of these characters by
looking for changes or developments in their natures
which their typicality and stylization will not permit, or
by hunting the single flawed faculty in each to which we
can consistently attribute his personal inconsistencies,
when the flaw in all of them turns out to be their limited
existence within literary artifices designed to generalize
aspects of human nature. Just as we share the author's
knowledge that his poem is a possibly useful illusion
which can be both true and not true without destroying
itself, so we know that while we experience Troilus and
Criseyde and Pandarus as three conventionalized modes
of poetic representivity, these (like all modes of discourse) always carry a variety of potential meanings,
realized only in differing particular applications.

Many readers worry about accounting for the "change"
in Criseyde, but are not at all troubled by the reversal
of attitude Troilus accomplishes in a couple of stanzas,
from devout scorner of lovers to fatally constant lover.
Of course the comparison is unfair. We cannot be
troubled by Troilus's character before he loved, because
despite our gleaning of a few facts about his earlier life,
he exists in the poem only in the style of the ideal lover.
The one point at which we might be disturbed by a
wavering in that style comes in his first *aubade,* and there
it is so brief and so contained in a conventional form
and situation that one cannot quite be sure. Perhaps, in
the Donne-like thrust and the faintly sardonic edge to
the imagery here, there is a suggestion that Troilus is
about to achieve a sophistication (in its old sense) which
would destroy him as an ideal courtly lover.

> "Allas! what have thise loveris the agylt,
> Dispitous day? Thyn be the peyne of helle!
> For many a lovere hastow slayn, and wilt;

> Thy pourynge in wol nowher lat hem dwelle.
> What profrestow thi light here for to selle?
> Go selle it hem that smale selys grave;
> We wol the nought, us nedeth no day have."
>
> (III. 1457–63)

Particularly the last two lines suggest a witty, satisfied, physical, sexual self-consciousness which pure courtly love lyric avoids, and which if it were developed would surely jar in Troilus's characterization more than Criseyde's turning to Diomede does in hers.

But the point is that these things are not solely, or even mainly, parts of mechanisms for defining individual psychologies. If, as in cases like these, when we say "character" we mean something like "a typical state of human feeling," then we must expect that the mechanism will work to define the state, not the person. If Criseyde is a way of saying something about the lovely vanity of human wishes, then she must be elusive or, as it could be put, treacherous. If Troilus is a way of expressing utter, ideal devotion to woman, then he cannot be allowed any real recognition of what the *aubade* seems to suggest, although the suggestion may serve the reader as an announcement that he has encountered one of the limits of this "character"—this way of feeling. It may also be one of the ways (others are more certain) of suggesting that his integrity is a kind of blindness, or at least a sharply limited range of vision, as the Boethian imagery of several of his set speeches suggests a limit at the other end of the range. If Pandarus is a way of talking about the directionlessness of pure practicality, then he should speak no language but proverbs—the formulae of a wisdom they do not contain. For proverbs achieve currency by generalizing insight to a degree dangerously near to indiscriminate applicability, and the truth of their utterance depends after all on what is understood by the user. That is the essential difference between the sententiousness of the author and the sententiousness of Pandarus. Chaucer's understanding, again like that of his audience, is ultimately from outside the poem, and based on his consciousness of it and of the uses of its deceptions.

Troilus and Criseyde, after all the close and natural similarities to the other pre-Canterbury poems are taken into account, is still a poem quite apart from them. Its return to a very conservative mode of narrative is its most obvious distinction, of course, but I think the difference which goes farthest toward accounting for its unique achievement is Chaucer's different exploitation of his (and our) awareness of limitation and uncertainty in a poetic which he still could not reject. In all the others except the *Book of the Duchess* (which seems a little flat without it), the uncertainty produced at best beautifully ironic definitions of itself, at worst the reduplicating tedium of Book III of the *House of Fame.* In *Troilus and Criseyde,* although allowed to define themselves with a similar irony, the ambiguities of poetics become controlled and useful elements in the poem. What in the other poems makes the perception of truth through art seem all but impossible, becomes in this poem a means of defining the *ways* in which we perceive through art, and of involving us along with the author in the perception.

The strategy by which we are lured into that involvement is beautifully subtle and fascinating to watch even as one is being taken in by it. It is made workable by the seeming openness with which the author shares his poem with us—keeps its making and working present as an agreed upon common concern among us. There has been much discussion of the role of the narrator in Chaucer's poetry, but very little of the role of the audience in it, and I think a close examination will reveal that the kinds of roles Chaucer creates for his narrators almost necessarily imply complementary roles for an audience which is nearly as much a created fiction within or around the poem as the narrator is. We have sometimes been too easily trapped by the ease and specificity with which Chaucer's poetry suggests an interested, aware, and sensitive group of immediate respondents, and have concluded that Chaucer must have read it aloud before a select court circle, and dropped the matter at that. Yet *Troilus and Criseyde* not only expresses certain concerns about its own preservation and the durability of language in general, extending at least its ambitions for an audience far beyond any fourteenth-century court circle, but the manner of the narrator's self-deprecatory ironies is such that any reader is made to feel specifically included in the audience, without exactly realizing that the feeling of inclusion is also an admission of qualities in himself which place him within the range of the poem's judgments. All the members of the audience specified by the poem possess the same few characteristics, but these characteristics seem somehow to fit us all.

The process begins at the very opening of the poem, as Chaucer declares himself no lover, but a servant of the servants of the God of Love, and possessed of only a second-hand knowledge of love's intricacies. It is nearly impossible not to feel included in his address to

> ye loveres, that bathen in gladnesse,
> If any drope of pyte in yow be,
> Remembreth yow on passed hevynesse
> That ye han felt, and on the adversite
> Of othere folk, and thynketh how that ye

Han felt that Love dorste yow displese,
Or ye han wonne hym with to gret an ese.

(I. 22–28)

The graceful comedy depends, as so often in Chaucer, on
a number of things, all of which are going to be very
important elements in his poem. First, our amusement
with this not quite clownish narrator is an amusement
of superiority, and since the obvious measure of superiority here is experience of love, we are drawn into an
illusion (for many of us a reality) of belonging to the
poem's select audience of lovers. But at the same time,
another set of our critical faculties is being amused at
watching the device work: the narrator analyzing in
neatly compact detail the feelings which he says he has
never had and doesn't know, but which we alone (his
select audience) are supposed to provide. So we are drawn
into a conspiracy with the author behind the narrator
to maintain his illusion and help make his poem work.
However, while we are permitted (or assigned) a superiority to him in feeling and a partnership in illusion, we
are kept firmly in our place with regard to history or
fact. We—that is, the audience the poem defines and
draws each individual reader into—do not know the
"olde storye." It is the poet who has knowledge (sometimes even a fussy and pedantic knowledge) of its details,
its sources, its various treatments by other poets. As we
become more and more aware of that knowledge, we
become more and more aware of the extension of experience and understanding; that is, that the meaning of this
emotional experience is not defined by the ability of us
old, experienced lovers to recognize it, or of us sensitive
and sophisticated readers to connive at the artifice of its
re-enactment. This poet-narrator, by his carefully differentiated relationship to the content of his poem, has

a kind of sense of its meaning which we do not have, and
if that is so the experience the poem records must have
a significance beyond its own emotional existence. Unless, of course, as the poet-narrator seems to suggest at
one point, the "fact" of history is itself deceptive, the
"olde bokes" delusions or lies, and his own remaking
of them the blind retouching of an imaginary portrait.

> For how Criseyde Troilus forsook,
> Or at the leeste, how that she was unkynde,
> Moot hennesforth ben matere of my book,
> As writen folk thorugh which it is in mynde.
> Allas! that they sholde evere cause fynde
> To speke hire harm, and if they on hire lye,
> Iwis, hemself sholde han the vilanye.   (IV. 15–21)

But in that case, what about the assertion, with which
we have already agreed, of the essential emotional truth
of this ancient fable?

We are not allowed to forget our initial assent, either,
and the constant agency of reminder is the authorial in-
terjection which asks us to help out the techniques of
illusion by drawing on our superior "sentement." The
further we develop our sophisticated awareness of being
above and outside the poem, the more we identify ourselves with the lovers it shows us. Since it is not exactly
possible to document the statement, one must simply
assert that he inevitably feels personally addressed when
Chaucer interrupts himself to ask that something he cannot write be supplied by "ye [that] ben wise," or "ye that
han ben at the feste," or "yow that felyng han in loves
art," or "thow, redere, [who] maist thiself ful wel de-
vyne / That swich a wo my wit kan nat diffyne." And
clearly, since all these requests are for things in the feelings of Troilus or Criseyde to which the author cannot
penetrate, our knowledge of them constitutes an identity

of ourselves and them, or at least a kinship far closer than the narrator admits to. At the same time, that other side of us which the poem amuses by ironically revealing its own tricks is able to note that the narrator's sympathies *are* engaged and that, disclaimers notwithstanding, he does identify, recognize, and participate just as we do. Our concern for the poem as a process, concurrent with our surrender to its effects, has often been discussed as a function of the self-conscious narrator and thus as a way of adding depth of perspective. But in addition it is a device for creating a self-conscious audience, and thus a way of making the reader's exercise of moral judgment become self-discovery. I think this is ultimately the difference between a poem which merely has a moral, and a poem which *is* moral.

All of these things—consciousness of a situation in which speaker confronts audience, awareness of an element of pretense as necessary to communication in the situation, agreement to tolerate specified artifices to keep the pretense working, identification of similarities and differences in speaker's and audience's reactions to a subject, the search for a larger ground of agreement between them (i.e. persuasion)—all of these things constitute a large part of what we mean by the term "rhetorical," even when it is used in a limited historical sense. In all these ways, a good deal more than simply in the configurations of its style, *Troilus and Criseyde* is a highly rhetorical poem—far more so than, say, Wyatt's "They flee from me," which pleads an offense and turns at the end (with calculated abruptness) to demand our judgment, because Chaucer's poem engages us in a continuing dialectic with the narrator which defines and locates both poet and audience. That is a kind of appeal from *ethos* which Aristotle's *Rhetoric* never foresaw, and of which no other English poet has made such capital.

What makes *Troilus and Criseyde* so much more than rhetoric is the alignment of these and other characteristics in such a way as to produce those almost endlessly expanding concentric ironies which constitute Chaucer's way of reconciling human wisdom with human limitation, and make of his whole poem an image of the conditions of moral knowledge *secundum Galfridum Chaucers. Deo Gracias.*

Bibliography

WITH GRIFFITH'S *Chaucer Bibliography* and the revised edition of Robinson both still relatively recent, it seems to me superfluous to include an extensive general bibliography here. However, since we have had little specific study of Chaucer's poetic theory and techniques, it may prove useful to append a selective list of the materials which relate most directly to the subject. In making this selection—always a fairly arbitrary procedure—I have tried to include all the important works which have to do (completely or in some considerable part) with Chaucer's poetics and the immediately preceding theoretical tradition, both taken in a relatively limited technical sense. The list reflects no systematic coverage of the field after 1960, and such obvious and generally known sources as Aristotle's *Rhetoric* and *Poetics* and the Platonic dialogues concerning rhetoric and poetry are not listed. The index provides a guide to materials used in the preparation of this study which may not appear in this selected bibliography.

L'Allemand, Évrard, *Laborintus*, in Faral, ed., *Arts poétiques*, 337–77.
Allen, Robert J., "A Recurring Motif in Chaucer's 'House of Fame'," *JEGP*, 55 (1956), 393–405.
Anonymous, *Cicero ad C. Herennium, de ratione dicendi, Rhetorica ad Herennium, with an English Translation*, ed. Harry Caplan, Cambridge, Mass., 1954.

Atkins, J. W. H., *English Literary Criticism: The Medieval Phase*, Cambridge, 1943.

Augustine, Saint, *De doctrina Christiana, liber quartus; A Commentary with a Revised Text, Introduction, and Translation* by Sister Thérèse Sullivan, Catholic University of America Patristic Studies, *23*, Washington, D.C., 1930.

Baker, Donald C., "Imagery and Structure in Chaucer's *Book of the Duchess*," *Studia Neophilologica, 30* (1958), 17–26.

Baldwin, Charles S., *Ancient Rhetoric and Poetic*, New York, Macmillan, 1924.

———"Cicero on Parnassus," *PMLA, 42* (1927), 106–12.

———*Medieval Rhetoric and Poetic*, New York, Macmillan, 1928.

Baldwin, Ralph F., *The Unity of the Canterbury Tales*, Anglistica 5, Copenhagen, 1955.

Baum, Paull Franklyn, *Chaucer: A Critical Appreciation*, Durham, N.C., Duke University Press, 1958.

———"Chaucer's 'The House of Fame'," *ELH, 8* (1941), 248–56.

Bennett, Jack Arthur Walter, *The Parlement of Foules; An Interpretation*, Oxford, Oxford University Press, 1957.

Bethurum, Dorothy, "Chaucer's Point of View as Narrator in the Love Poems," *PMLA, 74* (1959), 511–20.

Bevington, David M., "The Obtuse Narrator in Chaucer's *House of Fame*," *Speculum, 36* (1961), 288–98.

Birney, Earle, "The Beginnings of Chaucer's Irony," *PMLA, 54* (1939), 637–55.

Bloomfield, Morton W., "Chaucer's Sense of History," *JEGP, 51* (1952), 301–13.

Boccaccio, Giovanni, *The Filostrato;* ed. and trans. by Nathaniel E. Griffin and A. B. Myrick, Philadelphia, University of Pennsylvania Press, 1929.

Boughner, Daniel C., "Elements of Epic Grandeur in the *Troilus*," *ELH, 6* (1939), 200–10.

Bronson, Bertrand H., "Chaucer's Art in Relation to his Audience," in *Five Studies in Literature*, Berkeley, Calif., 1940.

———*In Appreciation of Chaucer's "Parlement of Foules,"* University of California Publications in English, *3*, no. 5, Berkeley, Calif., 1935.

———"The Book of the Duchess Reopened," *PMLA, 67* (1952), 863–81.

———"The Parlement of Foules Revisited," *ELH, 15* (1948), 247–60.

Caplan, Harry, "Classical Rhetoric and the Medieval Theory of Preaching," *Classical Philology, 28* (1933), 73–96.

Cicero, Marcus Tullius, *De inventione, De optimo genere, Oratorum, and Topica,* ed. and trans. by H. M. Hubbell, Cambridge, Mass., Loeb Classical Library, 1949.

Clemen, Wolfgang, *Der junge Chaucer,* Bochum-Langendreer, 1938.

Clerval, Abbé, *Les Écoles de Chartres,* Chartres, A. Picard, 1895.

Cummings, Hubertis M., *The Indebtedness of Chaucer's Works to the Italian Works of Boccaccio,* Cincinnati, 1916.

Curry, Walter Clyde, *Chaucer and the Medieval Sciences,* revised and enlarged edn., New York, 1960.

Curtius, Ernst Robert, *Europäische Literatur und lateinisches Mittelalter,* Bern, A. Francke, 1948; translation: Willard R. Trask, *European Literature and the Latin Middle Ages,* New York, Bollingen, 1953.

Dante, *De vulgari eloquentia,* in *Tutte le opere di Dante Alighieri,* ed. Edward Moore, Oxford, Oxford University Press, 1894.

David, Alfred, "Literary Satire in the *House of Fame,*" *PMLA, 75* (1960), 333–39.

Dempster, Germaine, *Dramatic Irony in Chaucer,* Palo Alto, Stanford University Publications in Language and Literature, *4*, 1932.

Deschamps, Eustache, *L'Art de dictier et de fere chancons,* in *Oeuvres complètes de Eustache Deschamps,* ed. Gaston Raynaud, Société des anciens textes français, *7*, Paris, 1891, 266–92.

Donaldson, E. Talbot, ed., *Chaucer's Poetry; An Anthology for the Modern Reader,* New York, Ronald Press, 1958.

———"Chaucer the Pilgrim," *PMLA, 69* (1954), 928–36.

Duffey, Bernard I., "Intention and Art in the Man of Law's Tale," *ELH, 14* (1947), 181–93.

Everett, Dorothy, "Some Reflections on Chaucer's 'Art Poetical'," *Proceedings of the British Academy, 36,* Oxford, 1950.

Faral, Edmond, *Les Arts poétiques du XIIe et du XIIIe siècle,* Paris, Champion, 1924.

Francis, W. Nelson, "Chaucer Shortens a Tale," *PMLA, 68* (1953), 1126–41.

Frank, Robert W., Jr., "Structure and Meaning in the 'Parlement of Foules'," *PMLA, 71* (1956), 530–39.

Garlande, Jean de, *Poetria,* ed. G. Mari, *Romanische Forschungen, 13* (1902), 883 ff.

Getty, Agnes K., "The Medieval-Modern Conflict in Chaucer's Poetry," *PMLA, 47* (1932), 385–402.

Gilson, Étienne, *L'Ésprit de la philosophie médiévale,* Paris, J. Vrin, 1932.

Glunz, H. H., *Die Literarästhetik des europäischen Mittelalters: Wolfram, Rosenroman, Chaucer, Dante,* Poppinghaus, 1937.

Goffin, R. C., "Chaucer and Elocution," *Medium Aevum, 4* (1935), 127–42.

Haarhoff, Theodore Johannes, *Schools of Gaul; A Study of Pagan and Christian Education in the Last Century of the Western Empire,* London, 1920.

Halm, Carl Felix, *Rhetores latini minores,* Leipzig, Teubner, 1863.

Hamilton, Marie P., "Notes on Chaucer and the Rhetoricians," *PMLA, 47* (1932), 403–09.

Harrison, Benjamin S., "Medieval Rhetoric in the Book of the Duchess," *PMLA, 49* (1934), 428–42.

———"The Rhetorical Inconsistency of Chaucer's Franklin," *SP, 32* (1935), 55–61.

Haskins, Charles H., *The Renaissance of the Twelfth Century,* Cambridge, Mass., 1927.

Hill, Mary A., "Rhetorical Balance in Chaucer's Poetry," *PMLA, 42* (1927), 845–61.

Hoffman, Arthur W., "Chaucer's Prologue to Pilgrimage: The Two Voices," *ELH, 21* (1954), 1–16.

Horatius Flaccus, Quintus, *Satires, Epistles, and Ars Poetica,* ed. and trans. H. Rushton Fairclough, New York, 1926.

Huppé, Bernard F., *Doctrine and Poetry,* New York, 1959.

Jordan, Robert M., "The Narrator in Chaucer's *Troilus,*" *ELH, 25* (1958), 237–57.

Kittredge, George Lyman, *Chaucer and his Poetry,* Cambridge, Mass., 1915.

Klaeber, Friederich, *Das Bild bei Chaucer,* Berlin, 1893.

Koch, John, "Chaucers Belesenheit in den römischen Klassikern," *Englische Studien, 57* (1923), 8–84.

Kökeritz, Helge, "Rhetorical Word-Play in Chaucer," *PMLA, 69* (1954), 937–52.

Kreuzer, James R., "The Dreamer in the Book of the Duchess," *PMLA, 66* (1951), 543–47.

Lawrence, William Witherle, *Chaucer and the Canterbury Tales,* New York, 1950.

Legouis, Émile, *Geoffrey Chaucer,* in *Les Grands écrivains étrangers,* Paris, 1910.

Lewis, C. S., "What Did Chaucer Really Do to *Il Filostrato?*" *Essays and Studies, 17* (1932), 56–75.

Lowes, John Livingston, *Geoffrey Chaucer and the Development of his Genius,* Cambridge, Mass., 1934.

Lüdeke, Henry, *Die Funktionen des Erzählers in Chaucers epischer Dichtung, Studies in English Philology, 72,* Halle, 1928.

Lumiansky, Robert M., "Chaucer's *Parlement of Foules:* A Philosophical Interpretation," *RES, 24* (1948), 81–89.

———*Of Sondry Folk: The Dramatic Principle in the Canterbury Tales,* Austin, University of Texas Press, 1955.

McKeon, Richard, "Rhetoric in the Middle Ages," *Speculum, 17* (1942), 1–32.

Malone, Kemp, "A Poet at Work: Chaucer Revising his Verses," *Proceedings of the American Philosophical Society, 94* (1950), 317–21.

———*Chapters on Chaucer,* Baltimore, Johns Hopkins University Press, 1951.

Manly, John Matthews, "Chaucer and the Rhetoricians," *Proceedings of the British Academy, 12,* London, 1926.

———*Some New Light on Chaucer,* New York, 1926.

Martianus Capella, *De nuptiis Mercurii et Philologiae,* ed. Adolphus Dick, Leipzig, 1925.

———*Liber de arte rhetorica,* in Halm, *Rhetores latini minores,* 449–92.

Meech, Sanford B., *Design in Chaucer's Troilus,* Syracuse, Syracuse University Press, 1959.

———"Figurative Contrasts in Chaucer's *Troilus and Criseyde,*" in *English Institute Essays,* ed. Alan S. Downer, New York, 1950.

Melkley, Gervais de, *Ars versificaria,* summary in Faral, *Arts poétiques,* 328–30.

Mizener, Arthur, "Character and Action in the Case of Criseyde," *PMLA, 54* (1939), 65–79.

Mroczkowski, Przemyslaw, "Medieval Art and Aesthetics in the *Canterbury Tales,*" *Speculum, 33* (1958), 204–21.

Murphy, James J., "The Arts of Discourse, 1050–1400," *Medieval Studies, 23* (1961), 194–205.

———"The Earliest Teaching of Rhetoric at Oxford," *Speech Monographs, 27* (1960), 354–57.

———"John Gower's *Confessio Amantis* and the First Discussion of Rhetoric in the English Language," *PQ, 41* (1962), 401–11.

Muscatine, Charles, *Chaucer and the French Tradition; A Study in Style and Meaning,* Berkeley, University of California Press, 1957.

Naunin, Traugott, *Der Einfluss der mittelalterlichen Rhetorik auf Chaucers Dichtung,* Bonn University Dissertations, *21,* 1929.

Osgood, Charles G., ed., *Boccaccio on Poetry; Being the Preface and the 14th and 15th Books of the "Genealogia deorum gentilium" in English with Introductory Essay and Commentary,* Princeton, 1931.

Owen, Charles A., Jr., "Chaucer's 'Canterbury Tales': Aesthetic Design in the Stories of the First Day," *English Studies, 35* (1954), 49–56.

———"The Crucial Passages in Five of the *Canterbury Tales*," *JEGP, 52* (1953), 294–311.

Paetow, J. L., *The Arts Course at Medieval Universities, with Especial Reference to Grammar and Rhetoric*, University of Illinois Studies, *3*, no. 7, Urbana, Illinois, 1910.

Patch, Howard R., *On Rereading Chaucer*, Cambridge, Mass., 1939.

Preston, Raymond, *Chaucer*, London, 1952.

Price, T. R., "*Troilus and Criseyde:* A Study in Chaucer's Method of Narrative Construction," *PMLA, 11* (1896), 307–22.

Quintilianus, Marcus Fabius, *The Institutio Oratoria, with an English Translation*, ed. H. E. Butler, New York, 1922.

Rashdall, Hastings, *The Universities of Europe in the Middle Ages*, new ed. in 3 vols., ed. F. M. Powicke and A. B. Emden, Oxford, 1936.

Robertson, D. W., Jr., "Chaucerian Tragedy," *ELH, 19* (1952), 1–37.

———"Historical Criticism," in *English Institute Essays*, ed. Alan S. Downer, New York, 1951.

Root, Robert K., *Chaucer's Troilus and Criseyde*, Princeton, Princeton University Press, 1926.

———*The Poetry of Chaucer*, New York, 1906.

Ruggiers, Paul G., "The Unity of Chaucer's *House of Fame*," *SP, 50* (1953), 16–29.

Sams, Henry W., "The Dual Time-Scheme in Chaucer's *Troilus*," *MLN, 56* (1941), 94–100.

Schaar, Claes, *Some Types of Narrative in Chaucer's Poetry*, Lund Studies in English, *25*, Copenhagen, 1954.

———*The Golden Mirror; Studies in Chaucer's Descriptive Technique and its Literary Background*, Lund, Gleerup, 1955.

Shain, Charles E., "Pulpit Rhetoric in Three Canterbury Tales," *MLN, 70* (1955), 235–45.

Shannon, Edgar F., *Chaucer and the Roman Poets*, Harvard Studies in Comparative Literature, *7*, Cambridge, Mass., 1929.

Shumaker, Wayne, "Alisoun in Wanderland: A Study in Chaucer's Mind and Literary Method," *ELH, 18* (1951), 77–89.

Siebert, Harriet, "Chaucer and Horace," *MLN, 31* (1916), 304–07.

Snell, Ada L., "Chaucer's Comments on his Method of Composition," *English Journal, 2* (1913), 231–34.

Spiers, John, *Chaucer the Maker,* London, 1951.

Stearns, Marshall W., "A Note on Chaucer's Use of Aristotelian Philosophy," *SP, 43* (1946), 15–21.

————"Chaucer Mentions a Book," *MLN, 57* (1942), 28–31.

Sypherd, Wilbur O., "The Completeness of Chaucer's *Hous of Fame,*" *MLN, 30* (1915), 65–68.

Tatlock, John S. P., *The Mind and Art of Chaucer,* Syracuse, 1950.

Teager, Florence E., "Chaucer's Eagle and the Rhetorical Colors," *PMLA, 47* (1932), 410–18.

Underwood, Dale, "The First of the Canterbury Tales," *ELH, 26* (1959), 455–69.

Vendome, Matthieu de, *Ars versificatoria,* in Faral, *Arts poétiques,* 109–93.

Vinsauf, Geoffroi de, *De coloribus rhetoricis,* in Faral, *Arts poétiques,* 321–27.

————*Documentum de modo et arte dictandi et versificandi,* in Faral, *Arts poétiques,* 265–320.

————*Poetria nova,* in Faral, *Arts poétiques,* 197–262.

Wells, Whitney H., "Chaucer as a Literary Critic," *MLN, 39* (1924), 255–68.

Woodbridge, Elizabeth, "Chaucer's Classicism," *JEGP, 1* (1897), 111–17.

Young, Karl, "Chaucer's *Troilus and Criseyde* as Romance," *PMLA, 53* (1938), 38–63.

Index

133, 145, 156, 159, 171–216, 217–
32; atmospheric decoration, 192–
96; human and divine love, 202–
16; lyric interpolations, 184–87,
192, 201–09; narrator as com-
mentator, 209–16, 220, 222–23;
poetics as theme-device, 217–32
passim; structure, 176–88; stylistic conventionality, 221–27; techniques of characterization, 182–
83, 197–201, 221–27
Tuve, Rosamond, 12 n.
Twelfth-century Renaissance, 42,
51–52

Underwood, Dale, 163 n.
Universities, 28 ff.; Latin literature
in curriculum, 30–31, 34 ff. *See
also* Quadrivium; Trivium
Usk, Thomas, 107 n.

Vendome, Matthieu de, 36 n.,
181 n., 189 n.

Vergil, 25, 31, 59, 80, 84, 117
Vernacular poetry, 18–19. *See also*
Latin and vernacular poetry
Vincent of Beauvais, 32, 113
Vinsauf, Geoffrey of, 16, 18, 34–35,
36 n., 43, 48–49, 50, 51, 53 n., 54,
119 n., 173, 174 n., 180, 185–86,
188, 189 n., 194
Visions. *See* Books-dreams-experi-
ence

Wells, Whitney H., 84 n.
Whitehead, Alfred N., 113
Wife of Bath, 13; Prologue, 66;
tale, 157
Woolf, H. B., 52 n.
Wotton, William, 29
Wyatt, Thomas, 231

Yeats, William Butler, 19, 20, 22,
60, 61, 83, 90, 217
Young, Karl, 172, 193 n.